ECONOMICS, DEVELOPMENT AND THE QUEST FOR ALTERNATIVES

Economics, Development and the Quest for Alternatives

Essays in Honour of Professor M. A. Oommen

Editors

K. K. GEORGE

V. SANKARAN NAIR

JOSE JACOB

CONCEPT PUBLISHING COMPANY, NEW DELHI

ISBN: 81-7022-678-3

First Published in 1997

Published by
Ashok Kumar Mittal
Concept Publishing Company
A/15-16 Commercial Block
Mohan Garden
New Delhi 110 059
Phones: 5554042, 5504042
Fax: 091-11-5598898

Layout by
Institute of Social Sciences
B-7/18 Safdarjung Enclave
New Delhi 110 029

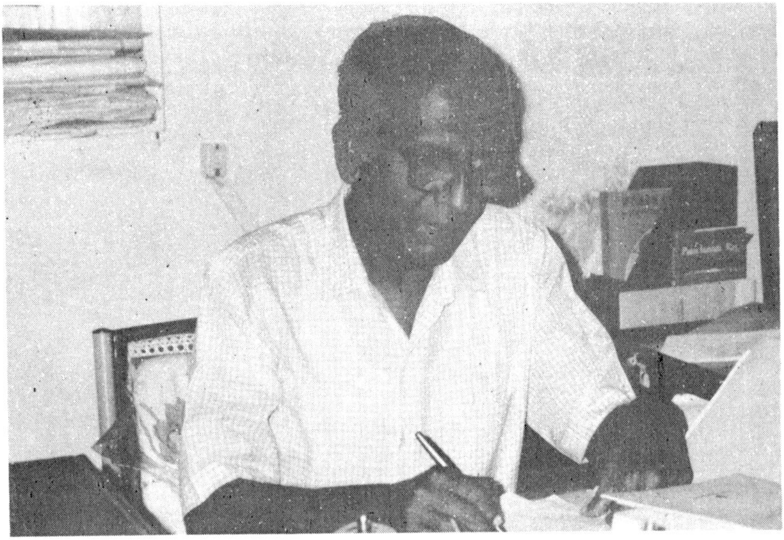

Prof. M. A. Oommen

Contents

The Contributors

1. **C.T. Kurien**
   Emeritus Professor, Madras Institute of Development Studies, Madras

2. **S. Umadevi**
   Professor of Economics, University of Kerala, Trivandrum

3. **M. M. Thomas**
   Formerly Governor, Nagaland.

4. **Koilpillai J. Charles**
   Professor of Economics, Lakehead University, Thunderbay, Canada

5. **Kamal Nayan Kabra**
   Professor of Economics, Indian Institute of Public Administration, New Delhi.

6. **Amitava Mukherjee**
   Formerly Professor, The London School of Economics and Political Science, London and Director ACTIONAID, Bangalore.

7. **Dalip S. Swamy**
   Professor, Department of Business Economics, University of Delhi.

8. **Malcom Adiseshiah**
   Founder Chairman, Madras Institute for Development Studies Madras and former Deputy Director General UNESCO.

9. **I.S. Gulati**
   Hon. Fellow, Centre for Development Studies, Vice-Chairman, State Planning Board, Kerala

10. **K. V. Sundaram**
Development Consultant to FAO/UN and formerly adviser, Planning Commission.

11. **Christopher C. Benninger**
Professor and Executive Director, Centre for Development Studies and Activities, Pune.

12. **K. N. Reddy**
Professor, National Institute of Public Finance and Policy, New Delhi.

13. **T. K. Oommen**
Professor, Jawaharlal Nehru University, New Delhi.

14. **George Mathew**
Director, Institute of Social Sciences, New Delhi.

15. **K. K. George**
Professor, School of Management Studies, Cochin University of Science and Technology, Kochi.

Introduction

THIS volume is a tribute to a distinguished scholar of Economics, in the form of essays on behalf of his innumerable students, colleagues, friends and admirers.

Except for the four years he spent in the University of Botswana, the rest of Prof. Oommen's career as a teacher of Economics, which spanned nearly thirty years, was in two universities of Kerala. This enabled him to influence a whole generation of students of Economics in Kerala who now occupy important positions in academic institutions, government and industry from the mid-fifties. As a professor in the Institute of Management in Government (Thiruvananthapuram) from the mid-eighties, he could directly influence the thinking and attitudes of all cadres of the Indian bureaucracy, especially from Kerala. Throughout his academic career, Prof. Oommen assiduously worked for changes in the Economics courses and syllabi. The insights gained from teaching Economics over the years and his concern with changing the quality of Economics courses culminated in the book, *Issues in Teaching of Economics in Indian Universities*.

A teacher is enriched by his research. Prof. Oommen is no exception to this rule. His academic research interests cover almost all the major areas in Economics – monetary economics, public finance, planning, industrial economics and rural economics. He even co-authored a book on the economics of cinema, a field in which very few economists in the country have ventured. His fascination for the economic problems of Kerala is noteworthy. He has also undertaken both policy-oriented and action-oriented research. He has been an adviser to governments as well as to many non-governmental organisations and action groups. Prof. Oommen did not confine himself to publishing in professional journals alone. He deemed it his mission to influence public opinion through his popular writings, both in Malayalam and English.

It is perhaps a poor reflection on Kerala's academic scene that Prof. Oommen was able to actively engage in research on larger issues of development only after his formal retirement from the academic institutions of Kerala. May be the move from the provincial towns to the nation's capital helped. May be the changing times posed the required challenge. Prof. Oommen is one of the few economists who has not got swayed by the general chorus about liberalisation and globalisation which has been ringing loud from the early nineties in India. His contributions to the theory and practice of local finance, especially state-substate fiscal relations, are now well acknowledged.

The collection of papers in this volume does not focus on any single subject. Broadly, the essays cover the major areas of concern to Prof. Oommen. While not addressing any one issue, *Economics, Development and the Quest for Alternatives* has emerged as the dominant theme of most of the papers.

Four papers in this volume challenge the notion of market-mediated economic growth, which is emerging as the dominant ideology, with apparently no alternative. C. T. Kurien makes a theoretical critique of the 'pure' logic of the market and argues that the unbridled functioning of the market cannot lead to the kind of welfare conclusions derived from Walrasian logic.

S. Umadevi also takes a critical look at the developments in economic theory and its relationship with economic planning. According to her, the greatest disservice of economic theory is that both land and labour are studied largely in relation to capital. Consequently, economic planning which enables man "to work in order to live his life" or permits land to remain as land, that is, a free gift of nature, has not been attempted.

K. J. Charles raises the larger question of what is development and argues in favour of a more holistic approach. He rejects the practice of conventional economics equating development with economic development and the latter, in turn, with large scale industrialisation and urbanisation.

M. M. Thomas's paper is part of the search for a new holistic paradigm of modernisation and development. He rejects the modernity associated with a mechanical materialistic world-view and highlights the destructiveness of high technology.

K. N. Kabra makes a survey of the literature on the informal sector, a subject of great interest to Prof. Oommen. He comes to the conclusion that the theoretical and conceptual tools of conventional development theories, which were essentially rooted in the neoclassical paradigm, are quite inadequate to deal with such complex realities as represented by the informal sector. He builds a case for a multidisciplinary approach to the study of informal sector, on the basis of which alone can appropriate developmental policies for this sector be devised.

Amitava Mukherjee takes a critical look at Amartya Sen's 'entitlement and deprivation thesis' and argues that food security may elude individuals even if Sen's conditions are satisfied. In addition to those discussed by Sen, three more conditions need to be met before an individual becomes food secure. These are: (*a*) the extension of institutional sanction to access to available food, (*b*) the exercise of choice of access to the food that is available, and (*c*) the presence of a secondary food system.

Three papers in this volume challenge the new economic policies being implemented in the country. Dalip S. Swamy traces their evolution from the eighties and pinpoints the nexus between these policy changes and the initiatives of the Bretton Wood twins. In his view, the new liberal reconstruction begun in 1981, when implemented in full, is bound to increase unemployment and drain the country's real resources.

Prof. Malcom Adiseshiah critically examines the move towards the privatisation of public enterprises. He finds that the supposed superiority of the private sector over the public sector is not grounded in any economic theory. While conceding the need for reforming the public sector, he warns against the present attempts at throwing out the baby with the bathwater.

I. S. Gulati also takes on the new economic policy for undermining the country's self-reliance. However, Gulati is not an unstinting admirer of the Nehruvian model. Nor is he a champion of the *status quo*. He holds that the concept of self-reliance has to be extended to the village level, for it to have real meaning. Decentralised and participatory planning must replace centralised planning.

There are two other essays in this volume on decentralised planning, a subject on which Prof. Oommen has done substantial work in recent years. K. V. Sundaram's paper is at once a critique of the present development paradigm and a plea for an alternative path calling for mass action at the local level. Christopher Benninger's essay starts from where K. V. Sundaram leaves. Drawing from his experience in rural Maharashtra, he attempts to give shape and form to participatory governance by preparing detailed guidelines.

Social justice can be ensured only if social development encompasses all sections of the people. This, according to the Indian federal Constitution, is the responsibility of state governments, who however are handicapped by the mismatch between their fiscal capacity and expenditure responsibilities. The Finance Commission in India has been bestowed with the task of correcting this imbalance under the Constitution. Prof. K. N. Reddy takes a look at the poor record of this constitutional body in this regard, and offers some useful suggestions for bringing about both vertical and horizontal equity in the Finance Commission's transfers from the Centre to the states.

T. K. Oommen surveys the several types of deprivation and their causes in a complex society such as ours. In view of the large number of the underprivileged in India and the limited resources, he advocates that the state should give first priority to the victims of cumulative deprivation. In this context, he examines the case for extending protective discrimination in favour of Dalit Christians and Muslims who suffer simultaneous disabilities and are therefore the most vulnerable among the deprived.

Two authors in this volume discusses important aspects of Kerala society and economy, on both of which Prof. Oommen has done substantial work. Kerala has been able to develop a unique model of community living. Is this model on the wane if not already destroyed? This is the question which George Mathew poses in the light of events since 1990.

As in the case of community living, Kerala's economy too has followed a unique pattern, often referred to as the 'Kerala model' of development. The unsustainability of this paradigm, despite the laudatory reference to it from different quarters, is highlighted by K. K. George. He also examines the options available to the state despite its numerous constraints.

We hope that the papers in this volume will help in providing a better understanding of the current issues in development in this country. This volume should also be particularly useful to those who are seeking alternatives to the market-mediated economic development strategy which is being projected as the only viable one. Much time has elapsed since the preparation of the volume got under way. Three of our contributors, Prof. Adiseshiah, K. N. Reddy and Dr. M. M. Thomas, passed away during this interval. We pay our deep respect to these eminent scholars, who were indeed great well-wishers of Prof. Oommen.

We will be failing in our duty if we do not acknowledge the various types of help rendered by the Institute of Social Sciences and its Director, Dr. George Mathew, in bringing out this volume. The editors are also grateful to Mr. P. N. Kuttappan and Mr. P. Nandakumar of the Institute for their support in processing the manuscript. We are highly indebted to Concept Publishing Company for the excellent job they have done for bringing out this volume.

Cochin and
Thiruvanathapuram
May 1997

K. K. GEORGE
V. SANKARAN NAIR
JOSE JACOB

1

The Market as a Social Institution

C. T. Kurien

M. A. OOMMEN is among the few economists in the country who have found it necessary to make a critical appraisal of the market even as most others have joined the general chorus about the newly discovered "magic of the market". His recent piece, "Economics, Economy and the Market Friendly Paradigm",[1] has rightly received a great deal of attention. As a tribute to him I propose, in this chapter, to clarify some issues which may be helpful in arriving at a better understanding of the role of the market in society.

Let us begin with two aspects of the market which are non-controversial. The first, of course, is that the market is one of the oldest of human institutions. The study by Karl Polanyi and his associates has documented the functioning of markets from as early as the seventeenth century BC.[2] But surely, as an institution it must be even older. Second, over time the market must have changed its characteristics. The changeover from barter to transactions mediated through money was one of major significance. However, the transition was gradual, and, barter in various forms is probably continuing even now in many parts of the world. Of equal significance was the linking of local and long-distance trade, though that too is far from complete. In fact a major thrust in this sphere is being witnessed today in the setting up of the World Trade Organisation.

While all these may be accepted as facts, economists in general tend to view the market not as an institution that has been changing over time, but as one whose logic is timeless and which is universally valid. In its elementary version, it was put forward as "the law of supply and demand", mainly by Marshall. It was an attempt to demonstrate the logic of the clearing of particular markets through the price-quantity adjustment mechanisms, price adjustments in the short run, and quantity adjustments in the long run. Surely, this logic of the markets adds a new dimension to the understanding of markets, which no amount of description in terms of the goods and parties involved or their location and other attributes provide. Indeed, a still deeper understanding of markets can be obtained through the Walrasian general equilibrium model which was put forward prior to Marshall's partial equilibrium models. Walras in his *Elements of Pure Economics* (written in French in 1874, and which remained relatively unknown to the English-using world till it was translated into English in 1954) tried to establish, with the help of mathematics, the interconnectedness of markets – of *all* markets – in an economy. Thereby, he also provided a new understanding of the concept of the "economy" – that it is essentially a system of interrelated markets. The underlying logic, again, is that of the law of supply and demand, which Walras spelt out in simple prose as follows:

> Let us imagine a market in which only consumers' goods and services are bought and sold. Once the prices of the ratios of exchange of all these goods and services have been cried out at random in terms of one of them selected as *numeraire*, each party to the exchange will offer at these prices those goods or services of which he thinks he has relatively too much, and he will demand those articles or services of which he has relatively too little for his consumption during a certain period of time. The quantities of each thing effectively demanded and offered having been determined in this way, the prices of those things for which the demand exceeds the offer will rise, and the prices of those things of which the offer exceeds the demand will fall. New prices having now been cried, each party to the exchange will offer and demand new quantities. And again prices will rise and fall until the demand and the offer of each good and service are equal. Then the prices will be current equilibrium prices and exchange will effectively take place.[3]

This is the basic Walrasian model of interrelated markets. Walras then extended the model to show that production can also be analysed in this manner because it is the offer of productive forces by landowners, workers and capitalists, which entrepreneurs demand to convert into consumer goods. Thus, all economic activities – production, distribution, etc. – can be thought of as a flow of commodities, of sales and purchases, each in its own market, prompted by the desire of every participant to get what he wants and to get rid of what he does not want in pursuit of his own most satisfactory position. This is how the entire economy can be shown to be a system of prices and quantities held together by the logic of supply and demand. In other words, the law of supply and demand is not only the logic of the market, but also of the economy, thus establishing the close link between markets (or prices) and the economy. The economy, therefore, is not merely a system of markets but of prices as well. No wonder, then, that attention shifts from institutions to logic, whether the subject under consideration is the market or the economy.

The power of this logic to grip the mind is not surprising. Who can easily give up the claim that there is a *single principle* underlying *all* market transactions and *all* economic activities? Is it not a great achievement to show that something as complex as the economy can be understood in terms of a single and rather elementary principle? No wonder, Schumpeter considered Walras' representation of the economy to be one of "revolutionary creativeness", that it was "the only work by an economist that will stand comparison with the achievement of theoretical physics."[4]

The logical underpinnings of the Walrasian system were further reinforced by the discovery, in subsequent years, of the relationship between competitive equilibrium and Pareto optimality. The latter is defined as a position where no participant in any exchange (recalling that all economic activities can be basically thought of as forms of exchange) can be better off in terms of his own preferences without making someone else worse off. According to the Fundamental Theorem of Welfare Economics, under certain specified conditions (in particular the absence of interdependencies that are external to the market), every perfectly competitive equilibrium is Pareto optimal, and under other conditions (especially the absence of economies of large scale), every Pareto optimal social state is also a perfectly competitive equilibrium. When these are also taken into account, the market, competition and efficiency become closely related. This, then, leads to the conclusion that the best of economic system is one where self-interested individuals try to maximise their own welfare by operating through competitive markets, because then the most efficient possible utilisation of resources is achieved.[5]

If one were to go by this logic alone, one would be tempted to say: "Thou hast conquered, Oh, Market!" And, frankly, a great deal of modern economic theory, especially neoclassical theory, is of this variety. Also, recalling what Keynes once wrote, mad men in authority in different parts of the world would appear to be fully and powerfully endorsing the ideas of some of these economists.[6]

But is the logic of the market "pure logic" or does it have institutional implications? Consider the statement from Walras quoted earlier. Arriving at equilibrium prices calls for an auctioneer who cries out prices. And if the prices called out initially are not equilibrium prices, he has the power to cancel *all* contracts, announce a new set of prices, and to repeat the same processes till the set of prices balance supply and demand in every market. Logically, these processes can be thought of as iterative steps of moving towards equilibrium. And, of course, there is no auctioneer steering the markets towards equilibrium. The real point, however, is different. What the Walrasian statement really implies is that among the parties to the transaction, there is no one with enough bidding power to stop the processes midway and thus scuttle the move towards equilibrium. But in this sense the iteration implicit in the Walrasian groping is not exactly similar to what a computer would do if all the supply and demand equations are fed into it. For, as Oskar Lange has pointed out, "the disadvantage of the market as a servo-mechanism is that its iterations cause income effects. Any change in prices causes gains and losses to various groups of people."[7]

Walras himself had not given much thought to this problem.

It surfaced in the attempts to link competitive equilibrium and Pareto optimality. In these exercises, it became clear that a set of equilibrium prices arrived at through the competitive processes would be dependent upon the initial endowments of the participants; and that all that the Fundamental Theorem of Welfare Economics would (and could) claim is that corresponding to *any* pattern of initial endowments, there would be a set of prices which could be considered to be efficient. It implied too that competitive prices claimed to be efficient may not satisfy considerations of distributive fairness on which the analysis was completely silent. Even extremely unfair distributional consequences arising from the market processes could still be considered to be "efficient", in other words.

Now, this certainly raises some questions because while the market may have some logic, it is not merely or even mainly a logical proposition. It is a functioning social institution. If its logic leads to the kind of implications mentioned above, can it be, more importantly, should it be, left to its own logic? This, though, is not the proper way to formulate the problem, although frequently that is how it is done. One has to search for the social counterpart of the logic of the market. From what has been stated already, it is clear that when translated into societal conditions, the logic of the market implies that as a social institution the market functions on the basis of the relative bidding power of the participants, which is a derivative of their overall resource power or economic power. The logical derivations, thus, depend crucially on the (social) assumption that resource power among participants is so distributed that no one party or a subset of the participants can prevent exchange from arriving at the postulated conclusions. It also means that in the real world, purchases depend on purchasing power! This is seen not only when one participates in an auction, but also when one bids for fish in the fish market or for property in the real estate market. Now one can appropriately formulate the real issues. Where there are known to be glaring differences in the distribution of purchasing power, should the market be allowed to function solely on the basis of this power, whether the good concerned is drinking water, food grains, medicine, education, or even a ticket for a movie theatre or an aeroplane? Interpreted in this manner, even the most ardent supporter of the "logic of the market" is likely to concede that there are many situations where the market cannot be and should not be left to its own devices.

Let us turn to another aspect which can also be picked up from the Walrasian illustration. The imagery that Walras provides is one where all the participants and the goods to be traded are assembled in one place, so that contracting and recontracting can be done with ease. Like the auctioneer, this too is not to be taken literally and the mathematical formulation makes it unnecessary to have space as part of the analysis. But as in the case already dealt with, the imagery communicates a crucial condition necessary for market equilibrium to be arrived at, and to be retained when arrived at. This condition refers to the information that the participants should have about the goods to be traded. It is assumed that the participants have perfect knowledge about the goods and about the offers that other participants are making.

This raises two sets of problems. The first is that, as Akerlof has pointed out in his widely cited paper, it is not true that under all circumstances, information available to buyers and sellers will be symmetric.[8] The seller of a used car will certainly have more information about the good being offered than a potential buyer can possibly have. Even in the case of a new car, the chances are that the seller will have more information than most potential buyers. In fact, this can be considered to be the most likely scenario for practically all manufactured goods. Where there are informational asymmetries, there is no reason to believe that the Walrasian processes will lead to equilibrium conditions. If informational asymmetries must be taken as part of societal processes, what implications do they have for understanding markets as social institutions?

Closely related to this is the second problem. The Walrasian logic of generalised exchange presumes a direct interaction between buyers and sellers. But it is impossible to generalise exchange without intermediaries – merchants – who buy from those who have to sell and sell to those who wish to buy. The presence of the intermediaries will lead to further asymmetries in information. On the one hand, the intermediaries make information available to the basic participants because that is necessary to promote exchange. But the intermediaries are not disinterested parties in this process. Their concern, certainly, is not to promote exchange as such, but to make profits out of the deal. Hence, whenever it is to their advantage to distort information, they should be presumed to do so.

If such is the case, we must draw the inference that as exchange increases and markets proliferate, it will become more and more difficult to concede the condition that all participants have the required information to lead to the Walrasian general equilibrium. We arrive at a somewhat awkward corner if we proceed along this line. But there is no alternative because it is impossible to envisage markets as a social institutions without providing a role for merchants. Incidentally, we now understand why even contemporary scholars who have done very rigorous work, with a view to critically scrutinising the Walrasian general equilibrium, have kept merchants completely out of the analysis.[9]

I shall touch upon one more aspect which is of special significance in the context of the emerging global markets, whose logic is considered to be an application of Walrasian analysis to the global situation although, strictly speaking, space (and time) is not a factor in that logic. Walras himself and those who have in more recent years tried to refine his analysis suggest that the main function of the market is to facilitate the exchange of goods and services. For instance, Koopmans, commenting on the Arrow-Debreu restatement of the Walrasian system, says that "it would be found best suited for describing a society of self-sufficient farmers who do a little trading on the side."[10] This is a very significant commentary on the nature of exchange and markets as envisaged in the Walrasian model. I shall deal with only •one aspect here. We can paraphrase Koopmans's comment to say that the social set-up that lies behind the Walrasian model is a system of petty commodity production.

But is it right to confine the "universal" logic of the market to just one social order? How about the capitalist system which, quite rightly, has been claimed to be the most market-friendly regime that humanity has known? What is the nature of the market in a capitalist order, and what is its logic? Now, unlike all other economic systems, capitalism has a logic of its own which Walras has not cared to address, but which Marx identified as that of accumulation. In order, therefore, to understand the market as a social institution in the capitalist order, the enquiry must be directed at examining the extent to which the market becomes an aid to the central objective of capitalism. The role of the market and of exchange in this context can be seen at different levels. First, it may be noted that the capitalist producer *realises* his profit not in production as such, but only by *selling* what he has produced; therefore, the capitalist *qua* capitalist cannot function without the market. (Unlike the self-sufficient farmers for whom exchange is only a kind of hobby!) But the capitalist is not a mere merchant; he is a producer too and the source of his profit lies in production. Production becomes profitable because one of the inputs that goes into production, viz., labour power, is capable of generating a surplus over what is required for its own maintenance. The source of profit for the capitalist is this surplus that he appropriates. This process too is done via the market because it is not production as such that gives the capitalist his profit, but the facility that the system provides him to *purchase* labour power along with the material and inert inputs for production. This, then, is the second level of market involvement in the capitalist system – that it can function only if labour power is also available for sale and purchase. Third, in this context, the appropriation by the capitalist of the surplus generated by the owners of labour power is made to appear like a normal exchange between the owners of two goods, or a horizontal transfer, although in effect, it is a vertical transfer similar to the transfer of grain from the cultivator to the landlord, who claims a share of the output solely on the strength of his ownership of land. A major role of the market in a capitalist system is this illusion of presenting a vertical transfer as though it is a horizontal one. Fourth, therefore, the crucial role of the market in a capitalist system is not facilitating the exchange of goods for goods (or more realistically the exchange of goods for money), though that function is important too because of the first role of the market mentioned above. The critical role of the market in capitalism is to serve as the conduit through which capital (abstract purchasing power or economic power) reaches out to concrete labour power.

The metamorphosis of the market from a facilitator of exchange of goods to an instrument of the relationship between capital and labour is a major transformation of the market as a social institution. However, its significance is not grasped because the claims of the market are still presented in terms of the logic of its former role. This is either a matter of ignorance or of deliberate deception. Since the Walrasian logic cannot be applied to the role of the market in its relationship between capital and labour, an attempt must be made to deduce the logic of the new role. However, the insights gained from the earlier discussion of the Walrasian system can be useful in the task.

First, recognising that exchange is basically a transaction between two owners, let us consider the nature of the two sides in a capitalist transaction. One of the parties to the transaction possesses economic power in the abstract, made completely homogeneous and exceptionally mobile. The other party possesses a specific skill, located within a human being and hence not having the mobility that capital, especially in its liquid form, has. With rare exceptions, therefore, it is reasonable to presume that the former will have much greater bargaining power. However, there is already a built-in bias in the transaction. This will become more pronounced if the owner of the specific skill does not have anything else that is saleable. Second, since abstract economic power can easily come to have control over technology and information, an informational asymmetry is also built into the transaction. Third, in view of the command that abstract economic power has over technology, information and virtually everything else in the economic sphere, the owners of capital also have the power to use the system itself in their favour. This power usually manifests itself in the system declaring from time to time different forms of labour power as redundant and hence not capable of commanding any exchange value. The social counterpart of this, of course, is unemployment, especially the manner in which those already employed (i.e., those within an exchange contract) are thrown out. It is the right of those who own capital to do this that is euphemistically referred to as the "exit policy".

These considerations will make it clear that the functioning of the market under these conditions cannot lead to the kind of "welfare" conclusions derived from the Walrasian logic. In that logic, the crucial assumption is that no participant has control over the mechanism of the market itself, whereas what we have seen is that in the context of the capitalist system, the market considerably comes under the sway of the owners of capital.

The new emphasis that the market has come to have globally in recent years becomes intelligible now. It is the counterpart of the global spread of completely homogenised and highly mobile abstract economic power, manifesting itself in the form of financial capital frantically rushing from place to place in search of profits through the operations of the market. That markets all over the globe are now completely integrated is the slogan that the owners of financial capital are propagating. "Leave it to the market" is their demand, not because of any concern for the logic of the market, but because of the conviction that they have control over the market as a social institution.

The range of issues that have been dealt with in this chapter has shown, I hope, that it is not necessary to jettison the logic of the market to understand it as a social institution. Instead, when that logic is properly made use of, it can become a powerful aid in this understanding.

NOTES

1. M.A. Oommen, "Economics, Economy and the Market Friendly Paradigm", ISS Discussion Paper, Delhi, July 1992.

2. Karl Polanyi *et al* (eds.), *Trade and Market in Early Empires*, New York: The Free Press, 1957.

3. Leon Walras, *Elements of Pure Economics*, tr. by William Jafee, Homewood: Richard D Irwin, 1954, pp. 40-41.

4. J. A. Schumpeter, *A History of Economic Analysis*, New York: Oxford University Press, 1954, p. 827.

5. See T. C. Koopmans, *Three Essays on the State of Economic Science*, New York: McGraw Hill, 1957, lecture one.

6. The passage reads as follows: ..."The ideas of economists and political philosophers both when they are right and when they are wrong, are more powerful than is commonly understood. Mad men in authority, who hear voices in air, are distilling their frenzy from some academic scribbler of a few years back." J.M. Keynes, *The General Theory of Employment, Interest and Money*, New York: Harcourt Brace and Co., 1936, p. 383.

7. Oskar Lange, "The Computer and the Market", in C.H. Feinstein (ed.), *Socialism, Capitalism, and Economic Growth*, Cambridge: Cambridge University Press, 1967.

8. G. Akerlof, "The Market for Lemons", *Quarterly Journal of Economics,* Aug 1970.

9. See Kenneth Arrow and Gerald Debreu, "Existence of an Equilibrium for a Competitive Economy", *Econometrica,* July 1954; Koopmans, *Three Essays*; K. J. Arrow and F. Hahn, *General Competitive Analysis*, San Francisco: Holden-Day, 1971.

10. Koopmans, *Three Essays*, p. 62.

2

Economic Theory and Practice

S. Umadevi

DEVELOPMENTS in economic theory have from time to time influenced the concept and techniques of planning. The popularity of the idea of planning even in the capitalist countries was a direct offshoot of the Keynesian revolution and of research in related fields of economics.

We will briefly summarise some of these developments in economic theory and then see how they have affected planning, particularly in an underdeveloped country like India.

In the thirties, three major contributions were made to economic theory. These were: (*a*) the ordinal utility concept, which in turn ushered in the new welfare economics; (*b*) the theory of imperfect competition; and (*c*) the Keynesian revolution, followed by the emergence of the theory of growth, macro-economics, social accounting and econometrics.

The switch-over from cardinal utility to the ordinal utility concept purged welfare economics of interpersonal comparisons.[1] It was held that economic welfare can be said to have increased only if some are made better off without making anyone else worse off – the famous Pareto optimality criterion.

In this kind of a theoretical context, economic theorists – mainly the positivists – refrained from talking about distribution because they shied away from interpersonal comparisons. They would not say that a rupee's worth to a poor man is more than its worth to a rich one. Hence, in our first four Five Year Plans, we were still hoping to increase total welfare by simply increasing production, so that if at least some people's welfare (usually of the top few) increased, other's welfare remaining the same, the total welfare could be said to have increased, using the Pareto optimality criterion.

Our planners had at the back of their mind the new welfare economics devoid of interpersonal comparisons and value judgements – not the Pigovian concept of welfare economics – which, according to Prof. Dobb, used "formal sophistication as a cloak for deficient logic and plain confusion."[2]

However, in the sixties, it came to be accepted that welfare economics could not do away with value judgements and interpersonal comparisons. At the same time, political forces in the less developed countries (LDCs) were pushing the problem of distribution to the forefront. Growth without justice, that is without a better distribution of wealth, was no longer acceptable. Hence, better distribution of wealth became a major objective in planning. This objective has not been fully achieved; it can never be attained unless value judgements and institutional factors are explicitly taken into account.

In the twenties, Pigou had talked of "two different ways in which economic welfare could be increased." The first of these is "any cause which, without the exercise of compulsion or pressure upon people to make them work more than their wishes and interests dictate, increases productive efficiency, therewith the average volume of the national dividend (income)."[3]

Hence, a mere increase in national income cannot be the aim of planning, which should be in accordance with the "wishes and interests" of the working people. When distribution becomes a major objective, employment should not be seen in isolation from the total welfare of man. The wishes and interests of a people depend upon the particular institutional set-up, value system and ethos. Veblensque factors cannot be ignored in a plan where the objective is to increase the welfare of the people. Tastes will have to be moulded by social forces.

This brings us to developments, in the thirties, in the theory of imperfect competition. Much was made of the incompatibility of perfect competition and increasing returns. Now we are back where we started. Namely, even those who had propounded the theory of imperfect competition feel disillusioned about its applicability.[4] There are others who feel that "it is perhaps a pity that the developments in the 1930s were to some extent to turn away from the insights into the competitive process contained in Sraffa's work", and that the "so-called imperfect competition revolution might have had a greater chance of success had it been more firmly rooted in a Sraffian framework."[5]

The developments in the theory of imperfect competition had a direct bearing on the question of planning. The fact that the market is imperfect meant that if the producers were left to decide what to produce and how to produce on the basis of market prices, it would lead to the misallocation of resources. When the market is imperfect, the system of prices that comes into existence does not reveal the true social cost. Further, because the producer is a price maker under imperfect competition, it is to his advantage to leave a part of the plant's capacity unutilised and to charge a higher price than that would have prevailed under conditions of perfect competition. Considering these, it was prescribed that monopolies should either be taken over or regulated by the government.

Increasing the role of the government in production was also justified in the case of those goods whose private profitability was lower than their social profitability. Individuals normally are likely to discount the future more than what is warranted from the point of view of the society as a whole. That is, the private or market rate of discount (as reflected in the market rate of interest) was considered to be higher than the social rate of discount. Based on this, sophisticated methods of project evaluation were suggested. The rate used in all these calculations was the social rate of discount which, in other words, is the shadow price of capital. Such methods of project evaluation came to be used in the selection of projects. By taking a lower shadow price for capital, the present value of projects using more capital was shown to be higher than what it would be if it was computed using the market rate of interest (as shown by the sum of discounted flow of future earnings expected). On the other hand, by assuming the existence of surplus labour in agriculture, the shadow price of labour was taken to be zero. The low imputed price of capital led to the selection of those projects whose import content was higher, while the low shadow price of labour belittled the cost of transferring labour from the agricultural to the industrial sector.[6,7]

The consequences of applying these project evaluation techniques to planning in the context of the LDCs can be understood better if we view them in the context of the growth theory which emerged in the wake of the Keynesian revolution. These theories laid greater emphasis on the factor of production capital. This was natural because the causes of the trade cycle in the mature capitalist economies (which already had a large stock of fixed capital) were found to be related to the pattern of demand for fixed capital; that is, the booms and depressions were found to be systematically related to the years of high demand for fixed capital and vice versa. Planning, therefore, meant making investments in such a manner that they did not lead to sudden spurts in economic activity in one year, followed by a fall, leading to recession, in the next.

It would not be an exaggeration to say that in the last fifty years or so, economic theorists have to a greater extent engaged themselves in studies of the factor of production capital. The theories of growth have been used to show that the foremost task of planning is to step up the level of investment and to accumulate capital. Capital has come to be considered superior to other forms of wealth because of its power of giving employment to labour.

Marshall long ago had tried to correct this wrong notion in the following words:

> Nor can we avail ourselves here of the notion that capital is distinguished from other forms of wealth by its superior power of giving employment to labour. For infact, when yachts and carriages are in the hands of dealers and are thus counted as capital, less employment is given to labour by a

> given amount of yachting or carriage driving than when the yachts or carriages are in private hands and are not counted as capital. The employment of labour would not be increased but lessened by the substitution of professional cookshops and bakeries (where all the appliances are reckoned as capital) for private kitchens (where nothing is reckoned as capital).[8]

Capital was considered to have the power of giving employment because employment itself has been defined as work done for a wage. Marx describes this figuratively. He says that for vulgar economists:

> Only Labour which produces capital is productive labour. A writer is a productive labourer, not in so far as he produces ideas, but in so far as he enriches the publisher who publishes his works, or if he is a wage labourer for a capitalist. The use-value of the commodity in which the labour of a productive worker is embodied may be of the most futile kind.[9]

Marx shows that in such a society, a criminal can be shown to be more productive as he produces the professor who speaks on criminal law, arouses moral and aesthetic feelings in the public, helps the production of "locks" to reach a high degree of excellence. Here he quotes from Mandeville: 'Fable of the Bees'.

> That what we call Evil in this world, Moral as well as Natural, is the Grand Principle that makes us sociable creatures, the solid basis, the life and support of all Trades and Employers without exception . . . there we must look for the true origin of all Arts and Sciences; and . . . the moment, Evil ceases, the society must be spoliers if not totally dissolved.

No doubt, in recent years several studies on labour have been undertaken. In fact, manpower planning has grown into a new branch of study. However, it is our contention that labour has been studied from the point of view of capital.

According to Marshall, "from some points of view, but not from all, the phrase Land, Labour and Capital would be more symmetrical if labour were interpreted to mean Labourers i.e., mankind."[10] A study of labour in this sense cannot leave out 'ecological, economic and sociological factors affecting labour. Such a study is bound to be humane rather than mechanical.

It can be shown that even the studies on "learning by doing", or skill formation, do not study labour independent of capital. "Learning by doing" refers to the speed gained by a labourer in performing a task by a process of repetition.

A proper measure of skill formation should be able to see whether a new economic activity enables a worker to (*a*) increase in general the command over the use of his fingers which in turn is the result of nervous strength and self-mastery; (*b*) be full of sagacity and energy; (*c*) "bear in mind many things at a time, to have everything ready when wanted, to act promptly and show resources when anything goes wrong, to accommodate oneself quickly to changes in detail of the work done, to be steady and trustworthy, to have always a reserve of force which will come out in emergency."[11]

Productivity of labour has not yet been measured in these terms, nor are new economic activities planned with a view to the development of these faculties of the worker. Simply because a worker handles an automatic machine, it does not mean his productivity in the above sense has gone up. Just as growth without justice is no longer acceptable, so is mere employment creation not the only goal. Sooner than later, there will be a demand for freedom to engage in work which is satisfying in itself – where the worker has scope to produce an effect on his work rather than be affected by it. Economic theory has always accepted this to be a goal, for, the very definition of economics says that it "is a study of wealth but on the more important side a study of man." Planning has yet to march towards this destination.

Marshall had reckoned organisation as a separate factor of production. His definition of capital was itself very broad. The rationality for considering organisation as a factor of production is given by him in the following words:

> Capital consists in a great part, of knowledge and organisation and of this some part is private property and other part is not. The distinction between public and private property in knowledge and organisation is of great and growing importance: in some respects of more importance than that between public and private property in material things; and partly for that reason, it seems best sometimes to reckon organisation apart as a distinct agent of production.[12]

The realisation that perfect competition and increasing returns are incompatible led theorists on the one hand to study the case of imperfect competition. On the other hand, theorists like D.H. Robertson undertook research into the nature of modern industry. One of his conclusions was that in the modern industry, control and risk are getting separated.[13] The function of the owners of capital theoretically lies in organisation. Profit is a reward for organisation, which in turn involves risk taking. But today, the owners of capital – whether private owners of capital in capitalist countries or the governments in socialist countries – retain control over industry without performing the second task, namely risk taking. Who then takes the risk? A further examination of the system will reveal that it is the unemployed who take risks, even as they have no control over the industry. The tendency towards horizontal and vertical integration is leading to an increase in the size of industry, but capitalists are shying away from taking risks. Through tacit agreements, monopoly power, or multinational corporations, they are reducing their risks to the minimum.

The capitalists have lost the spirit of enterprise. So is the case with socialist countries. Planners or those who take decisions at various levels are not answerable to anyone; even if their policies go wrong, their salaries are assured.

Hence, the economic activity planned should (*a*) give scope to both labour and capital to be enterprising, (*b*) raise the quality of the product, and (*c*) satisfy wants which have themselves been generated by the activity. The third criteria needs to be briefly elaborated.

Wants are of two types: (*a*) those which lead activity, and (*b*) those which arise in the course of activity. The latter may be termed as activity-led wants. The first group refers to the grosser wants, those which merely satisfy the appetite, while the second category refers to finer wants, which satisfy the desire for distinction and excellence. These have been spelt out by Marshall in his theory of demand. Preoccupation with the ordinal utility concept has prevented economists from giving any operational significance to the Marshallian theory of wants in the process of planning.

When activities are planned keeping in view the welfare aspect of society, rather than the mere quantitative aspect of production, then activities and wants will have to be seen in an integrated manner. This will be possible only if the "standard of living" is not bracketed with the "standard of comforts".

Most of our planning exercises have taken recourse to the optimising problem, which tries to maximise the terminal capital stock where "there is no question of intertemporal preference." According to Hicks, planning of this sort has a "war mentality, Stalinist mentality, and one might be forgiven for finding it distasteful."[14] The other type of optimising problem is more suited for us – namely where the consumption is to be maximised.

Having examined the nature of the three factors of production, capital, labour and organisation, and the place that should be accorded to them in planning, let us turn to the fourth factor of production – land.

Land in the sense of a free gift of nature is no more available, partly because it has been worked upon by man's labour and partly because it has been turned into capital. The process of capitalisation of land has gone so far that now there is a great deal of concern about the depletion of natural resources. It is being realised that the erosion of the natural resource base can threaten the very survival of the human race.

Land as the factor of production is the greatest victim of the development of modern industry which gives prominence to exchange value rather than use value. Capital has come between land and labour, between Nature and Man.

Planning has so far meant turning land into capital, and not letting land remain land – a free gift of nature to be enjoyed by all irrespective of a title to it. Nor has it attempted to enable man to "work in order to live his life, physical, moral and mental strengthened and made full by work."[15] Instead, we find that the inner life of the worker is overwhelmed by his work.

Finally, a word about the use of economic methods in planning. Macroeconomics emerged after the Keynesian revolution. It became fashionable to measure the macroeconomic parameters quantitatively and use them in planning and policy formulations. Recently, Hicks has tried to assess the role of macroeconomics and the quantitative methods in economics. He was motivated to examine this question because of his disappointment with the deliberations at the International Economic Association's Conference on the Micro-foundations of Macro-Economics. His conclusion about the use of econometric methods has serious implications for the use of these methods in planning.

According to Hicks, sampling and the methods of testing a hypothesis involve the use of the theory of probability. There are two probability theories: (*a*) the frequency theory and (*b*) the axiomatic theory. The latter is wider in scope and requires a judgement of probabilities, while for the former, probability is a property of random, repeated experiments. Hicks says that "it is the frequency theory which has become orthodox."[16] Although the use of quantitative methods in economics and planning became popular after Keynes, it was the frequency theory which found greater applicability, not the axiomatic theory of probability which Keynes had in mind.

Hicks concludes:

"the usefulness of 'statistical' or 'stochastic' methods in

> economics is a good deal less than is now conventionally supposed. We have no business to turn to them automatically; we should always ask ourselves, before we apply them, whether they are appropriate to the problem in hand. Very often they are not....[17]

Thus, before economic theorists undertaken the planning exercise, they need to chisel their tools and concepts. They should first put their own house in order by purging it of the myths accumulated over the last fifty years.

NOTES

1. A. K. Sen, *Collective Choice and Social Welfare*, Macmillan, 1970.

2. M. H. Dobb, *Welfare Economics and the Economics of Socialism*, Cambridge: 1969.

3. A. C. Pigou, *Economics of Welfare*, Macmillan, 1920.

4. Joan Robinson, *Contributions to Modern Economics*, Oxford: Basil Blackwell.

5. R. Clarka, "Sraffa's Laws of Returns – A reappraisal", *The Indian Economics Journal*, Jan. - Mar, 1981.

6. S. A. Marglin, *Public Investment Criteria*, George Allen & Unwin, 1967.

7. I. M. D. Little and J.A. Mirrlees, *Project Appraisal and Planning for Developing Countries*, Oxford and IBH, 1974.

8. A. Marshall, *Principles of Economics,* 8th edition, Macmillan, 1890.

9. K. Marx, *Theories of Surplus Value*, Pt. I, Moscow: Progressive Publishers, p. 158.

10. Marshall, *Principles of Economics*, p. 206.

11. *Ibid.*

12. D. H. Robertson and Dennison, *The Control of Industry,* Cambridge Economic Handbook Series.

13. J. R. Hicks, *Capital and Time*, Oxford University Press, 1973.

14. John Hicks, *Causality in Economics*, Basil Blackwell, 1979.

15. *Ibid.* p.121.

16. *Ibid.*

17. *Ibid.*

3

Eco-Justice and the Struggle for Social Justice in India

M. M. Thomas

ADMITTEDLY, we encounter a fragmented and unjust world. The pattern of so-called modernisation is highly lopsided. This chapter is part of the search for a new holistic paradigm of modernisation and development. It is sought to be illustrated by briefly analysing the struggle for eco-justice and social justice in India.

Modernity under a Mechanical-Materialistic World-view

The three forces which create modernisation are: (*a*) the revolution in science and technology; (*b*) the awakening of the peoples to a new concept of justice based on self-determination and equality, and their revolt against existing social structures in the name of fundamental human rights; and (*c*) secularism, denoting the break-up of traditional religious integrations of society and state, in the name of the autonomy of different realms of life. The lopsidedness has arisen as a result of interpreting and dealing with these forces within a mechanical–materialistic framework which denies the organic and spiritual dimensions of humanity and the universe. This framework seeks to make the law of dead matter in the natural sciences the norm in all sciences and all dealings with organic aspects of life and the spiritual aspects of selfhood. As a result, humanity's relation to the dynamics of community life has been reduced to mechanical proportions. Society, thus, becomes a collection of atomised individuals unrelated in their inner beings to each other and to nature in an organic way. This destroys the spiritual essence of society and nature. Atomic individualism and mechanical collectivism thus become the only alternatives for humanity.

Economic Development Interpreted Solely as Economic Growth

In the economic sphere, the mechanical–materialistic approach has led to economic development being equated with economic growth. This has meant neglecting or reducing to secondary position the other goals of economic development, namely social justice, self-reliance and protection of the ecological basis of life. In India, Nehruism sought to give some real consideration to the social welfare of people and national self-sufficiency by adopting a pattern of democratic planning for development, modifying the monocriterion of growth. But as C.T. Kurien[1] and M.A. Oommen[2] have shown, under the present regime of liberalisation in India, economic growth has become the sole criterion of development.[4] This entails risking increased unemployment and poverty and cutting back welfare measures for the weaker sections to limits set by the demands of electoral politics. Oommen shows that this is in line with the World Bank–IMF approach, which warns against "any uneconomical or populist redistributive measures that may impair the welfare of the non-poor on whose savings potential growth depends", and that "extra spending on education can be built up gradually so that increased burden of taxation on the non-poor is paid entirely out of increment to income."[3] Globalisation is seeking to remove all checks on the exploitation of Indian labour and markets by transnational corporations in the name of market-friendly capitalism. The disintegration of the socialist economies of Eastern Europe has made the profit-driven market economy the dominant development paradigm. No doubt, socialism eventually degenerated into a command economy, neglected the growth dimension, and produced political totalitarianism. But, the failure of Stalinist socialism does not mean the end of socialism. Social justice must find new forms in more holistic patterns of economic development. Because of the ideology of unlimited exploitation of nature and the overemphasis on material production, both capitalism and socialism failed to take the ecological question seriously. Any new paradigm of economic development must be able to integrate economic growth, social justice, self-reliance and eco-justice without letting any one of them eclipse the rest.

The Destructiveness of High Technology

The mechanical–materialistic world-view has resulted in the economics of high technology, which is not a means neutral to the ends of life. From the very beginning, high technology has been oriented to domestic and imperialistic exploitation. Motivations of profit and values of consumerism and aggression have been integral to the momentum of high technology generated in the modern world. So, one may say that modern high technology itself has an exploitative and imperialistic character, which gets exacerbated by the process of globalisation. The destructiveness of the false ends inherent in modernisation through high technology has now become evident to all who seek to go beyond the phenomenal form.

Let us examine the five destructive aspects of high technology. First, the high productive potential of technology has been instrumental in destroying the integrated subsistence economies of traditional societies. It has helped create mass poverty and unemployment and widened the gulf between the rich and the poor among nations and among classes within the nations. The promise of modern technology to liquidate mass poverty in the world remains an unrealisable dream.

Second, the relentless march of technology has destroyed not only the subsistence economies but also community structures, the sense of mutual responsibility, and the attitude and practice of interdependence among nature, humanity and spirituality. These have been replaced by the individualism and material consumerism that go hand in hand with urbanisation and industrialisation. The result has been a thoroughgoing mechanisation of life. Further, by empowering the oppressors, technological advancements have accentuated caste, ethnic, patriarchal and other forms of oppression of traditional society.

Third, untrammelled technological development has led to a situation where today it is capable of seriously threatening all organic life, of which human life is a part. It is in a large measure responsible for polluting the air, water and soil, wasting non-renewable natural resources, and doing violence to nature's efforts to renew itself.

Fourth, the culture of high technology has produced the technocrat and the bureaucrat and enhanced the functions and powers of the state. The structures of democratic participation of the people in the decision-making processes of modern society and state, which affect their lives, have been weakened. This has led to the further marginalisation of the weaker sections of society.

Finally, military technology, especially nuclear weapon technology, has made wars destructive to an unprecedented degree. The world is faced with a very real threat of a nuclear holocaust, which has the potential of destroying the human race and producing radical dislocation of cycles of organic nature. Even though this threat has diminished somewhat with the elimination of Big Power tension, high-tech wars like the one waged on Iraq show that mass killing of civilians has become an invariable corollary of technological military strikes and that ecological disasters are an inevitable consequence. Such wars now continue in different parts of the world.

Thus, the character of technology itself needs to be changed radically. It needs to strive towards the more wholesome goal of producing and reproducing life in accordance with the laws of organic life and its sustenance. It must also do justice to the struggle of the poor for food security, personal dignity, and social participation. This involves reshaping the technological-cum-cultural agenda so as to make it an instrument of justice for the self-awakening of oppressed peoples and the marginalised sections of society like women, Dalits, tribals, fisherfolk, etc. This self-assertion must find expression not just in their struggle to protect their rights to sustenance and survival. It should also be reflected in their attempts to realise their traditional self-identities in the modern historical setting, and to secure the right of self-determination through active participation in those decision-making processes of state and society which affect their lives. The main thesis presented here is that eco-justice and conservation of nature should not be treated in isolation but should be a part of the struggle of the underprivileged for social justice.

This point may be explained further. The vulnerable sections of society have certain common characteristics. First, they all are groups who have been eking their livelihood from one or another part of wild nature through their traditional labour. For their subsistence, tribals depend on forests, fisherfolk on the sea, the Dalits on the land, and women on their role as producers of life and sustenance. For this very reason, they all have been considered to be polluting and impure by the orthodox sections of Indian society and marginalised or excluded from religious functions of significance, and consequently from the social and cultural hierarchy and the governmental power structure.

Second, as noted earlier, these injustices have been exacerbated by the forces of high-tech modernisation and under the mechanical–materialist momentum of modernity. They have destroyed these groups' traditional rights over the forest, sea, land and home, their means of sustenance and livelihood, and thrown them into the labour market of a capitalist economy and industrial urbanism. The process has also atomised their traditional community life through individualized culture and forced them to migrate to cities where most of them become slum dwellers and join the army of the unemployed or the lumpen proletariat. In India while this process has gone rather far, it has not succeeded in dissolving all traditional social structures. It is to resist this onslaught that these weaker sections have become awakened to a new sense of their respective traditional cultural self-identities. They seek to protect and renew their traditional means of livelihood through appropriate technologies and thus forge a counter-culture of resistance to lopsided modernity.

Capitalists and socialists have tended to assume that the modern capitalist and working classes alone will matter in a fast modernising world, and that traditional societies will disintegrate. But that has not happened. Not only in the so-called Third World, but even in the USA and erstwhile USSR, traditional ethnic identities have survived the destructive impact of the modernisation process. The advocates of fast modernisation through high technology have been forced to rethink the character of modernity, its technical instruments, and its ideological framework. The global concern for eco-justice, as a part of a wholesome ideology and pattern of modernisation, reflects this pressure to reconceive the parameters of modernity. This is a growing consensus among the advocates of new socialism in India that the fight against caste, ethnic and patriarchal oppression cannot be subsumed under the class struggle against economic oppression. The view that the crusade for social justice is a pluralistic one, comprising simultaneous and interrelated struggle at the economic, social, ecological and religio-cultural levels, points to the same need to rethink the means and ends of modernisation.

The renewal of interest in the thought of Lohia and Ambedkar is significant, because they had advocated comprehensive ideological approach to new society long time ago. Vandana Shiva sees the Chipko movement for the protection of trees as embracing the movement of women for justice and calling for a redirection of the idea of development.[4] Gabriele Dietrich says:

> It is therefore crucial that the working class incorporates the survival values of women and nature and ecological and women's struggles resist the upward mobility syndrome and orient themselves towards the poorest and most exploited sections like Adivasis, Dalits and workers of the unorganised sector, of which women anyway form the majority.[5]

It is also possible that since the "working class" may have lost its nerve for struggle in view of the breakdown of socialist regimes in Russia and Eastern Europe and with their own willing cooption into the consumerist value framework, "the workers of the unorganised sector", that is, Adivasis, Dalits, fisherfolk and women, may even have to take the initiative for creating a counter-culture to destructive modernisation and shaping the nature of the new post-modern socialism.

Here are a few statements regarding the vision of the future development of tribals, Dalits and fisherfolk. They show how eco-justice and social justice are integral to each other.

Verrier Elwin who advised Prime Minister Nehru on the development of tribals in India and influenced the formation of Nehru's Tribals Panchsila says:

> My whole life has been devoted to fighting for the freedom of the aboriginal, to restore to them their ancestral jungle and mountain country which is their home and to enable them to live their own lives, to have their own diet and to refresh themselves with their traditional recreations. We have no desire to deprive the aboriginal of the blessings of civilization, but we do desire to save them from that parody of civilization, that economic exploitation, and that cultural and moral death which is invariably their lot when they come into contact with the degraded adventures, the lawyer's touts, the money-lenders, the grasping landlords, the exploiting merchants and the corrupt subordinate officials which are practically the only representatives of civilization that they ever met....We have never opposed intelligent, planned and regulated advance among the aboriginal ....(We) have only one desire, that as they move into the modern world, they may do so without economic loss, moral degradation and psychic despair....to study how this delicate and intricate problem of acculturation can best be solved.[6]

Regarding fisherfolk's development, Thomas Kochery, Chairperson, the National Fish-worker's Forum, says:

> Sustainable development is a multifaced concept including biological, human and technological dimensions. Fish being a renewable resource, biologically it would mean that the rate at which the resources are harvested should be in harmony with the rate at which they multiply. Humanly, it means that principles of equity and basic needs get a higher priority. Technologically, it implies using means that augment rather than displace human skills, utilize

> renewable energy resources and methods which are environmentally appropriate and less destructive. From the organizational and employment points of view, the policy of increased people's participation and decentralisation of investments and planning will offer added impetus....If development processes have to be life-sustaining, then they have to place stress on nature-tasks that do not have immediate fruits and are certainly not profit-oriented in today's sense of the word. Nature involves protecting and re-creating the fish habitats, be they reefs, the mangroves or the breeding grounds. It means caring for the natural flow of nutrients to the water and preventing pollution. It means providing for need and not for greed, a perspective of more equitable distribution. Recognizing the crucial role women play in the distribution of fish and net-making in the marine sector it should be a balanced approach with a concern for conservation, maximizing exploitation of resources and improvement of the socio-economic condition of the traditional fisherfolk.[7]

The World Bank Report on the Sardar Sarovar Project is replete with passages which criticise the Narmada Valley Dam Project, not purely from the economic but also the broader human view point. Such a perspective acknowledges the integral links between economic, ecological, social, cultural and spiritual aspects of community living, as found in the dam-affected villages. Here is a passage from the chapter on the villagers of Madhya Pradesh who will have to leave their homes on the banks of Narmada river if the dam is to be built and operated.

> People's lives are not guided–especially in the tribal and scheduled caste communities–by and attachment to profit rather than to place. On the contrary, we were told repeatedly in many of the villages we visited, of the spiritual and social meanings of the river itself. In fact, the Narmada has immense spiritual importance to many Hindus. We were told about river rituals that the women conduct at dawn of every new moon... It is not surprising therefore that we had glimpses of the deep anxiety that the thought of moving away from the Narmada causes in the

> minds of the people of the area. Many identify with the river as a source of religious strength. They also see their communities on its banks as essential to their material security. Again and again the men and women of the landless families express to us their reliance upon a place in community life.... People attribute their economic security to a long- established web of human and geographical links within their community.[8]

The new paradigm of development should aim at a gradual renewal of traditional societies to create a new, higher level of integration between eco-justice, social and cultural community values, and spirituality. This can be achieved through appropriate technologies–those which are compatible with the holistic world-view of traditional societies.

NOTES

1. C. T. Kurien, *The Economy: An Interpretative Introduction,* New Delhi: Sage Publications, 1992.

2. M. A. Oommen, "The Political Economy of Globalisation," Discussion Paper, New Delhi: Institute of Social Sciences, 1993.

3. *Ibid.*, p. 19.

4. Vandana Shiva, *Staying Alive*.

5. Gabriele Dietrich, *Women's Movement in India*

6. Daniel O'Connoh, *Din-Sevak*, pp. 66-67.

7. National Fish Workers' Forum, 1991, pp. 44-50.

8. World Bank, Sardar Sarovar Project, pp. 182-83.

4

What is Development?

Koilpillai J. Charles

> WHEREAS for the philosophy of knowledge, the fundamental kind of rational learning is acquiring knowledge, for the philosophy of wisdom the fundamental kind of rational learning is learning how to live, how to see, to experience, to participate in and to create what is of value in existence.[1]

Conventional economics, and the market-oriented policy prescriptions that emanate from it, though commended to the poor countries with unabashed enthusiasm by the rich nations and the international institutions they control, have been conspicuously unsuccessful in bringing about any sustained improvement in the lot of the large masses of poor people in these countries. In spite of the mushrooming of skyscrapers, superhighways, ultramodern airports and multipurpose dams in several of these countries, the lives of the majority of people continue to be "solitary, poor, nasty, brutish and short." This patent failure has not dampened the proliferation of development conferences, development journals, aid agencies and development experts. This chapter argues that the reason for the stark discrepancy between effort and result can be traced to the development paradigm of conventional economics, which is fundamentally flawed. Unless this paradigm and the institutions and values associated with it are thrown overboard, authentic development which improves and enriches the lives of people will not occur. The first section of this chapter outlines the basic features of the conventional concept of development, and in the next section the consequences and effects of such a view of development are considered. In view of the abysmal failure of the conventional development paradigm, in the third section a radically reformulated conception of development is advanced, one which is holistic, multidimensional and people-oriented. In the succeeding section a discussion of the implications of such a conception of development follows. The final section of the paper briefly refers to the nature of the social organisation in which authentic development, as defined here, can be realised.

I

Conventional economics equates development with economic development, and economic development with large-scale industrialisation. It measures the pace of development in terms of the rate of growth of national income.

Let us denote real national income by Y, and the increment of that income by Y. Net increase of income results mainly from the operation of the following three forces:

1. The productive effect of gross investment, (1/v) I, where 'I' is the level of gross investment, 'v' is the technical incremental capital-output ratio, and its reciprocal '1/v' is the output-capital ratio, that is, the stream of additional output that would be generated by one unit of material capital.

2. The decline of income that regularly occurs due to the obsolescence, waste, inefficient use, loss or destruction of material capital, –aY, where 'a' is a fraction of income expressed as a percentage.

3. The increase of national income that results from organisational improvements, disembodied technical progress, and increased energy efficiency, skill and creativity of the work force, bY, where 'b' is a fraction of income expressed as percentage.

Therefore $\Delta Y = 1/V.1 - aY + bY$ .....(1)
or $G = \Delta Y/Y = s/v - a + b$ ....(2)

Here 'G' is the rate of growth of national income and 's' is the proportion of income saved and invested, expressed as a percentage. The rate of growth of real income of an economy can be increased by increasing the proportion of income saved and invested, by full and efficient use of capital so as to keep the value of 'v' reasonably low, by better care and maintenance of capital equipment so as to lower the value of 'a', and finally through organisational improvements, general technical progress, and increased dedication and efficiency of labour, so as to raise the value of 'b'.

Both mainstream economists and Marxian economists seem to accept the conventional definition of development. For example, Paul Baran, in a brilliant Marxist analysis of underdevelopment, defines development as follows: "Let economic growth (or development) be defined as increase over time in per capita output of material goods."[2] There is also a striking similarity between mainstream and Marxian economics in the perception of the basic mechanism of growth.[3] There is fundamental disagreement between them, to be sure, on the causes of underdevelopment, and the policy measures necessary to energise the motors of development. Mainstream economics believes in the efficiency of market forces in bringing about rapid development, and therefore favours capitalist solutions to economic problems. Marxists, on the other hand, find in the institutional and socio-economic structures of poor countries the most powerful brakes on the motors of development, and therefore regard far-reaching, social and structural changes as necessary pre-conditions for the generation of growth and development. They reject the notion that the pursuit of private profit would maximise public welfare, and therefore call for a planned economy in which development is spearheaded by the state. But both are in broad agreement on the definition of development, and on the mechanism of growth. Even in practice, both capitalist societies and centrally planned economies seem to be in the race for more or less identical goals – the acquisition of more and more material goods and the creation of social and economic infrastructure conducive to the production and expansion of these goods and services. The value systems underpinning both types of societies seem to have become remarkably similar, accounting in part, at any rate, for the breakdown of the socialist experiment in the erstwhile Soviet Union and Eastern Europe.

The wide disagreement between Marxists and conventional economists regarding the role of the state in the development process has already been noted. Among non-Marxist economists, those with neoclassical leanings are ardent believers in the efficacy of market forces in bringing about rapid growth and are lusty supporters of the capitalist system. To the developing countries, neoclassical economists recommend deregulation of industries, removal of barriers to international trade, free flow of foreign capital, balanced budgets, reduction of social welfare expenditures, and maximum scope for the working of market forces. Keynesian economists, except for a radical minority, support the basic tenets of neoclassical economics, though not with the same gusto. They generally assign the state a more interventionist role in the economy. But there is widespread agreement among economists of all kinds on the definition of development and the mechanism of the growth process as expressed in equation (2) above, though they may disagree about the relative values of the parameters in the equation and about the forces shaping them.

II

The consequences of the prevailing conception of development as a process of growth of the economy through industrialisation, measured by the rapid growth of real national income, may now be examined.

The Pre-Eminent Role of GNP Growth Rate

The conventional development paradigm has enthroned the GNP growth rate, that is, Y/Y, as the single most important measure of the performance of the economy. Clearly, the Indian Planning Commission, in fixing targets and formulating policies, has subscribed to this in no unmistakable terms. This obsession with the growth rate is a near universal phenomenon, and everywhere has had the effect of shifting attention away from the other goals of planning such as increase in employment, reduction of inequalities of incomes and wealth, and the eradication of poverty. While our planners are basking in the limelight of India's high growth rate, and have received a pat on the back from the World Bank for this, the shockingly inglorious performance of the Indian economy in terms of these other indices has hardly received attention. This is typical of the situation prevailing in most developing countries. To them, nothing else seems to matter as long as the GNP is racing ahead at a fast clip.

Elitist Character of Development

Development strategies based on the conventional view of development inevitably result in an elitist form of development. The rich and the super-rich are the major beneficiaries of this form of development while the wretched of the earth remain in poverty and degradation. If a country is small, in the course of development, the small size of its indigenous market makes it turn to foreign markets for the sale of its products and its pattern of development is set by an export-led growth strategy. Only a small rich minority in these countries working hand in glove with foreign capital, benefits by this form of development, as amply attested by the experience of the countries of South-East Asia, such as Taiwan, Singapore, Hong Kong and South Korea. This form of development has resulted in an increase in the incomes of the majority of their peoples but, with the exception of Taiwan, inequalities in incomes and wealth have also increased, and the ecological costs of development have been recklessly ignored. India, on the other hand, is a large country, the approximately 10 to 15 per cent of the population which derives the lion's share of the benefits of development constitutes a vast domestic market. Therefore, the development strategy adopted was one of import substitution. This elitist market in India, of a size in excess of 100 million people, is massive enough for the growing industries to focus on it, without too much concern for foreign markets. In fact, there are probably about only five other countries in the world with population of the order of 100 million. Thus, both these apparently opposite strategies have yet a common purpose – to mainly enrich the small class at the top that owns and controls the resources and means of production in these countries. Elitist development neglects the poor. It is development as if people do not matter.

Stress on Quantity and Neglect of Quality

When development is equated with the rate of growth of national income, it inevitably acquires a quantitative character and qualitative considerations tend to be neglected. The planners and the public tend to regard quantitative improvements as important because they can be measured and to neglect qualitative losses because they cannot be quantified. In the course of economic development, there is a measurable improvement in the quantity of capital equipment and material goods. But this entails considerable human misery, crime, congestion, pollution and environmental degradation. Since these are largely qualitative changes, they tend to get neglected. The Mathura refinery adds to our GNP, and so is considered important. The damage it does to the Taj Mahal is a qualitative change and is therefore neglected. In the name of economic development, much scenic beauty is destroyed, entire tribal populations uprooted, non-renewable resources recklessly depleted, and our air, water, soil and foods polluted. Thus, this conception of development causes us to ignore or undervalue the enormous ecological damage and environmental degradation that come in the wake of our mega-development projects, multipurpose dams and other grandiose schemes to bring about quantitative increases in our national income. Obsession with the growth rate of national income causes us to neglect essential "non-development" expenditures such as health, education, housing and social welfare. As a result, while India is in the forefront of nuclear and space research, she has stubbornly high rates of illiteracy and infant mortality, and persistent incidence of such diseases as cholera, tuberculosis, malaria and leprosy that have practically disappeared in the more affluent countries. Over 40 per cent of our population lives below the poverty line.

Domination by Technical Experts

When the level of per capita income is seen as the sole measure of economic attainment, then development becomes a process through which a poor country catches up with the rich country. And this catching up is made possible by the transfer of capital and technology from the developed country to the underdeveloped country mediated through development experts and foreign capital. Multinational corporations are then seen as the vehicles for the transfer of technology and capital. In fact, they do produce and patent a substantial chunk of technology. Very soon, the economy of the poor country comes to be dominated by multinational corporations and its self-reliance and independence lost. It becomes strongly integrated with the world capitalist system, and develops a neocolonial relationship with the developed countries. The latter dominate the former by their superior economic strength and power.

Independence is lost both at the national and the individual level. If economic development is perceived as the process of transferring knowledge from the rich to the poor countries, mediated by the technical expert, he then becomes a dominant figure on the development scene. The local people gradually lose their sense of independence and become dependent on him as the source of their knowledge. They do not think for themselves as long as the expert is there to give them all the answers. When the poor countries were under foreign rule, they used to invest the colonisers with superhuman powers and abilities and regard themselves as incapable and inferior. The same kind of psychology grips the masses as long as the expert is assigned the pre-eminent role in the development process. Since the expert is seen as the custodian of scientific and technical knowledge, he is able to disguise political and ideological issues as technical ones and his pronouncements on these acquire the halo of unchallenged truths. Indian agriculture has for long been hamstrung by an extremely inequitable distribution of land and by unjust relations of production. The expert has been able to convince policy-makers and the public that the green revolution is an effective surrogate for much-needed agrarian reform. The imposition of such a package on our inequitable social order greatly accentuated rural inequalities and increased the size and sufferings of the class of landless labourers. The green revolution has also thrown overboard centuries' old agricultural knowledge and practices and reduced the small agriculturist to a position of helpless dependence and subservience.

As early as 1891, Dr J.V. Voelcker in a monumental report

to the Government of India, paid tribute to the mastery of cultivation displayed by the Indian agriculturist. He wrote:

> On one point there can be no question, viz. that the ideas generally entertained in England, and often given expression to even in India, that Indian agriculture is, as a whole primitive and backward, and that little has been done to try and remedy it, are altogether erroneous. At his best, the Indian Ryot or cultivator is quite as good as, and in some respects the superior of the average British farmer... What does however, prevent them from growing larger crops is the limited facilities to which they have access, such as the supply of water or manure.
>
> But to take the ordinary acts of husbandry, nowhere would one find better instances of keeping land scrupulously clean from weeds, of ingenuity in device of water-raising appliances, of knowledge of soils and their capabilities, as well as the exact time to sow and to reap, as one would in Indian agriculture, and this is not at its best alone, but at its ordinary level. It is wonderful, too how much is known about rotation, the system of mixed crops, and of fallowing. Certain it is that I, at least, have never seen a more perfect picture of careful cultivation, combined with hard labour, perseverance and fertility of resources, than I have found in many of the halting places in my tour.[4]

But the Indian agriculturist's past mastery of his craft was based on organic farming in harmony with nature, and in a self-renewing relationship with it. The green revolution has changed all that. The use of chemical fertilisers, insecticides and pesticides, and new varieties of seeds has upset the old delicate balance of organic cultivation, poisoning the soil, water and foodgrains. Indians have the dubious distinction of having the highest concentration of DDT in their blood, and a large number of our foods have become contaminated with dangerous chemicals. Ever increasing amounts of fertilisers, insecticides, pesticides and energy from non-renewable sources are required to maintain our agricultural output resulting in soil exhaustion, desalination, deforestation, and a host of other problems. The upshot of all these changes is that the Indian agriculturist has lost mastery over his art. Today he is a passive recipient of information, knowledge and other essential inputs from so-called agricultural experts.

Devaluation of Indigenous Knowledge

When the process of development is viewed as a transfer of technology from the developed countries to the developing countries, indigenous knowledge is automatically devalued. Because of the technological dominance of the West in today's world, it is assumed that technology is a unique product of Western civilisation. Quite early, Francis Bacon recognised that printing, gun powder and the magnet had "changed the whole face and state of things throughout the world."[5] Writing much later, J.S. Bury in his *Idea of Progress* recognised the crucial role of these inventions, but it did not occur to him to point out that none of these was of European origin.[6] The widely-held view that technological ingenuity is a characteristically Western ability, rooted in some dynamic principle of Western culture, turns out on examination to be devoid of factual foundation. Though countries like China and India have impressive records of technological and scientific achievements in the past, developing countries have also accepted the mythical claims of the developed West to technological supremacy. As a result, there is a tendency on the part of poor countries to devalue their own technological and scientific achievements. The Ayurveda system of medicines is an impressive alternative medical system, based on sound scientific principles, capable of durably curing ailments that have so far eluded the allopathy system of medicine. Nevertheless, many Indians dismiss Ayurveda as a system without value, and brand its practitioners as quacks. If we look upon our own scientific and technological heritage with contempt, we will necessarily look to the West for every technological device. The result of this attitude is the absence of indigenous efforts to develop technologies suited to our conditions. Our technological dependence on the West has caused us to neglect local research to solve local problems with local resources. Though the tiffin carrier is widely used in India, we have not been able to produce a waterproof tiffin carrier. We have not been able to harness solar and wind power on a wide scale for producing energy. We have not been able to use human and animal wastes for producing energy and manure on a national scale. We have the world's largest reserves of coal. Had we devoted our research resources to finding possible derivatives of coal, we could have attained self-sufficiency in energy. Our defence and space technologies are quite advanced but are imported from or patterned after the technology of the West. In the Seventh Five Year Plan, roughly two-thirds of the total allocation for science and technology is for space and nuclear research – prestigious fields without local or indigenous appeal or relevance. As long as development is defined in terms of an increase in material goods, we will continue to look to the West for our technology, and we will neglect indigenous knowledge and local problems and issues.

Stress on Export-Driven, Free Trade and Market Solutions

The conventional development paradigm stresses international trade as a powerful engine of economic growth. In order to derive the benefits of international trade, developing countries are urged to open up their borders to increased trade and foreign capital. To remain competitive and increase its exports, a developing country is encouraged to cut expenditure on social welfare programmes and keep wages low. The greater role of foreign capital in the economy and the increased reliance on market forces have the effect of increasing external indebtedness and accentuating the inequalities of incomes and wealth. As privatisation, deregulation, inflow of foreign capital, and international trade increase, developing countries are becoming more deeply indebted to the developed countries. Far from foreign savings flowing into developing countries, they are actually being drained of their resources. According to estimates of the IMF, the total debt of the developing countries rose from US $850 billion in 1982 to $1,240 billion in 1988. Contrary to popular belief, net transfers of resources are from the South to the North. In 1982, this amounted to $18.2 billion. The figure rose to $43 billion in 1988. As a developing country enters into close economic relations with rich countries, there is an increased craze for the material goods and gadgets of these countries. The former comes under the grip of the psychology of consumerism and the desire to keep up with the international Joneses. It loses its economic independence and self-reliance, and becomes closely integrated with the world capitalist system at its periphery.

Militarisation of the Third World

An inevitable concomitant of this form of development is the scramble for markets and raw materials. In view of the limited nature of the resources of our plant and their uneven distribution, it necessarily breeds conflict among nations. Militarisation is the inexorable logical consequence. The drive for foreign markets and the search for increased economic power, political influence, and security are the hall-marks of a country embarked on economic development along conventional lines. Very soon, these cause it to divert an increasing share of its precious resources to the military. Barely a quarter of a century ago, India spent 3 per cent of its national income on defence and internal security. Today the corresponding proportion is 9 per cent. The Third World's defence spending rose from 3 per cent of its collective gross domestic product in 1955 to 12 per cent in 1975. Meanwhile, of the 17 million people who have died in war and war-related deaths since 1945, the overwhelming majority have been from the Third World. The poor pay for this increased militarisation in other ways too. As more and more of the developing economy's resources are devoted to defence, less is available for meeting the basic needs of the wretched of the earth. Nearly 800 million people in the world live in dire poverty, and half of them suffer the ravages of famine, hunger and malnutrition. Over 50 per cent of the world's population has no access to safe drinking water supplies and over 40 per cent are illiterate.

During the decade 1970-80, arms exports to the Third World, excluding Vietnam, increased from US $2.5 billion (in 1975 dollars) to US $9.8 billion. It is estimated that between 20 to 30 per cent of the Third World's external debt during this period was directly attributable to arms imports. Sadat Deger has calculated that a mere 11 per cent cut in the Third World's military budget would be sufficient to cover the cost of a comprehensive social development programme, including education, literacy and community medical care. Development along conventional lines necessarily leads to increased militarisation for which the poor pay dearly through hunger, malnutrition, ill-health and illiteracy.

III

In a famous passage, Marx said that the ruling ideas of a society are the ideas of its ruling classes. Objective conditions in capitalist societies favour the conventional definition of development because maximisation of economic growth will ensure the maximisation of private profits. In socialist countries too, first the need to achieve socialist goals and later the need to ensure their protection against attack by capitalist countries led to an identification of development with economic growth and military might.

The conventional development paradigm results in consequences that are damaging to the general welfare of human beings and to the health of the environment. Thus, there is an urgent need for a radically different conception of development, one which has at its centre the human being, and his multifarious needs.

Authentic development, then, is a holistic and multidimensional concept. It is a qualitative change in the lives of people. A process through which a liberating environment is created for the economic, social, cultural, physical, intellectual, moral and spiritual progress of the human being. On such a path of development, people gain increasing control over the forces which shape their lives.

Oscar Lewis, the American sociologist who had studied slums in Havana in 1947, returned to the island after the Cuban revolution and visited the same slum. The changes he noticed provide a good description of what constitutes authentic development:

> The physical aspect of the place had changed little. The people were as poor as before, but I was impressed to find much less of the feelings of despair and apathy so symptomatic of the culture of poverty in the urban slums of the U.S. The slum was now highly organised, with block committees, education committees, party committees. The people had found a new sense of power and importance in a doctrine that glorified the lower class as the hope of humanity.[7]

The *differentia specifica* of authentic development then is a change in the attitudes of people – their awakening from one of apathy to one of energy, from one of fear to one of hope, from one of helplessness to one of self-confidence. It has little to do with high-rise apartments, superhighways, computers, automated factories, and nuclear and space research. Development is a process of empowerment of the people – from the long slumber of misery, squalor and despair. When a people long accustomed to thinking of themselves as the helpless victims of a cruel fate, suddenly waken to the consciousness of their ability to control and change their environment, to overcome age-old injustices, and to hurl defiance at the barriers of caste, tradition, custom and entrenched authority, true development has been born.

Such a radical change in the consciousness of people cannot come about without a far-reaching and fundamental transformation of the objective conditions governing their lives, either by a social revolution or by a progressive government firmly committed to the uplift of the poor and the downtrodden. A government so constituted alone will have the will and ability to take the first decisive steps towards authentic development. That is, to set in motion the necessary structural and institutional changes to lift the country out of its dependent relationship in the periphery of world capitalism. The mechanisms of control and domination operate chiefly through foreign trade, foreign aid, foreign loans and foreign direct investment by global multinational corporations. It is only by drastically curtailing and controlling these forces that a country will be setting the stage for an autonomous and self-reliant form of development.

IV

The rejection of the conventional view of development and its replacement by a radically different conception of development, which is people-centred, holistic and multi-dimensional, will have profound consequences, the salient among which may now be considered.

Development as if People Mattered

Bringing people to the centre stage of the development process will make them the subjects of their own development. They will cease to be objects to be studied and manipulated. Such a society cannot be dictatorial, authoritative, or superficially democratic. It will be one in which there is genuine participation by the people in the decision-making process at all levels of government. Such a government will be highly decentralized, and the political leaders and administrators will be true representatives of the people and at all times be accountable to them.

The Goals of Development

In people-centered development, high rates of growth of national income will cease to be the major concern of development planning. Other goals will acquire primacy. Eradication of poverty, increase in employment, reduction of inequalities in incomes and wealth, checks on environmental degradation, improvement in the health, education, housing and social welfare of people will be regarded as the primary goals of development. In our different Five Year Plan documents, there is indeed mention of several of these goals of development, but due to our obsession with the rate of economic growth, these have received little attention in practice. When the superficial and spurious conception of development of conventional economics is abandoned, the energy, intelligence, creativity and enthusiasm of the people fuel a more authentic development process. There will be an inevitable surge in economic growth, but this growth will not be the major goal of development planning. It will be the result of a concerted effort of the people to bring about all-round improvement in their lives. This will also be reflected in a different composition of the national income. A large share of it will be devoted to health, education, social welfare, rural uplift, cottage industries, and care for the environment, and a smaller proportion will be allocated to defence, urbanisation, and luxury consumption.

Quality of Life

Since the overriding goal of true development is improvement in the quality of life of the people, the growth rate of GNP is a poor index of such improvement. Indeed, quality-of-life changes cannot be easily measured, though of course, such changes are quite perceptible, as the above-quoted account of the Cuban people by Oscar Lewis testifies. While at present we lack a satisfactory measure of the quality of life, there are several reliable measures of the physical quality of life of a people – degree of inequality in income distribution, percentage of population below the poverty line, infant mortality rates, life expectancy, overall literacy rates, and female literacy rates. The experience of several countries clearly shows that enhancement in these social indices can be brought about even at low levels of per capita GNP and that at higher levels, the physical quality of life does not necessarily improve.

Development Policy and Decentralisation

Since people-centred development rejects the neoclassical view that the pursuit of private profit will automatically ensure maximisation of social welfare, it assigns a central role to public control and policy in the development process. The rejection of capitalism that this type of development necessarily entails does not mean the automatic acceptance of centralised planning. The experience of centrally planned economies clearly shows that this kind of socialism results in the accumulation of too much power in the hands of the state and the administrative apparatus, and creates a strata of bureaucrats determined to preserve and promote its own interests and welfare. In people-centred development, public control will be exercised through decentralised decision-making at all levels of government. Since planning will be from below, and public agencies at all stages are accountable to the people, this form of development will not result in the accumulation of vast powers in the hands of the state that has been the bane of centralised socialism. Under market capitalism, not only is too much power exercised by large capitalists, but richer nations exercise undue control over developing countries. The fundamental principle of authentic development is self-reliance of the individual and the state. This means increasing the control of the individual over himself and over his environment. For the state, this means reducing dependence on foreign capital, foreign debt, foreign aid, and foreign trade.

Rejection of Unlimited Industrialisation

Conventional development recognises no limits to the possible levels of per capita income because it accepts no limits to industrialisation. It is now widely acknowledged that unbridled industrialisation is not possible because of the barriers of resource depletion, environmental pollution and social disintegration. Authentic development recognises the need to set definite limits on large-scale industrialisation, and promote cottage industries and small-scale production. Multinational corporations and indigenous corporate firms in their single-minded pursuit of profits deplete scarce non-renewable resources and cause irreparable environmental damage. Protection of the environment and promotion of eco-friendly development will receive high priority in any radically designed development programme. The unconstrained industrialisation path mainly benefits the rich, causes resource depletion and ecological damage, and harms the health and wellbeing of the people. So any people-centred development programme will drastically curtail production in the large-scale segment of the economy and replace it with production by the masses in decentralised, labour-intensive cottage industries. It will greatly limit the introduction of new capital-intensive technologies and new products because of the unemployment and environmental damage caused by them. In agriculture too the indiscriminate use of chemical fertilisers and pesticides will be rejected in favour of organic and biological alternatives and farming methods which are in harmony with nature and the environment.

Rural Development

In several developing countries, various strategies for rural development have been experimental with. These have not been conspicuously successful. The reason for this is not far to seek. Almost in every case, attempts at rural development have been made without an awareness of the dialectics of rural-urban development. No rural development scheme, however ambitious, will succeed as long as large-scale industrialisation is allowed to rage unchecked in the urban sector. Untrammelled industrialisation will inevitably suck the lifeblood out of the rural sector. Through a host of powerful levers of exploitation such as rural-urban migration, massive resource transfers, destruction of cottage industries, and the erosion of rural cultural values, it will sap the vitality of agrarian life. As long as these powerful structural forces are left intact, rural development efforts, however well-intentioned, are bound to fail.

Therefore, the first essential prerequisite of authentic rural development is the rejection of unlimited industrialisation in the urban sector. Once the pace of industrialisation is regulated by considerations of employment creation, ecological safety, and social need, the conditions necessary for the sustained growth and promotion of cottage industries will be created, and genuine decentralisation of the economy becomes possible. When large-scale industrialisation is controlled and production in decentralised cottage industries is promoted, a large number of these will naturally be located in villages where the resources and labour are available. In such an environment, authentic rural development will be possible, because the present exploitation of the village by the city through the transfer of resources and labour will cease. A more wholesome balance will be established between agriculture and industry and between the rural and urban sectors. This will lead to the regeneration of rural life and our villages will throb with new life and vitality. Once the green revolution based on monoculture, capital-intensive techniques, chemical fertilisers, herbicides and pesticides is stripped of its technological mystique and is shown to be what it really is – an environmentally destructive and wasteful form of agriculture, that depletes the soil, poisons the food, upsets the delicate balance of nature and man's immemorial relationship of harmony with it, the farmer will again regain his mastery over the art of agriculture. Human and animal wastes in town and country, instead of polluting our seas, rivers and lakes, can be converted into compost and help sustain organic agriculture in rural areas, based on diversified farming, crop rotation, and other methods of traditional agriculture. The myth that organic farming is less productive and less scientific than chemical agriculture will be laid to rest forever. And the question posed by the Japanese farmer-philosopher Masanobu Fukuoka will no longer be ignored.[8]

> I have demonstrated in my fields that natural farming produces harvests comparable to those of modern scientific agriculture. If the results of a non-active agriculture are comparable to those of science, at a fraction of the investment in labour and resources, then where is the benefit of scientific technology?

The green revolution generates and exacerbates rural inequalities and, as noted earlier, undermines the autonomy of the farmer by making him subservient to the agricultural expert and to domestic and foreign agribusiness interests. It was started in Third World countries as a surrogate for the much-needed agrarian reforms. Therefore, if the Green Revolution is to be reversed, it should be accompanied by the implementation of long overdue agrarian reforms. Only these measures can drastically reduce the incredible inequalities in incomes and wealth that exist in the rural areas and place land firmly in the hands of the tillers of the soil. This will ensure authentic rural development and the complete and sustained invigoration of rural life.

It is only in an environment of reasonable equality and social justice that the energy and creativity of the rural masses can be harnessed to the several tasks and functions of genuine rural development. At present, research is a high-powered activity restricted to members of the scientific community. When people become the authors of their own development, research will become the common activity of all those engaged in work. In rural areas, local people will be engaged in the solution of local problems with local resources. Local research will be aimed at collecting and critically examining the large fund of local knowledge accumulated over the centuries. It will attempt to improve on traditional knowledge and resurrect those portions which have been unjustly discredited or destroyed by so-called outside experts. When authentic, self-reliant rural development takes root, rural areas will be exciting places to visit and live in. The Gandhian vision of regenerated rural life will then become a reality. Gandhi wrote to Nehru in 1945:

> My ideal village will contain intelligent human beings. They will not live in dirt and darkness as animals. Men and women will be free and able to hold their own against anyone in the world. There will be neither plague, nor cholera, nor small-pox, no one will be idle, no one will wallow in luxury. It is possible to envisage railways, post and telegraph and the like.[9]

Again, in 1946 he gave another apt description of the village under authentic development:

> When our villages are fully developed, there will be no dearth in them of men with a high degree of skill and artistic talent. There will be village poets, village artists, village architects, linguists and research workers. In short, there will be nothing in life worth having which will not be had in the village. Today our villages are dung heaps. Tomorrow they will be like gardens of Eden, where dwell intelligent folk whom no one can deceive or exploit.[10]

But what of the town and city? Since there will be a balanced growth of agriculture and cottage industries in the villages, there will no longer be a large-scale exodus of people from rural areas to urban centres. Because of the slowing down of rural-urban migration, problems of congestion, overcrowding, growth of slums and shanty towns, transport bottlenecks and breakdowns, increase in crime and delinquency which bedevil city life today will gradually disappear, and our urban centres will become better places to live in. Thus under authentic development, there will be regeneration of both rural and urban life.

Stages of Development

The purpose of increasing material wealth surely should be to release human energies for the development and fulfilment of man's psychological, spiritual and creative potentialities. Abraham Maslow has suggested that the needs of human beings are hierarchical, and that as each level is satisfied, the subsequent level becomes salient. This order of needs is as follows:[11]

1. Physical requirements (food, shelter, clothing etc.)
2. Safety and security
3. Companionship and affection
4. Self-esteem and the esteem of others
5. Self-actualisation

Maslow's theory implies that as material wealth increases, the first two needs will be fully met; human beings then turn to the satisfaction of the other three higher needs. But the path of unlimited industrialisation followed in the West has not had this result. Instead, production of material goods and services has greatly exceeded the needs of physiological requirements and those of safety and security. Seductive and subliminal advertisement and the wilful manipulation of men's minds through powerful mass media have turned the desire for conspicuous consumption and the urge to keep up with the Joneses into two of the most powerful drives of the human psyche. As a result, with increasing standards of living, human beings instead of climbing up Maslow's ladder, have been deflected into the never-ending path of consumerism and increasing material wealth. Because of the permeation of material values, the needs of companionship and affection, can neither be appreciated nor be adequately met. On the other hand, the needs for self-esteem and self-actualisation have been re-defined almost wholly in material terms. Man's self-esteem and the need for other's esteem depend almost entirely on his position in the slippery pecking order of power and wealth.

Instead of being understood as one's ability to realise to the full one's potential, self-actualisation has come to mean scaling the heights of the material ladder.

In a society engaged in authentic development, material advancement will be only one among the several goals pursued by human beings. Such a society will provide the appropriate ambience and conditions for the satisfaction and fulfilment of the various needs delineated by Maslow. As people's physiological requirements and safety and security needs are met, they will naturally turn to the satisfaction of their higher needs.

Understanding, Action and Love

It was noted earlier that the so-called experts do not contribute to true development, because they distance themselves from the people, and create the false impression that they are the sole possessors of knowledge and wisdom. This robs people of the ability to think for themselves which is the *sine qua non* of true development. When authentic development is attempted, these experts will be banished from developing countries, and will be replaced by development workers, who will participate with work shoulder to shoulder with the people in the exciting tasks development. In such a context, research too will become fully participatory – the distinction between the researcher and the researched will vanish, and understanding and action will become inseparably joined. The distinctive attribute of the development worker will not be technical knowledge, but commitment to and compassion for the people among whom he works and lives.

V

The foregoing discussion on the nature and attributes of holistic development clearly shows that mere palliatives or cosmetic changes in society will not ensure such development. Nothing less than a radical and fundamental transformation of society and its values is needed to usher in the new development order. Both the society based on private profit and the society based on centralised socialism have demonstrated, in their separate ways, their extraordinary unsuitability for its nurture and growth. It has become increasingly clear that authentic development can take place only in a decentralised, fully participatory socialist society, built along the lines of Gandhian economics. In the affluent West too, there are signs that more and more thinking men and women are arriving at this conclusion. But by strong historical habit, the West traditionally likes to reinvent what it borrows from the East. So it calls the proposed paradigm 'New Age Economics.' By whatever name we refer to it, when society is reconstructed along the lines outlined here, the Gandhian vision will be a powerful beacon guiding its path.

NOTES

1. N. Maxwell, *From Knowledge to Wisdom*, p. 66.

2. Paul Baran, "The Political Economy of Growth", *Monthly Review Press*: New York, 1957, p.128.

3. See Michal Kalecki, "Theories of Growth in Different Social Systems", *Monthly Review*: October 1971.

4. J.A. Voelcker, "Report on Improvement of Indian Agriculture", 1891, quoted in R. Palme Dutt, *India Today*, London: 1940, p. 200.

5. Francis Bacon.

6. J. S. Bury, *Idea of Progress*, New York, Dover: 1975.

7. Oscar Lewis, "The Culture of Poverty", *The Scientifc American*, 215: 4, 1966, p. 25.

8. Masanobu Fukuoka, *The One-straw Revolution*, Rasulia: Friends Rural Centre, 1984.

9. Nehru, *A Bunch of Old Letters,* Asia Publishing House, London, 1960, p. 506.

10. *Harijan,* 28 July 1946.

11. Abraham Maslow, *Motivation and Personality,* New York: Harper & Row, 1970.

5

The Informal Sector: A Synoptic Reappraisal

Kamal Nayan Kabra

AMONG the concepts thrown up by the growth of development studies, particularly those on unemployment and poverty, the informal sector (IS) has evoked considerable debate. The present brief essay which is based on a broad survey of select recent works, attempts to systematise the insights provided by various studies.

The concept of informal sector (IS) emerged during the early seventies to facilitate a realistic evaluation of some aspects of the economies of the LDCs. It was designed to take into account the diversity of conditions concerning poverty, unemployment, and inequality and the multiplicity of organisational forms of economic activities. The concept appeared as an extension of the studies on "dualism" and enclave development. It amounted to, at least implicitly, a recognition of the need for giving the institutional-organisational factors, evolving as a result of historical processes and current compulsions, their legitimate place. However from the very beginning, there has been a divergence of views concerning the IS and its implications for development policy. As a result, the concept has acquired a certain degree of fuzziness.

To begin with, on the basis of some well-known definitions, we try to identify the basic features of the IS. This is followed by an overview of various empirical studies highlighting different facets of the informal sector. In the concluding part, we analyse these features in their historical context and attempt a generalised, overall conceptualisation of the IS, which may have some explanatory value as well.

The IS may essentially be regarded as a manifestation of dualism; it is taken as polar opposite of the formal sector (FS). It recognises so-called unemployed people as the working poor, rather than as good-for-nothing idlers. The informal sector is also regarded as one of the causes of low productivity in the LDCs. This places the causes of low productivity in a wider socio-economic, historical and organisational-institutional context.

It should be recognised that the IS extends to non-household sectors as well. Further, there are a large number of linkages between the IS and the formal sector, though the place of the former is normally subordinate. The IS also responds to demand-side factors arising from widespread poverty, which creates a specific pattern of demand for low-priced goods. The variety of sources from and forms in which the IS obtains its labour supply, and the variety of goods which are supplied by the IS, account for the great diversity visible in this sector. In fact, the diversity in the forms of organisation of economic activities, in all their significant aspects, constitute the essence of the IS. Building on this essential character, many eclectic and descriptive definitions and approaches to the IS were evolved. Based on a number of empirical studies, which started with a set of hypothesised characteristics, they produced a mixed bag of empirical evidence to support the existence of these characteristics. They failed to appreciate that the features of the IS are neither exclusive or exhaustive, nor necessarily uniform all over the informal sector. They could not highlight the variety in the forms of use and hire of labour, organisation of production, participation in various markets, and use of self-labour to earn a livelihood. In fact, these approaches could not identify the *differentia specifica* of the IS vis-a-vis the formal sector. Moreover, they were ahistorical. As a result, the empirically observed features could not be appropriately woven together to come up with a coherent concept. The IS was basically treated as the residual form of the organised formal sector.

A large number of studies (see References), in many different countries and continents, of several industries in the informal sector, mostly in urban areas, have been carried out. On the basis of these studies, one can arrive at an understanding of the features characterising the putative IS in various countries at different stages of their development.

IS activities generally make use of various inputs supplied, to a very large extent, by the owner-operators themselves. Hired resources and/or purchased inputs are also used to some degree. To the extent external finance is required, it is generally obtained from the informal money market, though lately some public financial agencies have also started extending assistance to the IS. While the LDCs recorded a high rate of growth during the fifties and sixties and generally continued to expand even afterwards. The number of persons engaged in the IS, and the value of their output and capital stock, has been constantly increasing. The informal activities have also shown greater variety over time. This implies that the IS has less to do with the rate of growth of economies and more with the pattern of growth.

Notwithstanding the great deal of diversity in various aspects of the IS, one can find some common features. Similarly, though the IS is characterised by relative isolation, it has a number of linkages with the formal sector. In fact, the IS is not a new phenomenon. It has its origins in the colonial period, when it was recognised as the bazaar sector. With colonial penetration and the attendant influx of new technology and capitalist forms of organisation, pre-colonial economic activities and forms of organisation began to decline. However, since the process of capitalist growth was inadequate, lopsided and non-symbiotic, (in one word, involutionary) a number of conventional economic activities survived, even as a number of new ones emerged to absorb the labour released by the declining occupations but unutilised by the formal sector. Thus, the IS growth is associated with important changes in the occupational structure of LDCs.

Viewed a little differently, the new technology and products introduced in the colonial era could not wholly displace their predecessors. Thus, the IS became an arena of surviving conventional technologies and products, though in somewhat adapted forms, based on limited amounts of modern capital goods, markets and finance, and responding to local demand. However, the bulk of IS technology was non-patented and non-marketed, and was generally evolved by the worker-entrepreneurs themselves.

It is incorrect to consider the IS as a non-market sector. Most of the activities in this sector are market-based, involving circulation in the commodity sphere. However, the circulation sphere often does not extend to the entire range of inputs and their production. In a way, one can say that the IS represents protomarket or embryonic market relations. Alternatively, the IS often operates in local, segmented markets, with limited linkages or on a limited circuit. It is generally involved in community circulation, rather than full-scale commodity production. The IS-FS linkages are generally through various markets. Thus, IS leads to fragmentation of the market, thereby limiting its size and growth. IS entities are the relatively weaker partners in market transactions. Their activities are more labour-intensive. Labour is generally obtained from family circles and rarely goes beyond the local labour market. In fact, one can say that there is not a very marked technological differentiation among the IS activities. With the survival of older and adapted technologies, and the introduction of new ones, the IS may be taken to represent a technological continuum.

IS entities neither seek nor are accorded registration by state agencies. In the absence of any requirement to report to such agencies, they can easily bypass government regulations. In fact, there are hardly any regulations which strictly or exclusively apply to IS activities.

In terms of the range of goods and services produced, the IS presents significant sectoral diversity. It is neither exclusively urban nor rural. For example, small peasants working with family labour and recorded as paying land revenue constitute a key component of the rural IS. Even as more advanced capitalist agriculture develops, small peasant farming as a lower form of production survives. Small retailers, home producers of various goods, craftsmen, and informal moneylenders in rural areas also form a part of the IS.

Generally, IS entities have few opportunities for political participation. They have limited direct access to the public systems. Such access is usually obtained by means of intermediaries. For economic, political and administrative reasons, the planning and policy intervention system have rarely been designed to reach them directly.

The IS can be said to represent small and limited entrepreneurial response to special conditions prevailing in the LDCs. The informal sector is an instance of incipient entrepreneurship. However, it is incorrect to regard the IS as a consequence of the suppression of entrepreneurial response by means of public policies.

Nor is it correct to say that all microenterprises belong to the IS. Most LDCs have a small-scale, registered sector, which uses modern technology, and has capitalist forms of organisation, wide linkages with the formal economy, and official registration. Such activities, simply because of their small scale of operations, such enterprises cannot be regarded as a component of the IS.

Since the IS generally caters to the demands of the poor, it often supplies low-cost recycled goods, or goods based on recycled inputs. However, many luxury and artistic items are also produced in the IS. The IS labour market is not a fully developed one. It is a mixture of self-employment and family work along with some amount of hired labour, involving different, mixed modes of payment. Generally, one finds that piece-rate wages prevail in the IS. The variety in forms of labour use in the IS shows that the dichotomy between wage and non-wage labour is often overstated. Broadly speaking, based on labour market relations, there are two types of IS enterprises: (*a*) those based on hired labour, and (*b*) those. usually small establishments, which mainly rely on their own labour and other factors of production. Their activities can, therefore, be regarded as intermediate forms of production during the period of transition of domestic industry to either capitalist or post-capitalist or even socialist industry. In most of the LDCs, the involutionary pattern of growth leads to a segmentation of the labour market and the growth of informal enterprises. In the early industrialising countries, service enterprises dealing with maintenance, repairs, transport, etc., tend to follow the IS pattern.

On the basis of various features discussed above, the IS can be regarded as a mini-capitalist or petty capitalist sector. Categorising the informal sector as just a residual form ignores its analytical, evolutionary, systemic and mixed features.

However, none of the features discussed above is sufficient by itself to make a particular unit or its activity informal. Similarly, the absence of anyone of these factors does not exclude a unit or activity from the IS. In other words, no single feature defines the IS. Before a unit or activity can be classed as informal, a combination of these features has to be identified. Thus, an analytical framework which provides an operational *differentia specifica* of the IS has to be developed.

Another question is the supposed illegality or supralegality of the informal sector. It is clear that non-recognition, non-recording and non-monitoring of IS activities cannot by themselves make these activities illegal. It is therefore, incorrect to identify the IS with the black economy. Practices which are not strictly legal are not confined to the IS. They can do exist within the formal sector as well. For example, the corporate sector (a legal entity par excellence) adopts many devices like under- and over-consumption expenditure by promoters-controllers, falsification of accounts, etc., which infringe economic regulations, to generate black incomes.

On the other hand, some IS activities may be legal. They are undertaken with the help of loans from the FS, and taxes are paid on the incomes they generate. Thus, there is an overlap between the IS and the black economy. Actually it can be argued that illegality is the consequence of informality.

This is a connection between widespread poverty and the existence of a sizeable IS. This is because poverty makes for a pattern of demand which only the informal activities can satisfy.

It also generates labour supplies which only the IS can absorb, particularly in the context of mimetic, involutionary growth experienced by the countries of the South. However, within the IS itself, there are large income differences, as there are between the formal and informal sectors. The IS owes its emergence more to large and persistent inequalities in incomes (a factor critical to the prevalence of widespread poverty) than to absolute poverty. These inequities give rise to multifaceted differentiation and patterns of growth which are incompatible with the adequate and equitable incorporation of people into the structures of the economy, polity and society.

One can see many different motivational and behavioural patterns in the IS. This diversity makes for the IS-FS continuum, rendering their dichotomisation an abstraction. The IS derives its overall character from the predominant features of the economy. Generally, one can see both symbiotic as well as parasitic relationships between the two sectors. The two sectors do not seem to follow different laws of production and reproduction. They condition and influence each other.

The IS is found not only in LDCs but also in the developed industrialised countries, as well as those claiming to follow the socialist path. However, the relative role, significance, and some of the key characteristics of the informal sector will differ depending on the context. In developed countries, the IS is mainly an instrument which affords flexibility in the use of labour, supply of goods and services, and in bringing about adjustments in the face of rapid technological change. From this it follows that by not permitting informal activities to be undertaken legally, the industrialised 'socialist' countries denied themselves an instrument for imparting flexibility to the operation of the system.

Some of the important characteristics of the IS can be inferred by a comparative historical analysis of the origin and growth of the IS in the colonial and the post-colonial periods. During the colonial period, the IS emerged as an adjustment to the superimposition of capitalist institutions and industrialisation on the economies of the LDCs. However, in the post-colonial phase, the IS has become strong and diversified in response to the involutionary economic growth and industrialisation, particularly owing to the inability of these processes to absorb both the surplus labour from the agricultural-rural sectors and the internal growth from the urban-industrial sectors. As a result of this pattern of growth, differentiation in the economy increased.

People with very little command over capital, and financial and technological resources devised a multitude of activities to complement their labour power. Depending on their location on the socio-economic ladder, they produced certain goods and services to eke out a living. Naturally, they could not adopt advanced forms of production, characteristic of the dominant mode of production – one which had marginalised them. Thus, many activities with varying degrees of informality emerged in the LDCs.

Given the variety, dispersal and large number of these activities, their administrative recognition or recording is extremely difficult and costly. Further, given the constraints of rather limited access to resources and a hostile environment, owing to the dominance by a few, the marginalised have to take recourse to informal activities to meet their subsistence needs. The number of IS units engaged in such activities are naturally legion. Thus, the IS shares with the black economy the characteristic of being non-recorded.

Because of intrasectoral linkages and linkages with the organised sector, the IS is no longer a marginal or fringe sector. It involves a sizeable part of the labour force and contributes significantly to national output, though, its precise estimation remains difficult. On the basis of the above analysis, it can be said that the IS is an epitome of multiple unevenness and grassroots adjustment. It is a response of the vulnerable and sidelined sections of society to the inadequacies and limitations of a system which fails to take care of their basic needs. It indicates the simultaneous existence of many different forms of production.

This is a phenomenon, which can be seen both at the global level and within countries. The South may well be regarded as something akin to the IS. It represents an ensemble of different forms of production under the overall framework of the dominant mode of production. The conceptual and theoretical tools of conventional development theories which are essentially rooted in the neoclassical paradigm, adapted to a certain extent to the Keynesian macroeconomics, are quite inadequate to deal with such a complex reality as is represented by the IS. Hence, a multidisciplinary approach to its study is required, and organisational-institutional variables will have to occupy a key place. It is only on this basis that one can devise development strategies and policies for the regulation, development and integration of the IS.

REFERENCES

Banerjee, N., "The Unorganised Sector and the Planners", in A. K. Bagchi (ed.), *Economy, Polity and Society,* New Delhi: Oxford University Press, 1988.

Bienefeld, M., "The Informal Sector and Peripheral Capitalism. The Case of Tanzania," *Bulletin of Development Studies,* 6:(31) 1979, pp. 53-73.

Boeke, J.H., *Economic and Economic Policy in Dual Societies,* New York: Institute of Pacific Relations, 1953.

Bose, A.N., "Informal Sector: Problems and Prospects" *Nagarlok,* April-June, 1980.

Brandt, W., *North-South: A Programme for Survival,* The Report of the Independent Commission on International Development Issues, London: Pan Books 1980.

Breman, J., "A Dualistic Labour System: A Critique of the 'Informal Sector' Concept", *Economic and Political Weekly,* 27 November, and 4 and 11 December, 1976.

Brett, E.A., *Colonialism and Underdevelopment in East Africa: The Politics of Economic Change, 1919-1939,* 1973.

Bromley, R. and Gerry, C. (eds.), in *Casual Work and Poverty in Third World Cities,* Chichester, 1979.

Central Statistical Organisation (CSO), GOI (Government of India), *Economic Census, 1980*: *All India Report*, New Delhi: Hovernment of India.

CSO, *National Account Statistics: Sources and Method*, New Delhi: Government of India, 1980.

CSO, GOI, *All India Report on Economic Census* New Delhi, 1977.

Chakravarty, S., "Sharing the Urban Economic Space", in P. M. Mathew, (ed.), *The 'Informal Sector' in India: Critical Perspectives,* Eastern Books: New Delhi, forthcoming.

Chandavarkar, A., "The Informal Sector: Empty Box or Port Manteau Concept? (A Comment)", *World Development,* 16:10, 1988, pp. 1259-61.

Charmes, J., "A Critical Review of Concepts, Definitions and Studies in the Informal Sector", in D. Turnham, and others (ed.), *The Informal Sector Revisited*, Paris: OECD, 1990.

Chevalier, J.M., *Civilisation and the Stolen Gift: Capital, Kin and Culture in Eastern Peru*, Toronto: University of Toronto Press, 1982.

Davies, R., "Informal Sector in Subordinate Mode of Production? A Model" in Bromley and Gerry (eds.) in *Casual Work and Poverty*, 1979.

Duller, H.J., *Development Technology,* London: Routledge and Kegan Paul, 1982.

Dobb, M., *Studies on the Development of Capitalism*, London: Routledge and Kegan Paul, 1981.

Engels, F., *The Condition of the Working-Class in England in 1844*, London: George Allen and Unwin Ltd., 1952.

Fitzgerald, P., "Markets, Commodity Production and Indigenous Farmers in Colonial Algeria" in C. Dewey, (ed.), *The State and Market*, Delhi: Manohar, 1987, pp. 47-65.

Geertz, C., *Peddlars and Princes: Social Change and Economic Modernisation in Two Indonesian Towns,* Chicago: University of Chicago Press, 1963.

Gerry, C., "Small Scale Manufacturing and Repairs in Dakar: A Survey of Market Relations within the Urban Economy", in Bromley and Gerry, (eds.), *Casual Work and Poverty*, 1979.

Government of India, Dept. of Economic Affairs, *First Report of the National Income Committee,* Calcutta: Government of India, 1951.

Habib, I., "Notes on Forms and Process of Capital Accumulation" (mimeo), a paper presented at the Indo-Soviet joint Seminar on Modes of Production, Indian Council of Historical Research, New Delhi, 1989.

Hariss, J., "Urban Poverty and the Labour Market: A Study on the City of Coimbatore", in Mathew, (ed.) *'Informal Sector' in India*, forthcoming.

Hart, K., "Informal Income Opportunities of Urban Government in Ghana", *Journal of Modern African Studies*, II, 1973, 61-69.

Hill, Polly, *Development Economics on Trial,* Cambridge: Cambridge University Press, 1987.

Hugon, P., "The Informal Sector Revisited (in Africa)" in Turnham *et al.* (eds.), *Informal Sector Revisited*, 1990.

Illich, I., *Shadow Work*, Boston: Marion Boyars, 1981.

ILO, *Employment, Incomes and Equity: A Strategy for Increasing Productive Employment in Kenya,* Geneva: International Labour Organisation, 1972.

Jaganathan, V.N., *Informal Markets in Developing Countries,* New York: Oxford University Press, 1987.

Kabra, K.N., "The Urban Informal Sector and Development Policy: Growth and Equity", theme paper for the Seminar on Informal Sector, Institute of Applied Manpower Research, New Delhi, 1988a.

Kabra, K.N., "The Joint Existence of the Formal and the Informal Sectors. The Case of Indian Railways" (unpublished), Indian Institute of Public Administration, New Delhi, 1988b.

Kabra, K.N., *Black Economy in India: Problems and Policies,* Delhi: Chanakya 1982.

Khundker, Nasreen, "The Fuzziness of the Informal Sector: Can we Afford to Throw Out the Baby with the Bath Water? (A Comment)", *World Development,* XIV: 10, 1988, pp.1263-65.

King, K., "Research, Policy and the Informal Sector: African Experience", in Turnham, *et al* (eds.), *Informal Sector Revisited,* 1990.

King, K., "Kenya's Informal Machine Makers: A Study of Small-Scale Industry in Kenya Emergent Artisan Society", *World Development,* 1974.

Kotwal, O.P., *Indian Economy in Soviet Perspective,* New Delhi: Sterling, 1979.

Lenin, V.I., *The Development of Capitalism in Russia,* Moscow: Progress Publishers, 1977.

Levkosky, A., *The Development Countries' Social Structure,* Moscow: Progress Publishers, 1987.

Lewls, A., (1954) *Economic Development with Unlimited Supply of Labour,* The Manchester School 22, 1954, pp.139-91.

Leys, C. "The State and Crisis of Simple Commodity Production in Africa", in IDS Bulletin, 18: 3, 1987, 45-47.

Mathew, P.M., "*Development Theory, Planning and Information*", in Mathew, (ed.), *'Informal Sector' in India,* forthcoming.

Mathew, P.M., (ed.), *The 'Informal Sector' in India: Critical Perspectives,* New Delhi: Eastern Books, forthcoming.

Mathew, P.M., "The Industrial Informal Sector in a Developing Economy: An Inter-regional Study" (mimeo), ICSSR, New Delhi, 1987.

Menshikov, S., *The Economic Structure of Socialism: An Attempted Prognosis*, Moscow: Progress Publishers, 1990.

Miller, S.M., "The Pursuit of Informal Economics", *Economic Impact,* Vol. 63, 1988, pp. 23-26.

Morishima, M., *Why has Japan 'Succeeded'?: Western Technology and the Japanese Ethos,*Cambridge: Cambridge University Press, 1983.

Moser, C., "Informal Sector or Petty Commodity Production. Dualism or Dependence in Urban Development", *World Development*, 6: (9/1/10), 1978, pp. 1041-64.

Moser, C. and Judith Marsie-Hazen, *A Survey of Empirical Studies in Industrial and Manufacturing Activities in the Informal Sector in Developing Countries,* Vienna: UNIDO, 1984.

Nattrass, N.J., (1987) "Street Trading in Transkei – A Struggle Against Poverty, Persecution, and Prosecution", *World Development,* 15: 7, 1987, pp. 861-76.

Owens, E., *The Future of Freedom in the Developing World: Economic Development as Political Reform,* New York: Pergamon Press, 1987.

Peattie, Lisa, "An Idea in Good Currency and How it Grew: The Informal Sector", *World Development,* 15: 7, 1987, pp. 851-60.

Portes, Alejandro, "The Informal Sector and the World Economy: Notes on the Structure of Subsidised Labour", *IDS Bulletin,*9:4, 1978.

Sen, A.K., *Choice of Techniques: An Aspect of the Theory of Planned Economic Development,*Oxford: Blackwell, 1960.

Sethuraman, S.V. (ed.), *The Urban Informal Sector in Developing Countries: Employment, Poverty, and Environment*, ILO: Geneva, 1982.

Sinclair, Stuarat, W., *Urbanisation and Labour Markets in Developing Countries,* London: Croom Helm, 1978.

Smith, C.A., "Forms of Production: Fresh Approaches to Simple Commodity Production", *Journal of Peasant Studies*, II:49, 1984, pp. 201-21.

Soto, H, de. "The Informals Pose an Answer to Marx", *Economic Impact*, Vol. 67, 1989, pp.56-60.

Souza, P.R. and V. E. Tokman, "The Informal Sector in Latin America", *International Labour Review,* January-February, 1976.

Stressman, W. Paul, "Home-based Enterprises in Cities of Developing Countries", *Economic Development and Cultural Change,* 36:1, 1987.

Stuvel, G., *National Accounts Analysis,* Hampshire: Macmillan, 1986.

Tax, Sol, *Penny Capitalism: A Guatemalan Indian Economy,* Chicago: University of Chicago Press, 1953.

Todaro, M.P., *Economic Development in the Third World: An Introduction to Problems and Policies in a Global Perspective,* London: Longman, 1987.

Turnham, D. et. al, (eds.), *The Informal Sector Revisited,* Paris: OECD, 1990.

Wiles, P.J.D., *Economic Institutions Compared,* Oxford: Oxford University Press, 1977.

6

Institutional Sanctions, Choice and the Secondary Food System: Incompleteness of Sen's Entitlement and Deprivation Thesis as an Explanation for Hunger*

Amitava Mukherjee

Introduction

THE prevalent literature on the subject of food security, drawing from the "entitlement and deprivation thesis" (Sen, 1981 and Dreze and Sen, 1989), defines an individual to be food secure when there is enough food in the system that he can buy (food availability), when he has the capacity to buy that food (ability to buy food), and when the food that the individual buys provides him with the requisite nutritional value (World Bank, 1986). Where any of these conditions is not satisfied, the person's food security is endangered. That is, the person becomes food insecure.

We are of the view that individuals can be food insecure even when these conditions are satisfied and to that extent, there are gaps in the entitlement and deprivation thesis. There are three more conditions – namely, the existence of institutional sanction to access to available food, the exercise of choice of access to the food that is available, and the presence of a secondary food system – which must be satisfied before individuals can be guaranteed to be food secure. The principal concern of this chapter is to establish that the satisfaction of these three additional conditions are as essential as the ones emphasised by Sen, before individuals can become food secure.

---

* Thanks are due to Shri Upendranath, Policy Unit, ACTIONAID India, for very useful suggestions. An earlier version of the paper has been published in the Indian Economic Journal, September-December, 1996.

There have been other debates (for instance, Bowbrick, 1986; Sen's reply in Sen, 1986; Nolan and Sender, 1992; Sen's reply in Sen, 1992; and implicitly Dasgupta, 1993) about the entitlement and deprivation thesis, but additionality arguments have been in comparative neglect.

This chapter is divided into four parts. Because we wish to attempt a modification and extension of the entitlement and deprivation thesis, in Part II, we will examine the different concepts of entitlement and deprivation, and how they relate to food (in) security, based on Sen's thesis. In Part III, we will examine the gaps in the entitlement and deprivation thesis, and establish the conditions that need to be additionally satisfied for ensuring that individuals are food secure. We will also show, using certain evidence that in reality, when the additional conditions mentioned in Part III are not satisfied, food insecurity ensues. Finally, in Part IV, brief conclusions will be drawn.

Conceptual Specifications

According to food availability decline arguments, an individual is food insecure because there is not enough to eat. The entitlement and deprivation thesis, on the other hand, holds that food insecurity can also be seen as the characteristic of the person not having enough to eat, which is not tantamount to saying that "there isn't enough to eat." The latter could be the cause of the former, but it is not the only cause. It is argued that whether and how food insecurity is related to food availability is a matter for factual investigation and that food availability argument says things about food, considered on its own, whereas food insecurity statements are about the relationship of the person to food. Except in cases where an individual deliberately starves, so argues the entitlement and deprivation thesis, food insecurity statements translate readily into statements of ownership of food by the person, and to understand food insecurity, one has to go into the structure of ownership of food.

Ownership relations, according to Sen, are one among many kinds of entitlement relationships, which, as accepted in a private ownership market economy, typically include the following amongst others.

Trade-based Entitlement

An individual is entitled to own goods and services which he or she obtains by trading something owned by him or her with a willing party or parties.

Production-based Entitlement

An individual is entitled to own goods and services which he or she obtains by arranging production, and using resources owned by him or her or by hiring resources from willing parties which meet the agreed conditions of trade. Production-based entitlement may also be construed as an exchange with nature when considered in the context of food security.

Own Labour Entitlement

An individual is entitled to one's own labour power and thus to the trade-based and production-based entitlements related to his or her labour power. That is, an individual is entitled to whatever he or she produces with his or her labour, and or whatever he or she has command over by exchanging that labour.

Inheritance and Transfer Entitlement

An individual is entitled to own commodities that are willingly given to him or her by another who legitimately owns them. This could be either during the lifetime of the latter if the commodities are transferred as a gift, or after the latter's death, when they are transferred by way of a will, inheritance or bequest.

Commodities owned by an individual are called "endowment" or "direct entitlement". Goods and services which an individual receives by way of gift or charity are called "non-entitlement transfers".

In a market economy individuals can also exchange the commodities they own for another collection of commodities, either through trading (trade-based entitlement), or through production (production-based entitlement), or through some combination of the two. The set of all alternative bundles of commodities that an individual can acquire through such means has been collectively called "exchange entitlement" of what the individual owns. We shall discuss this in greater detail in the next section.

There can be, according to Sen, other forms of entitlements as well, such that an individual may be entitled to enjoy the fruits of some property without being able to trade it for anything else. For instance, individuals can use the river water for personal use, but cannot sell or buy a river. Or tribals living in forests in India can use forest products like honey, fruits and small timber, but cannot sell the trees. One can also inherit the property of a deceased person who did not "will" it to anyone, through some kind of kinship-based inheritance accepted in the country in question. One may also have certain entitlements related to unclaimed objects on the basis of discovery.

Exchange Entitlements

The exchange entitlement mapping is the relation that specifies the set of exchange entitlements for each ownership, which defines the possibilities that would be open to individuals corresponding to each ownership situation. An individual, according to the entitlement and deprivation thesis, will be food insecure if, for the ownership that he or she actually has, the exchange entitlement set does not contain any feasible bundle which includes enough food. Given the entitlement mapping, it is thus possible to identify those ownership bundles that must lead to food insecurity in the absence of non-entitlement transfers (such as charity). Based on an individual's ownership bundle (including labour power), Sen has identified the following five factors which determine an individual's exchange entitlement:

1. The individual's ability to find employment, the duration thereof, and the wage rate at which the individual will be employed.

2. The individual's ability to earn by selling his/her non-labour assets, and the costs to be incurred by the individual to buy whatever he/she may wish to buy.
3. The commodities that the individual can produce with his/her own labour power and the resources he/she can buy and manage.
4. The cost, to the individual, of purchasing resources or resource services, and the value of the products which he/she can sell.
5. The social security benefits which the respective individual is entitled to and the taxes, etc., that he/she may be enjoined by law to pay.

The extent to which an individual can avoid food insecurity will depend upon both his or her ownership of commodities and on the exchange entitlement mapping that he or she individual faces. A general decline in food supply may indeed cause an individual to be exposed to food insecurity through a rise in prices, with an unfavourable impact upon his or her exchange entitlement. Even where the food insecurity of the person is thus caused by food shortage, the immediate reason for the individual's food insecurity will be a decline in his or her exchange entitlement.

Significantly enough, according to Sen, an individual's exchange entitlement may worsen for reasons other than a general decline in food supply. For instance, consider an individual 'A' and two groups in an economy. Let 'A' belong to Group 1. Then given the same systematic total food supply, if the income of Group-2, to which 'A' does not belong, increases and it starts buying more food, prices can rise, worsening the individual "A's" exchange entitlement. Then again, some economic change, such as an IMF-World Bank enjoined structural adjustment programme leading to a cut in the size of government, may affect the employment possibilities of the individual if he or she is a government employee, thereby worsening his or her exchange entitlement. It is also possible that an individual's wages may fall behind prices, as it happened in India in 1991-92, when prices rose by upto 17 per cent on a month-to-month basis, but wages remained almost static, during the same period, on a month-to-month basis, particularly in the rural sector (Government of India, 1992). Yet another scenario in which the exchange entitlement of the individual can worse is when the commodities that he or she is engaged in goes up. This happened in India for the agriculture sector, following the 1991-92 budget of the Government of India, which raised the prices of fertilisers by as much as 30 per cent (*ibid.*) which is tantamount to raising the input prices for agriculturists. These diverse influences on exchange entitlements, according to the entitlement and deprivation thesis, are as relevant as the overall volume of food supply vis-a-vis the population of the country.

Food Supply and Food Insecurity

However, the discussion on food insecurity emanating from food supply falling behind population growth has attracted considerable attention in recent times. According to the entitlement and deprivation thesis, this gives only a partial picture because it is not merely falling food availability, but also food entitlement failure which is the cause of food insecurity. Sen summons evidence from accounts of some of the worst famines (acute cases of food insecurity) in history to establish that famines have occurred without any significant declines in food availability (Sen, 1981: chapter 6).

The entitlement and deprivation thesis thus holds that food insecurity depends not merely on food supply but also on its distribution, which has certain ramifications. The issues for examination in the domain of food security then revolve around the different factors which, determine distribution of food between different sections of the community. The Senian entitlement approach directs one's attention to questions dealing with ownership patterns and, less obviously, to the various influences that affect entitlement mapping. The influence of food supply itself on the prevalence of food insecurity works through the entitlement relations. If one person in eight are regularly food insecure in the world, this is seen more as the person's inability to establish entitlement to enough food, where the question of the actual availability of food is not directly involved.

Endowment and Exchange

Clearly, the entitlement approach to the food insecurity of an individual concentrates on his or her ability to command food through the legal means available, including the use of production possibilities, trade opportunities, entitlements vis-a-vis the state, and other methods of acquiring food. Individuals are food insecure either because they do not have the ability to command enough food, or because the ability to avoid food insecurity is not used. The entitlement approach concentrates on the former, to the exclusion of the other possibility, and it concentrates on those means of commanding food that are legitimate under the prevailing legal system. As Sen 1981 puts it:

> While it is an approach of some generality, it does not make any attempt at including all possible influences that can cause food insecurity, for example illegal transfers (e.g., looting) and choice failure (e.g., owing to inflexible food habits).

The entitlement approach concentrates on each individual's entitlement to commodity bundles which include food, and views food insecurity as resulting from a failure of the individual to be entitled to a bundle of commodities with enough food.

Normally, Sen 1981 argues, there is a menu before an individual to choose from. Suppose E1 is the entitlement set of an individual in a given society, in a given situation, where E1 consists of a set of alternative commodity bundles, any one of which the person can decide to have. In an open economy, with private ownership typical of a capitalist system, E1 can be characterised as depending on two parameters – the endowment of the person (the ownership bundle) and the exchange entitlement mapping (the function that specifies the set of alternative commodity bundles that the person can command respectively for each endowment bundle).

Suppose, a farmer has a piece of land, has his/her own

labour power, and has a few other resources, which together make up his or her endowment. Starting from that endowment, the farmer can either produce a bundle of goods, say food, that will be his/her own; or by selling his/her labour power, he/she can earn a wage, and with that wage buy commodities, including food. The farmer also has the option to grow some cash crops on the piece of land owned by him/her, which can be sold to buy food and other commodities that the farmer may need. There are many other permutations and combinations that the farmer may opt for. For instance, he/she can exercise the option of not cultivating the land at all. Instead it can be leased out, and the rent used to purchase different commodity bundles including food. The set of all such available commodity bundles to the farmer, in a given economic situation, is the exchange entitlement of his/her endowment. The exchange entitlement mapping, according to the entitlement and deprivation thesis, specifies the exchange entitlement set of alternative commodity bundles respectively for each endowment bundle.

In the case of a wage labourer, by exchanging the labour power he/she owns for wages (the exchange takes the form of employment), the labourer establishes command over some money, which can then be used to secure control over some commodity bundle or the other. The endowment of an individual is given by the initial ownership, namely, the labourer's labour power, the landowner's landholdings etc. These endowments can be used to establish entitlements in the form of holdings of alternative commodity bundles through trade. Instances of this include the labourer taking up employment and purchasing commodities out of the wages earned, or a landowner renting out land and purchasing commodities with the rent so earned, or the farmer selling off a portion of his crop to buy other goods and services, and so forth.

Direct entitlement failure can arise for individuals or groups who produce food. Trade entitlement failure, on the other hand, can visit those who produce commodities other than food – that is, those who sell their commodities to buy food – because of a fall in either the price of the commodities produced or a fall in quantity of commodities produced. The latter can occur either owing to an autonomous production decline, such as a cash crop being destroyed by drought or pest attack, or to an induced decline in output, caused by say insufficiency of demand. For instance, a mason may find himself involuntarily unemployed because of a slump in the construction industry. Or, jute growers in West Bengal may have had to cut down the output of jute as the demand has declined following the dismantling of the Soviet Union, the principal buyers of jute and jute bags.

In terms of the entitlement and deprivation thesis, it is possible for a occupation group to suffer both direct entitlement failure and trade entitlement failure, since the relevant group may produce a commodity that is both directly consumed and exchanged for food. An agriculturist in Bihar or West Bengal who grows rice, consumes this food article to meet his own food requirements but to meet his other needs, say of salt and sugar, sells the rice grown by him at favourable exchange rates.

An individual can face food insecurity if some economic change takes place in the system which makes it impossible for him or her to acquire any commodity bundle which has enough food to meet subsistence need. Such entitlement failure can be caused by a fall in the person's endowment (like alienation of land from a landowner, or the loss of labour power of a mason due to a limb injury caused by an accident while at work). It can also come about by an unfavourable shift in exchange entitlement (like loss of employment, fall in wages, rise in food prices, drop in the prices of goods or services the individual sells, decline in self-employment, fall in production and so on). Therefore, the relevance of seeing food insecurity as entitlement failures – which can occur even when food availability is not reduced, and even when the ratio of food to population rises rather than declines – cannot be overemphasised.

The entitlement and deprivation thesis further argues that an individual who is engaged in growing food, and succeeds in growing more than enough for survival, may concurrently be food insecure because he may not have the legal right to use the food so produced. In many cases of food insecurity during famines, the majority of the victims are indeed agricultural labourers. They are often engaged primarily in the production of food, but the legal nature of their contract, with the owner of the land or the farmer for whom they work entitles them to receive a wage payment from the farmer or the landowner in exchange for labour. Typically, they have no right to the food grown by their own labour, that is, no entitlement to the food produced. This is so notwithstanding the fact that the food so produced could be the basis of survival for the labourers and their dependent-households. Wages may be paid in foodgrains but wages so paid in kind (food in this case) as less than the food produced.

Where a labourer, whether employed in foodgrains production or otherwise, is paid a certain sum of money as wages, he or she attempts to become food secure by using the wages to purchase food in the market. The quantity of food which can be bought will, of course, depend on its prevailing price. Thus, if food prices rise very rapidly, without money wages rising correspondingly (and indeed wages nearly always lag behind prices), the labourers who themselves have grown the food may fail to acquire the food they (and their dependents) need for surviving. The food grown by the employer (typically the owner of the land) and the wage payment made to the labourer end the latter's (primary food grower's) right to the produce, irrespective of whether the wage so received by the does, or does not, yield enough food for the labourer (primary food grower) to be food secure.

Similarly, an individual who acquires food by producing some other commodity and selling it in the market to acquire food has to depend on the actual ability to sell the produce he or she has produced as also on the relative price of that product vis-a-vis food prices.

If either the sale of the commodity produced by the individual fails to materialise, or at the prevailing food prices, the person may acquire a quantity of food which is insufficient for his survival, he or she has no option but to be food insecure (go hungry).

It is also important to note that uncertainty and vulnerability can be features of subsistence production involving both "exchange with nature" and "market exchange". This precariousness is particularly visible in economies where a substantial proportion of the victims are frequently small and marginal farmers, hit *inter alia*, by a collapse of their "direct entitlement" to the food they normally grow. It would be misleading, according to the entitlement and deprivation thesis, to hold self-provisioning as being synonymous with being food secure. The peasant farmer, like the landless labourer, has no guaranteed entitlement to the necessities of life.

Extended Entitlements

While the concept of entitlement has so far focused on a person's legal rights of ownership, the entitlement and deprivation thesis accepts that there are some social relations that take the broader form of accepted legitimacy rather than legal rights that are justiciable. For instance, by a well-established convention, the male head of a household in several parts of traditional societies, such as in India, receives more favourable treatment in the division of the family's total consumption like having the first claim on, say, the meat or fish in the family's diet, or receiving better and greater medical attention in case of illness. Such claim to preferential treatment by the male head of the household, is accepted as legitimate and is thus effective, even though it is neither a claim enjoined by law established or justifiable in a court or enforced by the state.

This is more often the case in households where the male is the breadwinner. For instance, Greenough (1982) held that:

> the patriarchal values of Bengali Hindu society required priority to be given to the feeding of the male members of the household so as to ensure the continuance of the male line. The counterpart of this was a cultural expectation that women would sacrifice their food and ultimately their lives to enable their husbands and sons to survive.

Continuing this investigation further, it has been found that in many parts of South Asia, "even in normal times men are fed first in peasant households. Women eat after the men, receiving a smaller and poorer share of food." (Arnold, 1988, p. 89). Moreover, when food is short (or when disease strikes), the male children get more medical attention and food resources.

The foregoing are, according to Sen, legally weaker forms of entitlements. Nevertheless, such socially sanctioned rights may be extremely important in determining the intrahousehold availability and consumption of food, health care or other commodities, which too will play a part in the analysis of food security. For Sen, "extended entitlement is the concept of entitlements extended to include the results of more informal types of rights sanctioned by accepted notions of legitimacy." This notion is particularly relevant while examining the intrafamilial division of food availability and consumption, but it also has other uses in social analysis to which we shall presently turn.

The Additional Conditions

According to the entitlement and deprivation thesis, food insecurity afflicts people when they can no longer access enough food. It follows that different groups or individuals access food in different ways. Some avoid food insecurity through the cultivation of land which confers on them direct entitlements, while others shirk food insecurity by exchanging other possessions for food, thereby acquiring exchange entitlements. Clearly, the issue of food insecurity, analysed in terms of Sen's entitlement and deprivation thesis, is concerned with two basic conditions: First, availability of food; and second, the ability of people to access food either through endowment or direct entitlements or exchange entitlements. That is, if enough food were available and if people could access the food so available, then there would be no food insecurity. However, these two conditions do not guarantee food security in all cases; and even where these conditions are satisfied, individuals can be food insecure. There are three additional conditions, namely, existence of institutional sanctions, choice of food, and the existence of the secondary food system, which need to be met before individuals can be said to be food secure. We now proceed to examine each of the three conditions.

The Existence of Institutional Sanctions

A person's basic endowment or exchange entitlement have to be either objective goods like land, livestock, poultry, etc., or subjective goods like skill, knowledge, traits, etc. Sen's thesis laid considerable stress on possession-based ability, where ability is shaped by institutional sanctions, availability, and system of markets and prices. We will presently deal with all these briefly.

It has been rightly held that when individuals cannot access food, there is widespread food insecurity of severe intensity: hunger, starvation and even death caused by starvation. As pointed out by Sen, famines occurred when there were no systemic food shortages, in support of which the cases of the Bengal Famine of 1943 and the famine in Bangladesh of 1974 are cited as examples. In both cases, the inability of people to access food caused greater havoc than food shortage *per se*. Therefore, the distribution of food is a critical variable in causing or preventing famines. However, this is only a part of the story. There are other important factors, of which institutional sanction is an important one. It is best to start with an illustration to establish this point.

Even where the availability of food is not the problem and individuals have the ability to access food, a person's exchange entitlement can be seriously circumscribed by a fairly wide spectrum of legal, political, economic, religious, social and cultural elements, according to Sen's own theory. Possession of food (direct endowment), or of other commodities which can be converted into food (exchange entitlements), is important, but subject to certain constraints. What an individual has as basic endowment can be converted into exchange entitlements only subject to constraints, imposed, *inter alia*, by institutional sanctions. That is, the extent to which an individual can command food through exchange entitlements is determined also by institutional factors, which include but is not restricted to culture, religion, custom, usage, practice, beliefs and traditions. Exchange entitlements are not institution-neutral. This can be best explained by the following illustration.

Consider a village in India, say like Palanpur in Uttar Pradesh (Bliss and Stern, 1982) which has a mixed population of Hindus and Muslims. Both the communities have members who are engaged in agriculture and allied activities and therefore own cattle. Some of them grow crops, including food crops, which is consumed at the household level. Others sell their labour to acquire alternative commodity bundles, which includes food, to wipe out whatever food deficit they may have. The village is reasonably well serviced by grocers, butchers and a nearby bazaar.

Suppose a drought or a pest attack visits the village and completely wipes out all the standing crops. However, some food is available from the butchers who sell beef. The consequences of this scenario are twofold: First, the direct entitlements of the cultivators are all gone. Second, all those who used to rely on exchange entitlements (by sale of labour and non-food crop as well) will find that these have fallen sharply because not only have they no non-food crop to sell, but their employment opportunities have also shrunk owing to the destruction of crops (Mukherjee, 1993).

Suppose further that in keeping with the tradition of state action, a wage employment programme is launched and people earn wages in lieu of labour, which can be used to access alternative commodity bundles which include food. Now, the Hindus have the ability to access food in terms of the wages earned from the wage employment programme, but this food is available only in the form of beef in the village. While the Muslims will be hungry in the absence or destruction of food crops, they can still access some commodity bundle which will contain food by consuming the available supply of beef. The Hindus, on the other hand, will suffer food insecurity (starvation) because they cannot or will not access commodity bundles containing beef, as they do not have institutional sanction to do so. Here, religion is taken as an institution, and historically, the prevailing religious practices of Hindus forbid them to consume beef. (There is no expressed prohibition against the consumption of beef in Hindu scriptures.) Therefore, even where food is available, and people have the ability to access food, there can be hunger or food insecurity.

Alternately, some food insecure Hindus, either driven by hunger or not strict about adhering to the canons of religious practice, may opt to acquire commodity bundles containing beef. While the institutional sanction is obtained (in the breach) by one party to the exchange, viz., the buyer, the Hindus may still not be able to acquire commodity bundles containing food (beef) because the Muslims (vendors) will not sell them for fear of a reprisal. Typically, in a rural situation in India, such sale of beef by Muslims to Hindus can trigger widespread disturbance, since it may be interpreted as a valid attempt on the part of the Muslims to "defile" the Hindus or as an attempt to convert them to Islam. Indeed, preservation of the *status quo* in society is the responsibility of all the actors in the scenario.

A situation similar to the above can arise when the parties to the exchange are high- and low-caste people. Some years ago, Kusum Nair, who investigated the socio-economic scenario in Bihar, graphically illustrated this. Citing the case of one Gopal Prasad in village Mucharin, working on a bund on the river Mucharin, she quotes him thus:

> Thus, not very long ago, in the village of Mucharin, one Gopal Prasad went to work on a bund .... on the river Lilajana. According to him: "It became late and I decided to spend the night at the bund and not to return to the village. I am a Koeri ... by caste. Some other people also were camping here for the night but they were all Bhoomiyar Brahmins. Since I had not taken anything with me, they told me to cook and eat in an old earthen pot which was lying in the sand. I was told that pot has been used by a Koeri before, so I could use it. But it looked very dirty and old, and I thought to myself, how am I sure who used it. Since the Bhoomiyars were cooking their meal, I decided to eat the food cooked by them, and did so. They

> gave me some. Next day there was an uproar in the village. They called me insane and threatened to ex-communicate me; they wanted to beat me up. My family also turned against me. Not a soul would take my side. Even if a Harijan was working the latha ... on the well I could not bath there. All this because I had eaten cooked food by a Bhoomiyar. I was young then, and it made me angry. So I ran away to Gaya .... There I stayed with a tailor and learned to trade. For more than a year, I lived in exile. The *purohit* advised me to have *shuddhi* done, but I was obstinate. I decided to fight it out, even if it meant that I could never return to the village. Since I had become independent economically, I did not really care.
>
> Then fortunately for me, my grandmother dies, and the priest advised me to utilise the opportunity to undergo the rites of purification as well. I agreed and went to Vishupad Temple in Gaya and had my head shaved. I had to do that in any case for my grandmother, and then the *purohit* did my *shuddhi* also. Only then was I accepted back into my caste and family (Nair, 1979).

In anthropological studies, the issues centring around ceremonial purity of food in the rural areas of India, has been studied at length The ceremonial purity of food operates both ways. Just, as the case of Gopal Prasad indicates, the way a lower-caste person will not eat cooked food handed down by a higher caste person, a higher caste person does not have the institutional sanction to eat food prepared or served by certain lower caste people." Eating is actually a ritual and, like other Hindu rituals, has become associated with caste and status regulations" (Coon, 1948: p. 471). The ramifications, being too complex to be explored in detail, were avoided by Coon. Instead, he concentrated on indicating briefly the "rules of the game":

> The Thakur must closely observe the caste of anyone who prepares cooked food (*Kacha*) for him or touches it before it is eaten. He may take food fried in butter (*Pakka*) from the hands of all but eight low caste Hindu groups and four

> Muslim groups from the village. (Muslims, because they eat beef, are always capable of rendering the food and water of Hindus impure). But he can accept baked or boiled food only from one higher in caste than himself, namely, a Brahmin, or from another Thakur. Actually, the Thakur hesitates to take food from a Brahmin household, for in theory, the Brahmin is the one to receive service and alms, and it is considered in bad taste to accept his hospitality. Therefore, the Thakurs like other Hindus, actually freely inter-dine only with members of his own caste. He must be circumspect, also, about the identity of those from whose hand he takes water. In general, the rule is that he may take water served by those from whom he may receive fried food; thus the Thakur of Senapur may not take water from the Muslims of the village or from those Hindus of Senapur who belong to the eight low castes" (*ibid.*, p. 270-71).

Even Mushars, who eat rats and about whose food habits we will have occasion to reflect later in this chapter, "have their standards and insistencies. They decline to take cooked food at the homes of Chamars, Khatiks and Dhobis" (Coon, 1948: p. 488), as they are in popular conception, looked upon as belonging to castes lower than the Mushars.

This holds true even where people are on the verge of starvation. If food is provided or served by people to hungry individuals, the latter cannot accept it if institutional sanctions permitting such acceptance are not operative. Evidence available from the famine in Chotanagpur in 1866 is a pointer in this regard. The Santhals of the area had a long history of struggle against the Brahmins and their chiefs had issued fiats prohibiting any interface with the latter. During the 1866 famine, the government decided to undertake relief operations by way of distribution of cooked food amongst the starving Santhals. But the Santhals refused to eat the food so provided by the government because it had been cooked by the "hated" Brahmins.

> During the 1866 famine in Chotanagpur, British officials found to their astonishment that starving Santhals refused to

eat the food distributed by the relief committees because it had been cooked by the hated Brahmins (Guha, 1985: p. 120).

The starving Santhals did not access the food available, despite the fact that they had the ability to do so through non-entitlement transfers (in Sen's terminology), as the food was being distributed free by the government. This was because there was no institutional sanction to access the food. It had been cooked by the Brahmins, against whom a prohibition had been issued by the Santhal chiefs. Thus the Santhals went hungry despite food being available and despite the hungry Santhals having the ability to access the food in the absence of an institutional sanction to access the food.

Institutional sanction can also take the nature of food being actually withheld from people, on arbitrary criteria. In some societies, women may not have access to food, though food may be available. In such an event, the possibility of food insecurity looms large, even though there may be no paucity of food in the system and individuals have the capacity to access food. This is truer still during hunger periods. One instance of such discrimination is the Bengal Famine of 1943-44, when food was withheld from women, particularly in rural areas. Greenough has argued that "some kind of persons in Bengal are regarded as inherently more valuable than others and they will be favoured and protected from extinction during crisis" (1982: p. 214). He goes on to argue that as the economic situation deteriorated during the Bengal Famine of 1943-44, the head of the household (called *Korta*) "favoured more valued members at the expense of the less valued members. Since adults and males in Bengal are valued above children and females... the master tended to deny the latter in favour of the former" (*ibid.*, p. 217). Granted the foregoing, it seems *"that during the Bengal famine, food was deliberately withheld from women and given to men"* (Arnold, 1988: p. 89, emphasis added).

Arguably, there can be alternative interpretations of the facts stated by Greenough. Thus, food was seemingly available, but there was no institutional sanction for a section of society, namely, women, to access the food so available. Indeed, our economic history, as well as that of other developing countries, is replete with instances of gender discrimination in matters of accessing food, health and education, as reflected in greater malnutrition, higher illiteracy and poorer health among women (World Bank, 1989). These are all, at least in part, on account of the absence of an institutional sanction available to the women, to access these functions, without demur or recourse, at par with men.

The essential point that emerges from the examples cited above is that in a stratified society, it is not possible to access food even where food is available and the people have the ability to access it. In the absence of institutional sanctions, howsoever defined in the vocabulary of castes, food cannot be accessed and food insecurity will follow.

Sen was apparently aware of such eventualities when he said that what an individual can command in a society is constrained by a bundle of relationships covering legal, political and economic phenomena as well as social and cultural ones (Sen, 1981: p. 47). There is, therefore, an implicit admission of the fact that institutional sanctions are required, but their role and significance have been grossly underrated. In the entitlement approach to explaining food security and hunger, institutional sanctions at best indirectly influence an individual's ability to access food through either exchange entitlements or transfer entitlements; the position of institutional sanctions in the total scheme of hunger and food security is far from obvious. That is, an individual's ability to access food can be circumscribed by institutional sanctions. In the examples cited above, as in many other such cases of food insecurity, institutional sanctions may deny an individual the ability to access food notwithstanding the individual's possession of purchasing power, and thereby cause food insecurity and hunger.

The Issue of Choice

We further maintain that even in those situations where food is available, where people have the ability to access food, and the institutional sanction to access the food exists, there can still be food insecurity and hunger if people do not choose to acesss the available food. That is, the element of choice has to be fitted into the picture to ensure food security or prevent hunger. Sen was fully aware of this problem but elected to relegate it to the background with a one sentence disclaimer:

> While it (entitlement approach) is an approach of some generality, it makes no attempt to include all possible influences that can in principle cause starvation, for example illegal transfers (e.g.owing to inflexible food habits)" (Sen, 1981: p. 45).

Apparently, Sen was emphasising that starvation (food insecurity in our semantics) will almost always be caused by the inability of individuals to access food. He argues that "there is indeed no evidence whatsoever of people starving because of unwillingness to change food habits" (Sen, 1981: p. 165). He summons the evidence of the great famine of Ethiopia in 1888-92, for example, to suggest that people will eat almost anything under the grip of starvation (Pankhurst, 1968).

This is probably true only in some cases of sustained food insecurity. Sen's thesis overlooks the distinction between choices people make about food before and after they are starving. Sen seemingly looked at the limiting case of extreme hunger, and his arguments therefore may apply in cases of severe food insecurity. If one were looking at the causative factors in food insecurity (famines in Sen's terminology), then one of the more relevant issues, particularly so from a policy framing perspective, relates to choices made about food prior to the threat of death due to starvation. The evidence from the Bengal Famine of 1943 shows that people were not willing to change their food habits even in the face of famines. That is, the people chose to ignore the available food and risked starvation, despite the fact that food was available, they had the power to access the food, and there was institutional sanction for (or, more accurately an absence of any institutional sanctions *against*) accessing the available food. It was thus reported:

> During the famine, large supplies of wheat and millet were sent to Bengal and helped to relieve food shortage. They were supplied to rice eaters through the free kitchens but efforts to persuade people to eat them in their homes in place of rice met with little success" (Government of India, 1945).

Thus, food insecurity (starvation in Sen's terminology) may persist despite the fact of food being available and people having the ability to access it, and there were non-entitlement transfer, since the starving individuals did not choose to consume the food. This was so because the individuals deemed the available food (wheat and millet in the example of the Bengal Famine of 1943) to be something which they would not normally regard as acceptable food.

It is worth pointing out that rats are eaten by a class of people called Musahars in Bihar (Grierson, 1926) as food. The situation remains almost unchanged to date. Thus it was reported:

> The scorching summer sun beats down on the ground relentlessly. But the bunch of emaciated half clad children don't care... for the children of Musahar village near Bodhgaya in Bihar, the search for food is almost like trailing God. Some 5 kms away in Sarvodaypuri village... another group of starving children too forages around the countryside for food. A half-crazed look comes into their eyes as they spot some holes in the fields. Bending over the mouth of the holes, they burn cow dung cakes while anxiously watching the black smoke billowing out of the other end of the tunnel-like space. The reason for this peculiar behaviour soon becomes clear as an army of rats scampers out. The villagers triumphantly bludgeon them with sticks, roast them and eat them as part of their mid-day meal (Ahmed, 1992).

Rats, therefore are accepted as food by at least a section of the people in some parts of Bihar even today as they used to be nearly half a century ago. Rats are eaten by Musahars in UP as well. (Coon, 1948: 488). But, if during even acute food insecurity (starvation), rats are provided to the people of West Bengal, they would rather starve because rats do not find a place in their menu of edibles. The element of choice in food security or starvation cannot thus be ignored, without leaving the canvas incomplete, except in very limiting cases.

In traditional societies where tradition, practices, customs and beliefs about food and work are powerful, failure to adhere to these are fraught with dire retaliation, either by society or by nature embodied in deities and gods. The influence of such practices, traditions, customs and beliefs and adherence to them may be calculated and principled so that the actions of the poor people (who are most vulnerable in matters of food) are so chosen that they are consistent with the deep rooted cultural practices and traditions, religious beliefs and customary law, and therefore, they are in one sense incapacitated in acting differently. Sen's thesis needs to widen its scope to take account of this eventuality as well. If it is maintained that food insecurity (famines or starvation) is caused by the failure (inability) of the people to access food, then it is very important to explore, in all their dull details, the reasons for this failure. Not infrequently, people's failure to access food, can be traced to the impact of tradition, practices, customs and beliefs.

Existence of Secondary Food Security

In the context of a developing country, it would be unfair to define food security, as both the protagonists of food availability decline arguments (FAD) and Sen tend to, in terms of food produced by the application of technology in the economic sense, which here we will call "primary food". Food security has also to be informed by the existence of what we call "the secondary food system". In contradistinction to primary food, a whole range of food is available from forests (FAO, 1982, 1983, 1984a, 1984b), from common property resources (Jodha, 1989 and 1990), and from microenvironments (Chambers, 1990), to which the people have access without the application of technology in the strict economic sense. Fruits, nuts, tubers, leaves and mushrooms gathered and harvested from forests;

animals, birds and insects hunted from the jungles; fish, crabs, snails, etc., caught from rivers, ponds, waterbodies and sea; fruits, nuts, food and leaves collected from common property resources are the core constituents of the secondary food system.

Foods derived from the secondary system, "for most rural people... provide essential vitamins, proteins and calories" (Falconer, 1989). In several cases, as in the semi-arid regions of India, in absolute and in percentage terms, the quantities of food culled from forests, common property resources, and microenvironments may account for as much as 30 per cent of the total food consumption of rural households (Jodha, 1990). More importantly, the essential nutrients, otherwise missing in the primary food system, are vital not only in themselves but in terms of when they are available (Falconer and Arnold, 1989). Such food provides cover during periods of extreme stress – temporary scarcity of primary food during certain parts of the year, which have been rechristened "hungry seasons", when stored food supplies are dwindling and the next harvest is as yet unavailable, particularly in the rainfed areas; or peak agricultural periods when labour is in short supply and the disposable time available to women for cooking falls dramatically.

The secondary food system also provides lifeline to poor people during what is called "famine periods": times of natural and man-made calamities such as floods, earthquakes, famines, droughts (when additional energy-rich foods such as nuts, roots and tubers and rhizomes are an indispensable buffer), riots (Arnold, 1991), and even wars such as the one raging in Somalia over the last few years. That is why these foods have also been given the appellation "famine foods".

Our own findings in Midnapore district, West Bengal, show that during the two "hunger periods" that people face every year, food from the secondary system plays a critical role in helping them to tide over the difficulties. (Mukherjee and Mukherjee, 1994). This occurs year after year, on a fairly regular basis. Moreover, is not a recent phenomenon in the Indian context. As far back as in 1908-15, during the survey and settlement operation, it was found that the people of Hazaribag, Bihar, depend on food from the forest for a part of their requirements (*Final Report of the Survey and Settlement Operation of the District of Hazaribag, 1908-1915*). Although no quantitative data appertaining to such food are available, there is little doubt that it occupied a substantial portion of the common man's diet.

It is true that "famine foods" from forests, common property resources, and microenvironments are different from food derived from these same sources during normal times and are more complicated to gather and process. Nevertheless, they are characteristically energy-rich and, not infrequently, remain the only food available to the poor during famine periods. Additionally, gathering and processing foods from forests, common property resources, and microenvironments provide valuable income during these difficult times, which helps the rural poor to augment their (primary) food intake by accessing them in the market. And fortunately, a secondary food system exists, in some form or the other, in almost all economies: there may only be variations, at the margin, in the contributions made by the secondary food system to the overall food security of a society.

Thus, there will be *no absolute* food insecurity (starvation) if a secondary food system exists, even should the following prevail:

1. A decline in primary food (grown by the application of technology) availability, following the food availability decline argument.
2. Entitlement failure.
3. Institutional sanctions against accessing food available.
4. People choose not to access the food thus available.

Though there may be systemic hunger, it would be far less acute than what would prevail in the absence of the secondary food system. If one were to lay down an "absolute axiom", given the state of the art and the resources available, hunger will persist (or hunger will be more severe) in the rural areas of developing countries and there food insecurity will ensue, despite the steady supply of primary food, in the absence of food generated by the forests, common property resources, and micro-environments. Neither Sen's works nor the FAD arguments seem to have taken cognizance of the secondary food system. To that extent, both these approaches need to be revised.

Conclusions

Thus, the elements of food security, in terms of the entitlement and deprivation thesis, ought to be rewritten to include the following five crucial variables:

1. (Primary) food availability.
2. Ability of the people to access (primary) food.
3. Institutional sanction to access that food.
4. Exercise of choice by the people in favour of the available (primary) food.
5. Existence of a secondary food system.

There is no denying that many famines have been avoided or their impact mitigated by the availability of a secondary food system.

Just as the entitlement and deprivation thesis argues that defining food security in terms of food availability alone (as is done by those who adhere to the food availability decline argument) will be erroneous, defining food security in terms of entitlements without having due regard for institutional sanctions, exercise of choice in favour of the available food, and the impact of a secondary food system, will leave the picture incomplete. Unless all the five variables are incorporated in any analysis of hunger or starvation, in Sen's semantics (food security, in our terminology), the theoretical constructs will not be able to explain a good deal of hunger and food insecurity. This is particularly true of societies which are strongly influenced by religious edicts and are sharply stratified. (Prof. David Arnold pointed this out to me in a personal conversation during my term as Visiting Academician, SOAS, University of London, in the fall of 1993).

It is therefore necessary that in the event of a famine, or in order to prevent an increase in hunger or starvation, over and above the conditions laid down by Sen, the following conditions be satisfied: (*a*) additional supplies of food that are brought into the food deficit areas should be chosen by the hungry; (*b*) access to forests, common property resources, and the microenvironment is kept open and unhindered; (*c*) access to all available foods should be backed by institutional sanctions.

Granted these, it follows from (*b*) above that property rights in respect of common property resources, forests and microenvironments need to be laid down clearly and unequivocally. Such property rights must explicitly recognise that those dependent on the secondary food system for starving off hunger have an inalienable right to the fruits of CPR, forests and microenvironments. It also stands to reason that these can be put to sustainable use only when the people dependent upon them are guaranteed access to their fruits/products. Such guarantee, *inter alia*, will prevent people from abusing these sources of food. The success of the Joint Forestry Management Programme in Midnapore, West Bengal, and of the Sukhamajri experiment in Haryana, are examples in point. One need not labour the point that without sustainable use, it would be difficult to ensure that CPRs, forests and microenvironments provide "hunger food".

In the context of "choice", the role of both procurement as well as distribution of foodgrains assume significance. If one looks at the procurement scenario, it becomes apparent that the procurement basket and prices relate principally to rice and wheat. Consequently, these are the foodgrains, in the main, which are distributed through the PDS. The "choice" of foodgrains by the people is thus influenced and/or reinforced by what is distributed through the PDS. This is indicative of the fact that there is a possibility of changing food habits in the *long run* and hence, altering the choice/preference of the public by supplying successively higher quantities of particular foodgrains through the PDS.

For instance, in West Bengal consumption of wheat was virtually non-existent till the era of controls and statutory rationing emerged, when wheat came to be supplied through the PDS together with rice. Although no statistics are available, the Bengali people, who previously consumed only rice, have been observed to substitute wheat for rice, whatever be the extent. Thus, it is possible to influence "choice" to a limited extent. It is important that food policy planners have a long-term perspective, such that during crises, famines and acute hunger periods, supplying foodgrains which are both easily available as well as acceptable to the people, through a public distribution system, becomes a relatively easy proposition.

REFERENCES

Ahmed, Farzand, "The Musharas: The Rat-eaters of Bihar", *India Today,* 15 October 1992, p. 21.

Arnold, David, *Famines, Social Crisis and Historical Change,* Oxford: Basil Blackwell, 1988.

Arnold, J.E.M., *Tree Products in Agroecosystems: Economic and Political Issues*, London: International Institute for Environment and Development, 1991.

Bliss, C.J. and N.H. Stern, *Palanpur: The Economy of an Indian Village*, Oxford: Clarendon Press, 1982.

Bowbrick, Peter, "The Causes of Famine: A Refutation of Professor Sen's Theory", *Food Policy,* May 1986, pp. 105-24.

Chambers, Robert, *Microenvironments Unobserved,* London: International Institute for Environment and Development, 1990.

Coon, Carleton S., *A Reader in General Anthropology,* New York, Chicago and San Francisco: Hold, Rinehart and Winston, 1948.

Dasgupta, Partha, *An Inquiry in Well-Being and Destitution,* Oxford: Oxford University Press, 1993.

Dasgupta, S., "Adivasi Politics in Midnapur, c. 1760-1924", in Guha, Ranajit (ed.), *Subaltern Studies IV,* New Delhi: Oxford University Press, 1985.

Dreze, Jean and Amartya Sen, *Hunger and Public Action,* Oxford: The Clarendon Press, 1989.

Dreze, Jean and Amartya Sen (eds.), "The Political Economy of Hunger", *Entitlement and Well-Being*, vol. I, Oxford: Clarendon Press, 1990.

Falconer, J., *Forestry and Nutrition: A Reference Manual,* Rome: Food and Agriculture Organisation, 1989.

Falconer, J and J.E.M. Arnold, *Household Food Security and Forestry: An Analysis of Socio-Economic Issues,* Rome: Food and Agriculture Organisation, 1989.

Food and Agriculture, Organisation (FAO), "Fruit Bearing Forest Trees", Forestry Paper No. 34, Rome, 1982.

FAO, "Food and Fruit, Bearing Forest Species 1: Examples from Eastern Africa", Forestry Paper No.44/1, Rome, 1983.

FAO, "Food and Fruit Bearing Forest Species 2: Examples from South Eastern Asia", Forestry Paper No. 44/2, Rome, 1984a.

FAO, "Food and Fruit Bearing Forest Species 2: Examples from Latin America", Forestry Paper No. 44/3, Rome, 1984b.

Government of India, *Economic Survey*, New Delhi: Ministry of Finance, 1992.

Government of India, *Famine Enquiry Commission Report on Bengal*, New Delhi: Government of India, 1945.

Greenough, Paul, *Prosperity and Misery in Modern Bengal: The Famine of 1943-44*, Oxford: Oxford University Press, 1982.

Grierson, *Bihar Peasants' Life being a Discursive Catalogue of the Surrounds of the People of that Province,* London, 1926.

Gadgil, Madhav and Ramachandran Guha, "State Forestry and Social Conflict in British India", in David Hardiman (ed.), *Peasant Resistance in India 1858-1914,* New Delhi: Oxford University Press, 1992.

Jodha, N.S., "Management of Common Property Resources in Selected Areas in India" paper read at the Seminar on Approaches to Participatory

Development and Management of Common Property Resources, held on 10 March 1989, at the Institute of Economic Growth, New Delhi.

Jodha, N.S., "Rural Common Property Resources: A Growing Crisis" London: International Institute for Environment and Development, Gatekeeper Series, 1990.

Mukherjee, Amitava, *Structural Adjustment Programme, Putting the First Things, Poverty and Environment Last,* New Delhi: Segment Books, 1993.

Mukherjee, Neela and Amitava Mukherjee, "Rural Women and Food Insecurity: What a Food Calendar Reveals", *Economic and Political Weekly,* 29:11, 12 March 1994.

Nair, Kusum, *Blossom in the Dust: The Human Face in Indian Development,* Chicago and London: Chicago University Press, Midway reprint, 1979.

Nolan, Peter and John Sender, "Death Rates, Life Expectancy and China's Economic Reforms: A Critique of A.K. Sen", *World Development,* 20:9, 1992, pp. 1279-303.

Pankhurst, R., *The Economic History of Ethiopia*, Addis Ababa: Artistic Press, 1968.

Sen, A.K., *Hunger and Poverty: Essays in Entitlement and Deprivation*, Oxford: The Clarendon Press, 1981.

Sen, Amartya, "The Causes of Famine, A Reply", *Food Policy,* May 1986, pp. 125-31.

Sen, Amartya, "Life and Death in China: A Reply", *World Development,* 20:9, 1992, pp. 1305-12.

Sistion, J.S., *Final Report of the Survey and Settlement Operation of the District of Hazaribag 1908-1915*, Hazaribag: Settlement Officer Chotanagpur, August 1915.

World Bank, *Poverty and Hunger: Issues and Options for Food Security in Developing Countries,* Washington D.C., 1986.

World Bank, *Gender and Poverty in India,* Washington D.C., 1989.

7

The World Bank and Globalisation of the Indian Economy

Dalip S. Swamy

UNDER pressure from the International Monetary Fund and the World Bank, the Indian economy has been opening up to global capital since 1981. Restructuring of the policy framework and industrial production, inflow of capital goods and technology, growing foreign collaborations and foreign credit have, to a great extent, tuned the economy to global developments. Although it is too early to assess the full ramifications of these changes, because the process of globalisation has not yet been completed, its major aims and thrust can be clearly identified.

Two phases of globalisation have already unfolded and the contours of the next phase are becoming visible. The first phase began with the IMF loan of SDR 5 billion in 1981 and continued in a sporadic manner until 1990. Broadly termed as a phase of "economic liberalisation", this period, saw a dilution of bureaucratic regulations and reduction in state intervention so that market forces could play a greater role in guiding the economy than hitherto. This decade long process of liberalisation essentially prepared the ground for the next phase of globalisation which began in 1991 with a structural adjustment programme/loan (SAP/SAL) from the World Bank. The new programme was outlined in a memorandum submitted by the World Bank to the Government of India in 1990. It cannot be predicted with certainty how long will this phase last. But, unlike the earlier phase of liberalisation, it has been marked, right from the beginning, by swift and sweeping changes in economic policies so that the new "structural reforms" have become almost irreversible. The basic ingredients of these (unfinished) reforms too are contained in the World Bank Memorandum to the Government of India. SAP has induced significant changes in the structure and ownership pattern of industries and encouraged the inflow of foreign capital. Such induced changes will determine the content and shape of the third phase of globalisation.

This chapter takes stock of the changes in economic policies and activities that have already taken place and those expected to occur in the near future as part of the on-going process of globalisation. It also considers some prominent effects of globalisation in the last section.

THE FIRST PHASE OF GLOBALISATION

The first phase of economic liberalisation in India as noted earlier, began in 1981 with the SDR 5 billion loan from the International Monetary Fund. The loan was conditional on an "adjustment programme" which militated against the growth of the public sector and increased the leverage of the foreign sector. As a result of these conditions, the government liberalised imports, relaxed price controls, deregulated industrial production, oriented industrialisation towards the export market, and toned down budgetary support for the public sector. These policies were consolidated in 1985 by sharply reducing taxes (income and wealth taxes were slashed and estate duty was abolished), introducing modified value-added tax (MODVAT), raising the MRTP limit, and liberalising the terms and conditions for foreign capital.

Initiated in 1981 and consolidated in 1985, the new policy regime had significant effects on the economy[1] and paved the way to the next phase. During the eighties, the growth in government expenditure, without a commensurate increase in taxes on the incomes of beneficiaries of this growth process, increased the budget (revenue) deficit by more than ten times. Import liberalisation unaccompanied by a corresponding growth in exports increased external (current account) deficit by more than six times, propelled mainly by the growth of imports of capital goods and military arms. To meet the growing current account deficit, external debt increased by more than three times (Table 7.1).

Table 7.1
Budget and Balance of Payments Indicators

(*Rs. Crores*)

	1980-81	*1990-91*
Budget deficit		
Revenue account	1,175	18,580
Balance of payments deficit		
On merchandise account	5,967	12,413*
On current account	1,657	11,382*
Imports		
Total	12,549	43,190
Capital goods	1,910	10,470
Exchange rate**		
Rs. per US $	7.9	17.95
Long-term external debt		
Total (US $ billion)	18.7	57.3

Note: *refers to 1989-90. **Exchange rate refers to December end, for example, December 1980 for 1980-81.

Source: Economic Survey 1992-93, Government of India.

The average rate of inflation was 9 per cent during the eighties. Employment of labour stagnated in the private manufacturing sector (Planning Commission, 1990; Gupta, 1992). Industrial relations also changed in favour of profit. While lockouts increased until 1988 and declined thereafter, the number of strikes came down significantly through the eighties (Table 7.2). Industrial lockouts and closures sapped the strength of trade unions so that real wages and conditions of work deteriorated. In the manufacturing sector, the share of wages, salaries and bonus in total cost declined from 14.8 per cent in the seventies to 11.5 per cent in the eighties (Sharma, 1991). As capital-intensive imported technologies began to be adopted by various industries, average capital per unit of labour went up. While average capital productivity declined, that of labour increased (Ajit, 1992).

Table 7.2
Industrial Relations in the 1980s

(Annual Averages)

	1979-81	*1980-90* (*Rs. Crores*)
Industrial disputes (number)	2,831	1,305
strikes	2,485	950
lockouts	346	322
Workers affected ('000)	2,120	938
in strikes	1,879	729
in lockouts	241	176
Mandays lost (lakhs)	341	135
in strikes	230	80
in lockouts	111	87
Intensity of disputes (days)	16.09	14.39
strikes	12.25	10.97
lockouts	4.61	49.43

Note: Intensity of dispute is indicated by the number of days that an average worker lost due to the dispute.

The new policy regime also intensified economic stress on farmers and small industrialists. Agricultural producers experienced a significant dilution of their green revolution prosperity as the terms of trade moved against them.[2] An alarming number of small industries became sick and non-viable. Between 1980 and 1990, small sick units increased ninefold (from 23,000 to 2,19,000).

In short, the new policy regime weakened the economy's overall structure and its traditional linkages.

Table 7.3
Foreign Investment and Foreign Collaborations

	Upto 1980		*Upto 1989*	
Country	*Rs. cores*	*Number*	*Rs.crores*	*Number*
UK	660	1,455	742	2,485
USA	592	1,221	882	2,587
West Germany	245	1,098	455	2,348
Japan	32	536	140	1,198
Italy	36	204	90	580
Others	654	2,086	1,065	4,171
All	2,219	6,600	3,374	13,369

Source: India Investment Centre, New Delhi.

The new policy regime in fact had a dual impact. On the one hand, it enfeebled the economy by creating conditions for a massive disengagement of production geared towards the domestic market. It also simultaneously oriented the pattern of production in favour of foreign markets. The relaxation of imports of technology and capital goods linked the production of new items (like personal computers and fax machines), and many elite-oriented consumer goods (like video recorders and colour television sets), to the world supply. Deregulation of the domestic industry imparted a new flexibility to the consumer goods sector; unshackled from domestic markets, it could, conditions permitting, serve export markets. The introduction of MODVAT lessened the cascading effect of indirect taxes on consumer goods, making some of them competitive in international markets. Depreciation of the rate of exchange and streamlining of the export administration after 1986 enlarged the basket of exports and pushed some non-exporting firms to the edge of international markets.

This was the first phase of liberalisation (1980-89). It weakened the economy's capacity to withstand external shocks; created the "preconditions" for export orientation; and facilitated the recomposition of the industrial sector in accordance with the needs of world capital accumulation.

THE SECOND PHASE OF GLOBALISATION

The economic measures initiated in 1991, closely monitored by the IMF and World Bank, constituted the second phase of a coherent programme designed to restructure the economy. These measures were based on the World Bank's structural adjustment programme (SAP).

The chief ingredients of this programme were derived from the Anderson Memorandum, dated 30 November 1990, submitted to the Government of India.[3] The memorandum charted out an "improved co-ordination" of all economic policies – fiscal, monetary, industrial, trade and labour – to reorganise the Indian industrial sector as an important source of cheap consumer goods for the global market.

The principal aims of this reorganisation were significant cost reduction and internal demand deflation. The former was expected to make exportables competitive in foreign markets, and the latter would release them from the internal market. Exportables can be cheapened by reducing material as well as labour costs. National production can be released for exports by reducing government expenditures or increasing excise duties or both. This, in brief, was the logic of the SAP policy package.

The first phase of liberalisation, brought about by relaxation of imports, deregulation of domestic industry, MODVAT, and depreciation of exchange rate, undoubtedly improved the comparative advantage of Indian consumer goods. However, their exports remained limited by the extent of cost reduction. For this purpose, the World Bank (1990) identified the share of the three chief subsectoral groups – basic metals, heavy chemicals and machinery – used in other sectors of the economy. For example, in 1989, the share of these three subsectors in total inputs used was 27 per cent in synthetic textiles, 45 per cent in motor vehicles, 67 per cent in metal products, and 51 per cent in rail equipment. The efficiency and pricing of these key input-supplying sectors determine the economy's cost structure. The World Bank, therefore, articulated the next phase of policy reform in terms of these three subsectors.

Interestingly, these three subsectors were highly sheltered from foreign competition. The average protective tariff rates (measured by the ratio of customs duty collection to value of imports) was 71 per cent on metals, 70 per cent on chemicals, and 63 per cent on machinery, as compared to 50 per cent for the entire industrial sector. In some key industries, the tariff rates were even higher; for example, 106 per cent in organic chemicals and 122 per cent in other chemicals, compared to 70 per cent for the chemicals group as a whole. Equally significant was the fact that these three subsectors, dominated by public enterprises, received a substantial share of fixed investment (26 per cent) and absorbed a large share of imports (45 per cent in 1987-88).

Import-dependent, highly protected, and public sector dominated, these three input-supplying sectors were indeed strategic, and became the focal points of the country's investment. The prevailing cost-price structures of these subsectors prevented the full benefits of deregulation from reaching foreign as well as national (upper class) buyers of manufactured consumer goods. A reduction in their costs, preferably through a lowering of import duties, would serve three objectives with one stroke. It would expand the Indian market for imported capital goods, subject the public sector to foreign competition, and increase the export-orientation of Indian consumer goods industries. It would also keep Indian industrialists and middle-class consumers happy. The former would find their profit margins (in short period) improving; and the latter, the basket of consumer goods expanding.

There could be no better strategy for globalising (and subordinating) Indian industries than one which effected cost reductions in these three subsectors. The Bank, therefore, advocated the slashing of customs duties on their competing imports, to the 20-30 per cent range, as the most important instrument for increasing competition and efficiency as well as for providing growing market to foreign suppliers.

Thus, the policy package put forward by the World Bank consisted of the following proposals:

> Redesign the import policy in concordance with the Harmonised System of Classification, create one negative (restricted) list, allow all items that are not explicitly on the restricted list also to be importable through REP licenses (World Bank, 1990: p. 179).
>
> Reduce protective tariffs on intermediates and capital goods initially to an average of about 30 per cent (with a range of 20-40 per cent) and then to 20 per cent with corresponding adjustments in the domestic tax-cum-expenditure system, extend the scope of the MODVAT to cover machinery and correspondingly adjust domestic tax and expenditure to offset potential revenue losses, coordinate the tariff reduction and domestic fiscal adjustment with exchange rate depreciation so as to maintain existing levels of current account deficit (*ibid.*, p. 184).
>
> Make consumer goods in the restricted list importable through REP licenses and then render the OGL stock and sale category (ibid., p. 179).

The World Bank advocated this policy package in 1990 and also suggested a three-phase implementation scheme. The first recommendation was to be implemented immediately; the second could be undertaken over the next three to four years; the last measure to be implemented thereafter.

The first recommendation was essentially cosmetic; its effect on the balance of payments or domestic industries was expected to be negligible. Nevertheless, it was important in providing a green signal and preparing the ground for the other two sets of measures to have their desired effects. The second set was a crucial one. It involved tariff reductions in intermediate and capital goods, from 51 per cent and 59 per cent to 31 per cent and 30 per cent, respectively. The highest tariff reductions proposed were in machinery.

In order to release national production for exports, reduction in protective tariffs should be accompanied by an upward adjustment of union excise-cum-countervailing import duties and/or downward adjustment in government expenditure. If excise duties were not increased, the benefits of reduction in protective tariffs could accrue to consumers. In the absence of a compensatory increase in excise duty, reductions in government expenditure were required to reduce aggregate demand and divert production for exports. Another alternative was to subject domestic goods to more competition by lifting the ban on the imports of consumer goods. But according to the World Bank scheme, this alternative was to be implemented last of all.

The hidden objective of the World Bank was not to stabilise prices, much less to lower them, but to compress real wages in dollar terms. If nominal wages did not decline, owing to trade union pressures, an exchange rate devaluation was required to raise prices and hence prevent an increase in real wages.

Also, the proposed reduction in import taxes (in phases) was to be combined with a reduction in fiscal deficit by 2 per cent of GDP in the first year of reform, and 1 per cent of GDP in the second year of reform. This contractionary fiscal policy would deflate prices and also improve export profitability, but would not reduce real wages in dollar terms. It was, therefore, crucial to reduce the rate of exchange.

In order to determine the rate of exchange, a macromodel with questionable parameters, developed by Pradeep Mitra and Suresh Tendulkar for the World Bank,[4] was simulated. It suggested that to achieve balance of payments neutrality and maintain the aggregate domestic output, a cut in real public expenditures of 3.7 per cent and a devaluation of 13.4 per cent would be required. This simulation exercise also implied a rate of inflation of 17.2 per cent. Taken together, a 30.6 per cent (13.4+17.2) depreciation of the nominal exchange rate was called for in the year of reform.

Public Sector Reform

It should be emphasised that the public sector was an important target[5] of SAP not only because its cost-pricing structure affect the entire economy, but also because it pre-empts resources with respect to the private sector. Over 1,000 public enterprises (244 at the central level) hold monopoly positions in many critical basic industries such as steel, oil and gas, coal, power, and petrochemicals, and in services such as financial institutions, railway transport, and communications. They account for the bulk of organised sector employment. Through steady increases in the statutory liquidity ratio (SLR), the government has been able to channel a growing proportion of commercial banks' demand and time deposits to the public sector.

The reform package for the financial sector was directed at removing all these deficiencies so as to transform it into a market-friendly system. This action programme consisted of:

1. Reducing the level of directed investments via SLR.
2. Reducing the scope of targeted credits.
3. Enlarging the sources of funds for banks and development financial institutions by the modifying tax treatment of financial instruments.
4. Promoting greater private sector participation in the banking and mutual funds industry.
5. Organising an adequate regulatory and supervisory framework to safeguard investors' interests and promote orderly growth of the market.

The World Bank also suggested that the remaining reforms regarding deregulation, import liberalisation, incentives to foreign capital, exit policy, etc., should be implemented in the early nineties. It proposed that all forms of capacity licensing for industry could be phased out completely over the medium term (five years). "In the interim, the investment size limits below which a license is not required could be substantially raised each year" (World Bank, 1989: p. 28).

In respect of large and/or dominant firms, the Bank

suggested that "the Government cease to use *ex ante* MRTP investment and production clearances to regulate firms." The criteria of control should not be the size of a unit *per se*, but its unfair or uncompetitive business behaviour and practices which could be controlled by the threat of import competition. "Thus, MRTP clearance, as a condition for entry or growth, could be phased out completely in the medium term" (*ibid.*).

> In the interim, "the asset limits, defining large or dominant firms, above which MRTP clearance is required, could be progressively raised to permit MRTP firms to grow at least to minimum economic scale (mes) in each of their plants... The definition of the product groups within which dominance may occur might be broadened... to include the relevant competitive substitutes (*ibid.*).

Articulating the World Bank's point of view, Ahluwalia had suggested that the asset limit for MRTP companies be raised from Rs. 100 crore to Rs. 500 crore, the entire industry be removed from the ambit of the Act, and a negative list be prepared showing only those firms subject to MRTP regulations. "This list could gardually be reduced in scope and, in the interim period, abolished" (Ahluwalia 1990).

It was suggested that FERA companies be subjected to the same diminishing need for clearances as MRTP companies. The case for easier clearances for non-MRTP FERA firms was considered even stronger. A. V. Desai (1990) proposed that the Europeans and Americans be given the freedom to invest in India in return for duty-free and barrier-free access to their markets. ASSOCHAM wanted to scrap FERA altogether from the statute book.

In respect of the small-scale industry, the World Bank (1989) recognised the need for some incentives for growth but denounced "perpetual and often absolute protection for small firms." To encourage their graduation from the SSI sector, the report suggested a framework that included tapering off of subsidies over a fixed period, phasing out of excise tax concessions, and gradual dereservation over the medium term. In the interim period, before dereservation was completed, growth could be encouraged by raising asset limits. Entry and growth could also be given impetus by allowing small firms to integrate with larger units. For example, in ancillary production, large units could be allowed to have an equity stake in small firms (*ibid.*).

Sick companies should be given "freedom to adopt as they see fit...measures such as retrenchment, mergers or closures and sale of assets." This would require modification of the Industrial Disputes Act and the bankruptcy and winding up procedures, and reform of trade unions.

Canalising agencies "should be open to competition from private traders on equal terms. The 'actual user' policy should be abolished. The re-emergence of import and export houses would follow automatically" (*ibid*, p. 39).

These measures would serve to offset the influence of the state, which controlled the financial sector, and broaden and deepen the capital market.

To recapitulate, the World Bank SAP combined macroeconomic stabilisation with structural reforms. It consisted of:

* Major fiscal adjustment effort.
* Further liberalisation of the trade regime.
* Public sector reforms.
* Reforms of domestic interest rates coupled with measures to strengthen capital markets and institutions.
* Further deregulation of domestic industry and promotion of foreign direct investment.

Push Towards Globalisation

World Bank experts relentlessly pressurised the government to implement these reforms. But till 1990, little was done to accelerate policy reforms. Trade union resistance held back the government in 1988. In the following year, the National Front government made attempts, albeit abortive, to alter the path of development. Moreover, government revenues depended heavily on import taxes, so that the required tariff reductions without compensatory revenue measures could lead to a worsening of the already alarming budget deficit.

Whatever the factors which held back the process of liberalisation, the World Bank persisted with its well-tried tactic for ensuring compliance. It decided to hold up the concessional aid and waited for India's credit options to sufficiently narrow down so that the SAL/SAC remained the only alternative.

The process of eliminating foreign credit options was already underway in late eighties. The Aid India Consortium (AIC), a rich nations' club was inclined to determine its aid pledges in the light of the World Bank recommendations. Until 1987, it offered higher credit than that recommended by the World Bank in response to India's acceptance of the suggested economic policies. In 1988 and 1989, when the process of liberalisation slowed down, the flows recommended by the World Bank were slashed by almost 25 per cent. In 1990, AIC refused to pledge itself to maintaining even the 1989 level of concessional credit, itself a sharp reduction over previous year's levels. In fact, it put a great deal of pressure without offering additional credit. Commenting on the decision taken by the AIC in June 1990, the *Economic and Political Weekly* stated:

> The Consortium tightened the screws, demanding policy reforms in the industrial, fiscal, trade, and financial sectors and making future aid flow contingent on their implementation... The US delegation declared that... India probably cannot rely on historical levels of concessional assistance...which is likely to remain static because of new claimants...but her task is removal of barriers to foreign direct investment, trade and modern financial markets and ensuring fair competition (EPW, 28 July, 1990, p. 1623).

The external commercial credit also declined. The *Economic Survey* of 1990-91 states:

> The increasing trend in approvals of external commercial borrowings witnessed during 1987-88 to 1988-89 was reversed in 1990-91...owing to the fall in the over-all availability of international credit...and downgrading of India's credit rating for long-term funds by international rating agencies (Government of India, 1991: p. 167).

Changing International Environment

Decline in the availability of foreign credit was a consequence of changes in the international environment which had drastically altered by 1991. There was a new conjuncture in international relations. Following its capitulation to the capitalist world, the socialist bloc was no longer a countervailing power in the world economy. The First World consequently acquired an unprecedented influence over the developing countries. Operation Desert Storm in the Middle East clearly established the unequivocal supremacy of the US on the international scene.

In the fifties and sixties, India could play off USA against USSR to strike a bargain for foreign credit; she could get loans from both, with minimum political interference. The detente between the superpowers changed this condition in the early seventies. Since then, her political leverage has been declining; it reached its nadir with the fall of the Berlin Wall in 1989. Since Operation Desert Storm and the collapse of communist states in USSR and East Europe in 1991, she has virtually no bargaining power.

The new world thus increased India's vulnerability by adversely affecting her prospects of trade and aid. The move towards total integration of the European market was expected to not only divert European trade from developing countries to East European countries, but also make the latter a major destination of American, Japanese and West European investors. Under these conditions, India could hope to get only a small fraction of the new trade generated by foreign investment and upgradation of technology in East Europe. This incremental trade would be offset by the diversion of foreign capital to East Europe.

Another important aspect of the international environment was the change in development ideology. Reagan and Thatcher inherited a world in which the "development consensus" had already broken down and the Bretton Woods institutions had come under enormous strain. Internally, in the OECD countries, Western capitalism had begun to shed welfarism and turned its back upon full employment.

Thus, the new international balance of power reduced the prospects of concessional and commercial foreign credit and consolidated the ideology of a new policy regime in the image of the West. This was the external backdrop which made India's big push towards the policy of globalisation feasible. The decisive moment, however, came when the foreign exchange crisis threatened default on debt servicing in 1991.

Foreign Exchange Crisis

The balance of payments (BOP) crisis had been deepening since the second oil shock in 1980. It worsened after 1985 owing to significant imports of military equipment (about $ 18 billion from 1985 to 1988). The government increasingly relied on borrowings from private international banks. As a result, the total external debt, outstanding and disbursed (DOD), increased from about $ 41 billion in 1985 to $ 70 billion in March 1991, raising the ratio of DOD to GDP from 19 per cent to 25 per cent. Much of this borrowing was in the form of relatively short-term and potentially volatile instruments such as foreign currency bank deposits from NRIs, with two to three years' maturity. Since NRI bank deposits can be withdrawn on demand (with only a small penalty), the weight of these deposits and the share of short-term commercial bank debt in the total stock of debt (about $18 billion or 25 per cent of the DOD in March 1991) made the country extremely vulnerable to a liquidity crisis stemming from a loss of private creditor confidence abroad.

These latent weaknesses were revealed at the time of the Gulf face off in 1990. This crisis disrupted the supplies and increased the prices of oil and petroleum products. It raised the country's cost of POL imports by 72 per cent, deepening trade deficit by Rs. 4,400 crores. The direct and indirect cost of the Gulf crisis was estimated at $ 2.9 billion (equivalent of Rs. 5,200 crores).

In view of the worsening BOP deficit, some international agencies suddenly lowered India's credit rating, restricting her access to the global money market. This drying up of international commercial credit occurred at a time when concessional credit was not available, and the Gulf crisis had adversely affected the country's foreign exchange reserves.

In any case, the foreign exchange crunch was so severe that even after using the reserve tranche position in the IMF, amounting to SDR 487 million (equivalent of Rs. 1,173 crores), from July to September 1990, the external payments situation did not stabilise. Reserves declined to $ 1.2 billion on 31 December 1990, equal to about two weeks' imports. On 18 January 1991, the government was forced to borrow again from the IMF, this time amounting to SDR 1.23 billion (equivalent of $ 1.78 billion or Rs. 3,334 crores). Subsequently, the decline in commercial credit and withdrawal of deposits by NRIs created panic, leading to a *de facto* depreciation of the rupee in the *havala* market.

The government resorted to emergency measures with respect to the BOP crisis, beginning January 1991. First, it availed itself of Fund resources, drawing almost $ 1.8 billion from the Contingency Compensatory Financing Facility (CCFF) and a first tranche stand-by credit. Secondly, it adopted import compression measures such as an increased interest rate on bank credit for imports.

Despite these initiatives, the decline in foreign reserves continued unabated. By March 1991, the reserves plummeted by $1.4 billion, an amount almost equal to the reduction in commercial bank loans over the year. As the country's credit rating continued to fall and foreign banks refused lending, the cost of short-term loans rose to a level which was 1.25 per cent above LIBOR (standard reference interest rate in the international money market) by May 1991.

The government also explored the possibility of fast disbursement of loans already sanctioned. In 1990, International Development Assistance (IDA) – the soft lending affiliate of the World Bank – cancelled some project loans. Still, credit of about $ 10 billion by the Bank and IDA for 120 projects was in the pipeline. Of these projects, 67 were in power, irrigation and rural development. Loans for these projects were not disbursed, presumably because the credit agencies were not satisfied with their implementation. This might be due to the lack of necessary infrastructure or the resource crunch facing the government. Whatever the reasons for the unsatisfactory implementation of the projects, the fact remains that their close monitoring would have enabled the government to draw upon $ 10 billion worth of credit by 1990.

In January 1991, the government initiated discussions with the Bank for utilisation of the undisbursed IDA loans ($ 3.3 billion). But the Bank indicated that important bases for fast disbursing assistance could be "reform measures contained in the 1991-92 budget, and in any policy related statements" (1991: p. 5). Nevertheless, it organised an informal donors' meeting in April 1991 to mobilise support, conditional on the country's willingness to adopt a structural adjustment programme. However, since the caretaker government at that time was not able to decide on policy reforms, neither the Bank released any portion of the undisbursed credit, nor did any donor provide new loans.

The April denial was sufficient to transmit shock waves to NRIs, who love their money more than their country. Gripped by panic, they began to transfer their deposits to foreign banks. The outflow from NRI deposits during April-June 1991 was $ 952 million and it continued, albeit at a reduced rate of $ 200 per month, in the next quarter. With this continuous attrition, the rupee depreciated by 16 per cent in the five months from mid-January to mid-June 1991.

The fourth fire-fighting operation on the BOP front was the sale of 20 tonnes of gold valued at $ 200 million. But this too was insufficient to break the spiral of expectations generated by crawling depreciation and the possibility of further devaluation. These expectations, by shortening the period for import payments and lengthening that for the realisation of export proceeds, exacerbated the foreign exchange shortage.

Reserves dipped again in June 1991. They fell below the previous bottom of $1.1 billion – less than sufficient for two weeks' import requirements. Since the next instalment of CCFF drawal was not due till July, default on deposit withdrawal and repayment of short-term loans loomed large on the horizon. The government was indeed pushed to the wall and, in desperation, decided to pledge an additional 47 tonnes of gold to garner $ 400 million in July.

This was the moment when all foreign credit options of the country were foreclosed. Default could be avoided only if credit was made available from the IMF or the World Bank.

Indian Government Succumbs

Cornered by the NRIs, foreign commercial banks, and the World Bank, the government approached the IMF and the Bank for structural adjustment loan/credit (SAL/SAC). The IMF then insisted on a nominal devaluation of 30 per cent – its leading weapon to test the government's pliability.

A devaluation of 30 per cent was not acceptable to the "new" government. The aversion to devaluation was not based on the philosophy of self-reliance. By 1991, "ideology" had been pushed to the political backwater; after almost fifteen years of atrophy of self-reliance globalisation had become the most cherished slogan. But devaluation of that order in 1991 would have upset the political (minority government's) apple-cart. The problem for the 'autonomous' decision-makers of India was, therefore, how to persuade the Bank and the Fund to agree to a politically acceptable rate of exchange.

The burden of salvaging the politics of devaluation fell on the Finance Minister, Man Mohan Singh, who cherishes market friendliness, notwithstanding his oft-quoted speech on behalf of the South-South Commission, accusing the North of unfair trade practices. His early researches on India's exports, conducted in Oxford University, were widely acclaimed, and his articulation and personal contacts with international academic bureaucracy were unparallel in India. He thought he would get away with a 9 per cent devaluation announced on 1 July 1991. But it was wide off the mark; it fell short of the World Bank target without adjusting for inflation. The simple rationalisation that the contemplated tight fiscal and monetary policies could reduce inflation was obviously unacceptable to the IMF experts, unless, of course the target rate of inflation was put on paper.

The Finance Minister could do no better than fix the target of inflation at 9 per cent, with a stipulated reduction in the budget deficit equivalent to 2 per cent of GDP by March 1992. Arithmetic was then simple. A real devaluation of 13 per cent with a targeted inflation of 9 per cent required a 22 per cent nominal devaluation. Within two days of the first devaluation, the rupee was again devalued, so that on 3 July 1991, foreign currencies appreciated by exactly 22 per cent.

This step immediately raised the ratio of external debt to GDP, from around 25 per cent in June 1991 to 31.4 per cent in July 1991 indicating the grip of external debt on the economy.

With the fall in the rate of exchange other policies proposed by the IMF and the World Bank followed without resistance. On 4 July, the government announced a trade policy reform package which, together with supplementary measures announced on 13 August 1991, aimed at significantly reducing the quantitative restrictions on imports of intermediate and capital goods, lowering the tariff rates, substantially eliminating the state monopoly on imports and exports, and making the rupee convertible for trade transactions in three to five years.

The New Industrial Policy

On 24 July 1991, the Union budget as well as a "Statement on Industrial Policy" were presented to Parliament. The budget announced the government's intentions of reducing its fiscal deficit by more than 2.5 percentage points of GDP in 1991-92 (as recommended by the IMF), despite the fact that only two-thirds of the fiscal year remained at the time.

The new industrial policy eliminated investment licensing requirements for all but 18 industries, which accounted for about 20 per cent of the existing manufacturing output. It drastically reduced the number of industries reserved for the public sector; eliminated restrictions on investments and mergers of large concerns under the MRTP Act; and opened up an extensive positive list of industries in which ownership of up to 51 per cent (and up to 100 per cent in special cases) by foreign companies was freely permitted. At the same time, the mandatory convertibility clause, under which financial institutions had the right to convert a proportion (up to 20 per cent) of their loans to the business sector to equity, was abolished for new projects. Thus, the new industrial policy marked a fundamental break with the past practices of capacity planning and entry regulation.

It was also announced that there would be no further phased manufacturing programmes (PMP) for new projects; and in October 1991 some initial steps were taken to remove constraints on firms already operating under PMPs. This process, taken to its logical completion would leave all decisions on the sourcing of inputs to individual firms, subject only to tariffs and any remaining controls on import of inputs.

Thus, many changes were introduced in a very short period, and more was promised. While the government recognised the need for further concessions to foreign investors, because of the delicate BOP situation, investors still required licence to import capital goods for projects in which the foreign exchange content was over 25 per cent of total investment or Rs. 2 crores; unless foreign exchange supply was ensured through foreign equity capital. Again, reflecting the acute BOP pressure facing the economy, dividend repatriation by companies with up to 51 per cent foreign ownership was linked under the new rules to their export earnings. Nevertheless, the government was aware that incentives for foreign direct investment would have to be strengthened, and planned to remove the provision linking dividend repatriation to export earnings once the external payments situation showed some improvement. It also realised that the 'only financing' requirements for capital goods imports needed to be modified to allow 'debt as well as equity financing' in order to facilitate the financing of large investment projects.

The government also promised to put in place a plan for comprehensive deregulation of the steel industry, the most important subsector still subject to price and distribution controls. It also committed itself to devising appropriate amendments to the Sick Industrial Companies Act of 1985, improve its functioning, and streamline and facilitate its procedures in order to strengthen the Board of Industrial and Financial Reconstruction (BIFR).

The government's commitment to economic reforms facilitated the IMF approval of the second drawing of the CCFF for SDR 166.2 million on 22 July 1991. The World Bank subsequently organised a lending programme spread over the next four year period, 1992-95, comprising the following (1991: p. 32):

* World Bank lending of up to $ 2.0 billion per annum.
* IDA resources of approximately $ 0.9 billion per annum.
* IDA resources of $ 0.65 billion from replacement of funds cancelled from the current IDA portfolio.

It should be noted that the last facility constituted about 20 per cent of the undisbursed IDA credit that was denied earlier and was extended after the Finance Minister submitted his letter on Development Policy on 11 November 1991.

This was the Bank's first policy-based loan, amounting to $12.25 billion spread over four years, to India. Its objectives are to support "India's efforts to restore macroeconomic equilibrium, accelerate structural reforms, and regain access to private credit markets abroad" (*ibid.*). These objectives will be ensured through a time-bound monitoring system.[6] The Bank would also "closely co-ordinate" its economic and sector work and policy dialogue with Fund staff, regularly review Fund staff briefing papers and reports, and frequently exchange views on recent development and policy options (*ibid.*, p. 39).

As soon as the Bank agreed to lend, other creditors also took their cue. AIC gave a positive but niggardly response to the request for exceptional financing – about $ 6.7 billion in overall pledges, an increase of about 6 per cent over the previous year's level. Pledges of quick disbursing balance-of-payments assistance amounted to $ 2.3 billion. Some creditors, especially Germany, expressed interest in associating their fast disbursing assistance with the proposed SAP. Several major MNCs, such as General Motors, IBM, Asean Brown Bowery and Hankel (of Germany), also responded enthusiastically to India's liberalised foreign investment regime.

The Government of India, on its part, did not fail the donors. In order to ensure continuing foreign assistance, it intensified the policy reforms. The foreign trade regime was made "market friendly." Almost all quantitative restrictions on imports were eliminated; customs duties were significantly brought down in April 1993 – in the case of certain capital goods, to levels proposed by the World Bank (1990); the rupee was made convertible on the trade account in two steps and then on the current account; significant tax concessions were provided to foreign institutional investors such as pension funds, mutual funds, investment trusts, etc., investing in the capital market (long-term capital gains tax rate on them was reduced to 10 per cent); and the FERA regulations were diluted so much as to render the Act toothless.

These policy decisions made it crystal clear to the World Bank and the IMF that the Indian government was committed to the SAP. Noting the "irreversibility of structural reforms", AIC pledged $ 7.2 billion of assistance for 1992-93, an increase of $ 500 million or about 7.5 per cent over that pledged in 1991. The quick disbursing component of this assistance was $ 1.79 billion, about 25 per cent of the total aid, which could be utilised straightaway. But it should be noted that in spite of an increase in the aid pledges, the rate of disbursement was quite slow. *The Economic Survey* for 1992-93 states:

> In spite of the larger pledges from the Aid India Consortium donors this year, the disbursements have been running at a much lower level than last year. Upto December 1992, the gross disbursements have amounted to only US$ 2 billion against US$ 3.16 billion during the same period last year – 36.7 per cent lower. As a result, for the first three quarters of 1992-93, net capital transfer under external assistance has been zero. This is in spite of the drawal of about US$ 625 million fast-disbursing funds during April-December 1992 – US$ 200 million as the last tranche of World Bank's SAL, about US$ 100 million from World Bank under Social Safety Net Loan, US$ 150 million from ADB under Financial Sector Loan, US$ 125 million from Japan under Hydrocarbon Sector Loan, and about US$ 50 million from Germany during 1992-93 upto December 1992 (Government of India, 1991: pp. 113-14).

Thus, the economy was caught in a cycle of debt. To tide over the crisis caused by the first phase of liberalisation, fresh injections of external life-saving aid were required. The World Bank loan was contingent on the acceptance of SAP which was designed to cheapen Indian commodities and factories in dollar terms. Lowering customs duties on capital goods and intermediates opened up strategic industries, producing basic metal, heavy chemicals and machinery, to face competition from transnational corporations. Reduction of subsidies and deregulation regimented rent-seeking activities. Privatisation of the public sector converted public purpose into private profit. Devaluation of the rupee ultimately made all commodities and assets cheaper in foreign currencies and tightened the grip of external capital (debt) on GDP.

FREEDOM TO TNCs

The blitzkrieg of reform measures since 1991 has also made the environment immensely favourable to transnational corporations. Allowing TNCs to increase their equity participation to 51 per cent or more, lowering capital gains tax on foreign institutional investors (FIIs) to 10 per cent and devaluation all enhanced the profitability of foreign investors. This process was reinforced by the next phase of restructuring which began in 1993. Its agenda was specified by Samuel Otoo (World Bank, 1993). It was designed to facilitate the expansion of transnational corporations in the power, telecommunications, oil and gas sectors. In order to make the environment more conducive to the entry and operation ot TNCs, plans were also formulated for reforming the financial sector, ports and internal transport facilities.

The government planned to spend more than Rs. 2,00,000 crores on infrastructure during the Eighth Five Year Plan (1992-97). Transnationals had special interest in this sector not only because a more efficient infrastructure would stimulate their expansion in general, but also because modernisation of this sector would generate demand for their equipment.

The electric power subsector was expected to absorb 38 per cent of the government expenditure on infrastructure. It was planned to increase installed generating capacity from 70,000 MW in 1992 to 1,18,000 MW by 1997, with half of the additional capacity (i.e., 24,000 MW) to be provided by the private sector. The government provided several incentives to the private sector to fulfil the targets of power generation. These included full ownership of power companies by the private sector (local and foreign); a (sovereign) guaranteed rate of return of 16 per cent in foreign exchange to foreign companies undertaking power generation; reduced import duty on power projects to 20 per cent; and a five-year tax holiday for new power projects. State electricity boards were induced to improve their plant load factor, reduce transmission and distribution losses, rationalise tariff, and clear arrears. These changes were expected to expand generating capacity and achieve a flow of high quality power services.

Transnational corporations require internationally compatible communications and port services. In order to modernise telecommunications, World Bank (1993) proposed a change in the structure of the Department of Telecommunications (DOT). The Department is engaged in regulation, direct provision of services, and promotion of telecommunications equipment manufacturing. The World Bank recommended, as a first step, that DOT be reorganised such that each of these three functions are handled by a separate body. The regulatory and policy making body should be independent of the one ensuring the flow of services to users; while the third body should concentrate on the provision of physical infrastructure (*ibid.*, p. 89).

The government has already allowed non-DOT firms to arrange lucrative wireless cellular services. The potential market for telecommunications equipment to serve rail roads, oil and export markets is estimated at about Rs. 50,000 crores. Once the third component of DOT becomes independent, it will be much easier for TNCs to capture a major share of the equipment market.

Improvement in port services also has been given high priority in the World Bank scheme. The cost of foreign trade depends upon, besides main line services, the speed of cargo clearance at ports. Container delays cost about $ 70 million per year, excessive ship waiting time costs about $ 100 million per year, and the cost of foreign trade moving in feeder services is about $ 250 million per year. The World Bank suggested that the various operating services of the ports, employing 104,000 workers, should be leased out or franchised to the private sector (*ibid.*, Ra'anan, 1992). These changes, along with mechanisation of cargo handling, will lead to the retrenchment of about 60,000 port employees.

There is no financial crisis in the telecommunications and port sectors. Their operating efficiency can be increased by rationalising administration and management. But the World Bank had stronger reasons for privatising important aspects of the country's infrastructures – "the reasons for reforming both ports and telecommunications have to do with integrating with global markets" (World Bank, 1993: p. 100).

The World Bank's reform model for railways was similar to that devised for telecommunications: "The first step is to separate the regulatory and manufacturing functions from that of providing commercial freight and passenger services" (*ibid.*, p. 93). Manufacturing and commercial operations could be subsequently privatised. The implementation of the first step will throw out of jobs 4 lakh workers (out of a total work force of 17 lakhs), considered to be redundant by the World Bank. The World Bank apprehended that the railways was inclined to solving its financial problems by raising rates on coal transport. But this, it argued, would merely transfer resources from one ministry to another and exacerbate the problems of the electric power subsector. It therefore suggested that a more efficient response would be to reduce subsidies on rail passenger services, responsible for congestion on the main lines, and promote an expansion of domestic rail container services (*ibid.*, p. 94).

Road travel dominates the transport system. It accounts for about 75 per cent of the intercity passenger kilometers traversed and about 60 per cent of the intercity goods kilometers covered. But owing to slack public investment, high density corridors (HDCs), which carry most of the traffic between major cities (about 23,000 km), have become congested. It is projected that another 10,000 km of HDC road capacity will be required by the year 2015. This entails expanding the existing two-lane roads of the HDCs to four-lane ones, with urban bypasses and the construction of a parallel limited access expressway. Given the increase in traffic intensity, about 1,350 km of such works are required by 2000. The World Bank hopes that "the private sector can be induced to undertake Build-Operate-Transfer (BOT) type operations" to make up the supply gap. A beginning has already been made in this direction. An MOU has been signed between the Ministry of Surface Transport, the Public Works Department of the Government of Maharashtra, and Infrastructure Leasing and Financial Services (ILFS which was involved in the security scam of 1992), to improve and widen the national highway linking Bombay to Pune (NH-4, 10.14 km) from the existing two to four-lanes. On 28 March 1994, ILFS awarded a $ 250,000 contract to Hume Industries (Malaysia) and Berhad and John Holland Aisa (Holdings) of Australia, which is part of one of the world's largest civil contracting firms towards design engineering and project cost.

POSSIBLE EFFECTS OF GLOBALISATION

Although it is too early to fully assess the consequences of globalisation, some immediate effects can be discerned. First, there has been a reduction in (real) public investment and government expenditure on education, health and welfare. As a result, the growth of infrastructural output has decelerated from 6.1 per cent in 1991-92 to 2.5 per cent in 1992-93, with adverse implications for manufacturing production.

Employment is going to be the second major casualty of globalisation. Restructuring of the economy through privatisation, import liberalisation, exit policy, and a deflationary fiscal policy can lead to an increase in unemployment at least by 2.8 million per year for the next three years. Mundle (1992) estimates a jump in the rate of unemployment from 4 per cent in 1991-92 to 5 per cent in 1992-93, assuming a high growth scenario; and to 5.9 per cent in 1992-93 and 6.6 per cent in 1993-94, assuming a low growth scenario. According to his estimates, the additional unemployment due to SAP will be 4 million and 10 million persons in the high growth and low growth scenarios, respectively. Growing unemployment in the organised sector, owing to increasing capital intensity, is likely to push workers into the informal and agricultural sectors.

The process of globalisation has important implications for workers' standards of living. As prices rise and recessionary impact on the economy spreads, their standard of living will decline. The stagflation generated by SAP is likely to aggravate poverty levels in rural areas.

Third, reductions in the budget deficit and customs duties, both of which directly support the expenditure of the centre (and not of states), will affect the centre-state economic relations. The centre's revenue losses from lower customs duties will have to be made up by greater revenue mobilisation from other instruments like income tax and excise tax which are to be shared with the states. The reforms underway will therefore weaken the centre's economic power or render the existing tax-sharing formula unworkable.

Fourth, lower effective protection has encouraged some international suppliers to resort to dumping. For example, a transnational corporation sold DAP fertiliser at $ 166 per tonne (in 1993) in India, when its international price was $ 186 per tonne and that in the US $ 240 per tonne. Dumping has rendered many fertiliser units sick. Other examples are PVC resins, monoethylene glycol, bulk drugs and capital goods. Bilateral aid projects, tariff reductions on capital goods, and provision of concessions to foreign (power) companies have reduced the orders for power turbines manufactured by BHEL, rendering more than 50 per cent of its capacity idle. This type of restructuring is obviously quite costly because not only is setting up new units is expensive, but the capacity of old units is wasted. Thus, these reforms have hit the very root of the country's indigenous strengths – the core sector – developed since Independence.

Fifth, the abolition of MRTP and FERA restrictions, specially the pre-merger scrutiny by the MRTP Commission, has accentuated industrial concentration. Merger and acquisition (M&A) activity has increased from less than 25 instances till 1990 to 33 in 1991 and 28 in 1992. The most striking of these is the takeover of Parle Exports by Coca Cola, which gives the latter access to 60 per cent of the market and the bottling, sales and distribution network which goes with it. Another notable case is the acquisition of Tata Oil Mills Company (TOMCO) by Hindustan Lever. This deal would enable the latter to control 70 per cent of the toilet soap market, 30 per cent of the detergent market, and 10 per cent of the detergent cake market. It is interesting to note that Uniliver's other two subsidiaries in India, Lipton and Brooke Bond, have merged. As a result, a conglomerate has been created with a turnover of Rs. 1,400 crores. This merger took place after Brooke Bond acquired Kothari General Foods, Tea Estates, Doom Doma, Kissan Food Products, and Cadburys' Dollops Icecream Division. Thus,

Uniliver will dominate the country's soap, detergent, tea and processed food markets. Similarly, Gillette has acquired a 26 per cent stake in Malhotra and Sons which makes shaving blades.

In the pre-1991 liberalising period, M&A activity was confined mainly to Indian companies. In the post-1991 period, foreign companies have begun to play an increasing role. About 40 per cent of the takeovers since 1991 have been by transnational corporations, most of which are directed at consolidating their hold on respective markets. The mergers took place in industries such as tea, food products, soaps and detergents, industrial machinery, chemicals and power. Having acquired a critical position in the economy, the TNCs can shape the structure and development of the entire industrial sector.

Industrial concentration is the direct result of deleting Chapter III of the MRTP Act, which deals with monopolistic trade practices. And the shift in the focus of control from indigenous big industrial houses to transnational corporations has taken place because of devaluation of the rupee and the liberalised share acquisition policy, at terms which involve relatively small costs in foreign currencies.

Sixth, allowing foreign equity participation to increase to 51 per cent or more has sharply increased the leverage of the foreign companies. In most cases, foreign controlled rupee companies have resorted to preferential allotments of shares to the foreign holders, based on an appropriate resolution of the general body meeting, rather than allowing the parent firm to purchase shares from existing shareholders, at prices much below the market price. For example, Colgate-Palmolive hiked its equity share in its Indian venture from 40 to 51 per cent at Rs. 60, when the market price was ruling at Rs. 615; Castrol acquired additional shares at a price of Rs. 110 against the market price of Rs. 1,000 and CP Tools at a price of Rs. 110 against the market price of Rs. 1,300. Discounts have been 78 per cent in the case of Asean Brown Bowery, 70 per cent in Lipton, 76 per cent in Alfa Lavel, and 80 per cent in Phillips. This requisition have conferred a whopping capital gain of

Rs. 2,390 crores to 23 FERA companies investigated by this author.

Seventh, the incentives to foreign capital have not resulted in any significant inflow of high technology. Foreign investment has taken place in low/intermediate technology areas like potato wafers, soft drinks and in the screwdriver technology sector (assembly of Zen car and IBM PCs). On the contrary, the inflow of portfolio investment has increased. This has intensified and amplified the fluctuations in equity prices because FII inflows are hot money, with a built-in expectation of outflow.

It is interesting to note in this context that Indian financial institutions already hold about Rs. 70,000 crores worth of shares in public limited companies. However, these shares yield a (cash) return of only 0.4 per cent on the current market value of the investment. If the opportunity cost for such investment is considered to be 10 per cent, a financial loss of about Rs. 6,600 crores is incurred by them, which is supposed to be covered when the reserves are converted into actual dividends. Thus, financial institutions, which hold these shares in the short term, sustain their current, artificially high prices and thereby subsidise the ownership stake of and control by private companies. The entry of FIIs, whose activities are governed by global rather than national considerations, can alter this cosy relationship. They can embarrass the management by unloading shares in the market at vulnerable times or gain control of the management. They are unlikely to subsidise the price of ownership for long.

The entry of FIIs is likely to lead to a bifurcation of stock market transactions into wholesale and retail trade. Since FIIs buy and sell in big lots, there is a likelihood of wide fluctuations in share prices. Under these conditions, investors are inclined to hedge through trading in futures market. An investor can circumvent and limit his risk by entering into a similar transaction at some future date. If buying (and selling) in the spot market is matched by selling (and buying) in the future market, then the implied rate of return is assured irrespective of the price at that future date. The Securities and Exchange Board of India (SEBI) has abolished *badla* transactions and replaced them by a sort of future trading. The experience of 1995 and 1996 clearly shows that FIIs with financial muscle have acquired dominant influence over the stock market.

To sum up, the path of neoliberal reforms and the process of globalisation begun in 1981, have reshaped the government apparatus, encouraged individual enterprise and distorted the economy. The process of globalisation, undertaken since 1991, will further distort the economy if the present market-oriented development strategy has time to mature. It will lead to growing unemployment and the destruction of small-scale industries. It will increase the control of transnational corporations on industrial production and of FIIs on the capital market, resulting in an unprecedented drain of the country's real resources.

There is no doubt, as Kaushik Basu (1993) has shown, that over the years, expansion of the bureaucracy, in the name of development, has led to intolerable corruption, rent-seeking activities, and structural inflexibilities. A change in the economy's structure was needed to deflate this unproductive rentier class. However, but what has happened in the name of liberalisation and globalisation is a total surrender to market forces dominated by multinational corporations. Behind the World Bank dictated structural adjustment programme, there are powerful TNCs with their sights set on public sector corporations like BHEL, SAIL, MTNL and ONGC.

Transnational corporations are keenly eyeing the country's large market for (power) turbines and telecommunications equipment. Through direct foreign investment in politicians and bureaucrats, they (World Bank and TNCs) already control the apex decision-making bodies. With the completion of the third phase of globalisation, they will control all the strategic production centres as well. The country is indeed getting recolonised without occupation.

NOTES

1. For a comprehensive analysis of the impact of new economic policies on industrial sector, see Swamy (1994), chapter 13 and Kumar, A (1993).

2. Since 1975, India has been in the throes of a Soviet style 'scissor crisis' which adversely affects the real incomes of farmers. However, its impact on the farming community was uneven. Richer farmers were better able to withstand the downward pressure on their farm incomes, by supplementing them through trade and services; those having links with industry could endure diminished farm incomes for a longer time. In any case the alienation of the farming class was growing.

3. In 1985, the World Bank initiated an in-depth research (the cost of which was about $25 million) on India's industrial and trade policy directed by Robert J. Anderson and Garry Pursell. This research effort generated 10 confidential reports, 2 research reports by Garry Pursell, 4 working papers, 2 major World Bank reports and many small confidential in-house research papers that fed into the Anderson Memorandum, see World Bank (1990).

4. Mitra P. and Suresh Tendulkar (1986). The parameters of this model are dubious, having no statistical base. They are guestimates of the authors: import and export elasticities as well as employment responsiveness of the model are higher than those suggested by historical data.

5. The World Bank's document on structural adjustment loan/credit (1991. p. 33) clearly states: "The Bank's policy dialogue ... aims at making private sector development and orderly public sector retrenchment dominant elements of the adjustment programme."

6. The SAL/SAC document states that the loan instalments "would be contingent upon satisfactory overall progress on programme implementation and the implementation of specific conditions detailed in the policy matrix (25 items). As part of the Bank's/Association's continuing policy dialogue with the Government, it will monitor the Government's macroeconomic programme".

REFERENCES

Ahluwalia, M. S., "Towards a Restructuring of Industrial, Trade and Fiscal Policies", *Financial Express,* 11 July 1990.

Ajit, D., "Industrial Growth and Employment: An Analysis of Labour Absorption in Manufacturing Sector in India", *RBI Staff Studies,* December, 1992.

Basu, Kaushik, "Structural Reform in India, 1991-93: Experience and Agenda", *Economic and Political Weekly,* xviii: 48, 27 November 1993.

Bhagwati, J. and T. N. Srinivasan, "India's Economic Reforms", *Economic Growth and Social Change,* September 1993.

Desai, A.V., "The M Document", *Indian Express,* 8 August, 1990.

Gupta, D., "Employment, Output and Productivity Trends in India's Small Scale Industry", *RBI Staff Studies,* August 1992.

Khanna, S., "Deregulation and Competition in the Indian Industry: Anatomy of Rent Seeking Behaviour in the Corporate Sector" (mimeo.), Indian Institute of Management, Calcutta, 1993.

Kumar, A., "New Economic Policies: Prospects for the Industrial Sector", *Economic Growth and Social Change,* September 1993.

Ministry of Surface Transport (MOST), *Development of a Long Term Plan for Expressways in India,* Final Report, New Delhi: Government of India, 1991.

Mitra, P. and Suresh Tendulkar, "Coping with Internal and External Exogenous Shocks, India, 1973-74 to 1983-84", CPD Discussion Paper No. 1986-21, World Bank, 1986.

Mundle, S. (1992), "Environment Effects of Stabilisation and Related Policy Changes in India, 1991-92 to 1992-93", in ILO-ARTP, *Social Dimension of Structural Adjustment in India,* New Delhi, 1992.

Planning Commission, *Employment: Past Trends and Prospects for 1990s,* Working Paper, May 1990.

Sharma, K.C., "Investment and Financial Behaviour of Public Limited Companies", RBI Occasional Papers, June 1991.

Singh, A. K., "Social Consequences of New Economic Policy with Particular Reference to Levels of Living of Working Class Population", *Economic and Political Weekly,* 13 February 1993.

Swamy, D.S., *The Political Economy of Industrialisation: From Self-reliance to Globalisation,* New Delhi: Sage Publications, 1994.

World Bank, *India: An Industrialising Economy in Transition*, Washington DC, 1989.

——, *India: Strategy for Trade Reform, Sector Report,* volume II: Main Report No. 8998-IN, Washington DC, 1990.

——, *India: Structural Loan/Credit,* Washington DC, 1991. *Economic Report–India: Progress and Challenges in Economic Transition* (11761-IN), Washington DC, 1993.

8

Public Enterprises and Privatisation: A Note

Malcolm S. Adiseshiah

THE title of this chapter is ambiguous. It could either suggest that the subject under discussion is the process of transforming public sector enterprises into private sector units, or it could imply that the relative merits of the public sector units vis-a-vis those in the private sector will be analysed. Implicit in the second connotation is the assumption that private sector units are superior to public sector undertakings when it comes to efficiency, functioning and profitability. Actually, the conversion of public sector undertakings into privately owned units is firmly based on this assumption.

Public Sector Performance

Belief in the superiority of private sector units is not founded on any theory, but on the empirical facts about the performance of the public sector enterprises. On five major counts, there is a growing dissatisfaction with their work, shared by the government, Parliament, academic community and the public. First, public sector enterprises at all levels seem to be working at higher and growing costs, resulting in heavy subsidies which have to be met from government budgets. Second, their output is of low and unsatisfactory quality. Third, the plants work well below the installed as well as their targeted operational capacity. Fourth, public sector enterprises, with rare exceptions, suffer from growing technological obsolescence. Finally, the financial performance of the enterprises is abysmal. (Of all the above, this perception is the strongest among the public and Parliament.) The majority of the units at the central (121 out of 220[1]), state (all electricity boards, transport undertakings, and irrigation works, as well as some state owned and operated units), and local government level (cooperatives with their growing overdues and the increasing sickness and deficits of small industries)[2] are working at a loss.

On the above, three comments may be made. First, a sizeable part of the losses sustained by public sector units at both the central and state levels are on account of units which were previously in the private sector and were nationalised under trade union and parliamentary pressure. The textile mills are classic examples of this. Second, since all public sector enterprises operate under a system of regulated and administered prices, and the markets in which they operate are closed ones in the sense they are in the inclusive domain of the public sector, the question of profits or losses is meaningless. Third, public sector enterprises at all levels – central, state as well as local – have social obligations. These include generating employment, including for the most backward classes, acting as a model employer in the areas of wages and housing, developing backward areas, and providing certain goods and services at prices below costs. This implies that their financial performance is not an accurate measure of their actual industrial and commercial status.

In most discussions on public sector undertakings, the principal object of Indian economic development – raising the standard of living of the people, particularly the poorest of the poor – is never referred to. All attention is focused on profits. A major if not the sole criterion for judging the success of private sector enterprises, it has now become the yardstick for measuring the viability of public sector units. This was never the *raison d'être* of the public sector. The fact that it is not generating enough investible resources is only an alibi for doing away with this very important instrument of social justice, and for turning over a major part of the economy to private enterprise.

The pervasive feeling of uneasiness and dissatisfaction with public sector undertakings has led to various reform proposals. Of these, the one regarding the transfer of most of these units to the private sector, through the process called privatisation, is one of the most recent.

Theoretical Framework

The theoretical framework of privatisation rests on a three-point configuration of the efficacy of the market, the role of private property in the market, and the relative efficiencies of different modes of productions by the state (public sector) and the market (private sector)[3]. Implicit in the argument advocating the conversion of public sector enterprises into private sector units are: (*a*) the automaticity of the market and the price system which regulates it, (*b*) transferable proprietal rights which guide it to the goal of profits maximisation, and (*c*) relative efficiency of its production. However, this theoretical underpinning contains many unproven assumptions and has inbuilt contradictions. Particularly for India, the role of the market and prices built into the theory is inapplicable. The condition on market equilibrium of Pareto optimality, and the functioning of the pricing system – based on the assumption of full information about supply-demand conditions and coordination of the activities of a mass of individuals and firms, all of which is costless – do not apply. In fact, this theoretical construct does not exist anywhere. Moreover, the latest World Bank publications[4] introduce some important limitations on their market friendly approach. The President of the World Bank, at its two-day annual World Bank/IMF meeting,[5] stressed the need for an efficient public sector as a promoter of sustainable growth. He said: "the private sector cannot do this alone. An efficient public sector is an essential partner to support basic infrastructure, and to enforce environmental protection without which there can be no sustainable development." Following him, the Managing Director of IMF made a strong case for evolving and applying social policies. He stated: "I include here policies to alleviate poverty, protect the most vulnerable and slow down excess population growth." These are important caveats from the two apostles of the market-friendly approach.

India – the Way Forward

The public sector in India has accumulated a lot of useless and excess baggage. This includes the loss-making units, originally in the private sector, referred to earlier, which have been taken over by the public sector, as well as some perennially loss-making public sector undertakings which are not part of the original texts and rationale or the founding resolutions of the Government of India,[6] be that of 1948 or 1956. I have shown[7] that 110 out of the current 211 public sector units which are the subject of the Annual Survey of the Bureau of Public Enterprises can either have all their shares sold in the open market, or merge with sound functioning public or private sector enterprises, or close down. But there is a core of over 100 public sector units which need to be safeguarded and which one leading industrialist in the private sector referred to in the following terms:

> I am one of those who has always believed that on our country attaining political independence, had not our government shouldered most of the infrastructural industries like coal, steel, rail, and air transport, power, fertiliser and number of other basic industries, the industrialists like Tatas, Birlas, Goenkas, Kirloskars and dozen of others would have found it extremely difficult to attain the extent of industrial development they have been able to achieve. In fact, they would not have found adequate resources for both basic and strategical important industries.[8]

We need always to bear in mind that public sector enterprises have been responsible for the country's rapid industrialisation (ranked 10th on among the industrialised countries of the world till recently[9]), for providing private sector enterprises with the infrastructural inputs that they need, and for promoting self-reliance in several critical areas. It stands in need of reform and continuous review. Little will be gained by throwing the baby out with the bathwater, which is what indiscriminate privatisation of the public sector will achieve.

NOTES

1. Bureau of Public Enterprises, *Annual Survey, 1975-76*, New Delhi: Ministry of Industry, Government of India.

2. Statements introducing states budgets and CAG comments on them, State Governments from 1975-76, New Delhi.

3. G. Stringler, "The Theory of Economic Regulation", *Bell Journal of Economics and Management Science*, 1971.

4. World Bank, *East Asian Miracle*, Washington DC, 1993; *Sustaining Rapid Development in East Asia and the Pacific,* Washington DC, 1993.

5. Annual meeting of the World Bank and IMF Development Committee, Washington DC, September 27-29, 1993.

6. Government of India, White Paper on Industrial Policies, New Delhi 1945. The Industrial Policy Resolution, April 1948; Industries Development and Regulation Act of 1951; The Industrial Policy Resolution, 1956.

7. Malcom S. Adiseshiah, *Privatisation and State Enterprises*, Monograph Series IV, Calcutta: Indian Institute of Management, 1989.

8. Navel H. Tata, "Rejuvenating the Public Sector", *Commerce,* 20, September 1986.

9. UNIDO, *Annual Report 1980-81*, Vienna, 1982.

9

The New Economic Policy and Self-Reliance*

I. S. Gulati

SELF-RELIANCE was one of the key elements of free India's economy envisaged during our national struggle against colonial rule. Decentralised development, balanced regional growth, and equitable distribution of the gains of development were the other issues of importance. We associate this pre-Independence vision with Mahatma Gandhi. In Gandhiji's thinking, self-reliant development had to proceed hand in hand with democratic decentralisation from the village level upwards. Indeed, national self-reliance required that the villages undertake their respective development, mobilise their own resources, and meet their own needs.

Nehru's Development Strategy

In giving practical shape to this vision of the economy after Independence, Nehru made some departures from the Gandhian notion of self-reliance. One of these was with regard to decentralisation. He favoured centralised planning as the route to rapid economic development and modernisation. Perhaps, in Nehru's assessment, this was of immediate political priority; that the country needed a strong government at the Centre, one which could hold the country together and face external challenges to its territorial integrity.

In a recent lecture, K.N. Raj, while speaking about the intellectual debate in the Planning Commission in the early fifties, recalled that on the one hand, persons like him were fully convinced that rapid agricultural development and promotion of small-scale industries, based on locally available raw materials

---

* I have chosen this topic keeping in mind the economic philosophy I share with Professor Oommen.

and catering to local markets, were the only channels along which income levels could be raised in the countryside and fuller employment opportunities created for the rural population. On the other hand, they were also aware that a hard core of modern, technologically advanced industries must be built in the country, not only to strengthen its defences and improve its competitive position vis-a-vis other countries, but also to support and sustain agricultural growth and rural development on a technologically sound footing.[1]

Nehru's departure from the Gandhian views should not, however, be misconstrued as an attempt to de-emphasise self-reliance. Nehru placed greater emphasis on autonomy at the national level, in the sense of the country becoming self-reliant with regard to basic materials, be it food, steel or technology. It was in pursuit of this view of self-reliance that the Nehruvian development strategy can be said to have deviated from Gandhiji's vision.[2] Whatever experimentation was attempted in the field of decentralisation was conspicuous by the absence of democratic component, and these experiments were largely unsuccessful. The Community Development Programme, taken up as part of the planning strategy, failed principally because it was a top-down exercise, with very little democratic decision-making. In fact, very few local bodies involved in the programme allowed to function without interference from above.

Indeed economic decision-making became more centralised with each successive Five Year Plan. Planning became an instrument for concentrating powers in the hands of the union government vis-a-vis the states. At the same time, the latter took over whatever powers the local bodies possessed at that time. In the process the economic system became deeply bureaucratised. Controls and regulations introduced in the name of optimal allocation of scarce resources led to increasing centralisation, widespread corruption and inefficiency.

Still, Nehru was firm on his model of self-reliant development. Some of the solid achievements of the Nehruvian model were self-sufficiency in domestic food output and several areas of industrial production.[3] Unlike several other developing countries, which could show higher rates of growth in income, India's, dependence on imports, particularly in critical areas such as food, steel or capital goods, became negligible.

Unfortunately, economic growth was not evenly spread over the different regions of the country, and regional disparities worsened. Also, poverty showed little signs of declining, leave alone being eliminated altogether. In most parts of rural India, land reforms were neither thoroughgoing nor fully enforced, with the result that the incidence of landlessness in the country is no less today than it was five decades ago. If anything, it is worse. Poverty and unemployment among the landless and nearly landless households have increased enormously.

Emphasis of the New Economic Policy

The new economic policy, with its emphasis on globalisation, is designed more to integrate the Indian economy with the world economy than to make it self-reliant. In this respects, the new policy will put the clock back even in the one area in which the Nehruvian strategy could be said to have shown solid achievements, namely, national self-reliance. If the new policy regime had been adopted five decades ago, the country by now would have presented a classic picture of neocolonial exploitation of the Latin American type, with the economy dominated by multinationals, extreme economic inequalities, high unemployment, and explosive class relations.

It is appropriate that we take note here of a claim often made by the authors, proponents and supporters of the new economic policy. They argue that the policy they advocate is also aimed at achieving self-reliance, in the sense of generating exports at a level and pace which will yield enough earnings to finance the country's import requirements. Obviously, there is a major shift in the meaning being given to "self-reliance". The term no longer implies making the country self-sufficient in basic commodities, be it food, steel or capital goods. All that is aimed at through this new interpretation of the term is the development of the capability to purchase goods, essential or non-essential, from other countries. This is not the sort of self-reliance that, for instance, impresses the Japanese who, in spite of substantial balance of payments surpluses, continue to resist attempts to make them open their shores to food imports; or even the USA which spends enormous amounts in support of not only domestic agricultural prices and incomes but also technological development.

The new economic policy currently being pursued in India is also bound to adversely affect the rural economy, with its greater emphasis on the commercialisation of agriculture and the relaxation of regulations related to dealings in agricultural land. The increasing accent on agricultural exports could lead to a shift in cultivation from food crops to export crops. To the extent this happens, the country's agriculture will become vulnerable to the vagaries of the world commodity markets, particularly since India has become a signatory to the new GATT treaty which is heavily biased against the developing countries. At the same time, we risk sacrificing the self-sufficiency in food which we currently enjoy.

Opening up the industrial sector in pursuit of globalisation has no less serious implications for the economy. In the short run, the new policy is bound to depress growth, as is already happening. Out of fear of competition from liberalised imports, domestic industrial investment and production have begun to stagnate. At the same time, foreign capital has started flowing in to take control of domestic firms. In the long run, the new policy will convert our industrial sector into a mere adjunct of the global economy, dominated as it is by rich countries and their multinationals.

Foreign Direct Investment

Great store is being laid by the new economic policy on direct foreign inflows as a source of finance for both increased investment in the country and meeting its growing import requirements. It is worth noting, however, that the success achieved so far in attracting such an inflow can at best be described as modest. Even assuming that the inflow does gather strength in the coming years, it is wrong, in my judgement, to speak of foreign direct investment in aggregative terms. We shall have to judge the inflow of foreign investment by the sectors it targets and the technology it bring in. The dangers to be guarded against are that foreign investment may: (*a*) crowd out private domestic investment; (*b*) acquire monopoly power; and (*c*) go to sectors in which domestic technology is already reasonably well-developed.

A highly undesirable scenario that an unregulated inflow of foreign investment could lead to is one in which industries producing major consumer goods, which are in demand by the urban elite, are taken over by MNCs; or domestic savings get channelled to the MNCs through the manipulation of the financial system (let us not forget the major role of a handful of foreign banks in the banking-cum-securities scam). Should such a scenario obtain, and given the scope for enormous profits, very soon the country will be faced with a massive outflow of funds in the form of profits and other incomes of these MNCs. Most of the Latin American countries had experienced similar situations in the past.

External Debt

In this context, it is pertinent to remind ourselves that India's external debt has almost quadrupled in dollar terms since 1980 and now stands approximately at $ 85 billion (or Rs. 265,000 crores). Normally, when a country resorts to external borrowing, it is a reflection of its current trade deficit, that is, when imports exceed exports. In our case, the trade deficit has lately been on the decline, mainly as a consequence of the drastic devaluation of the Indian rupee as against the US dollar and other currencies. Consequently, imports have become extremely expensive. On the other hand, even though export earnings have been maintained (they have started registering a substantial increase lately), it has been possible only at a high real cost, given the drastic decline in our terms of trade.

The loans taken in the first three years or so of the new economic policy have gone less towards financing current balance of payments or even repaying old external debts falling due, and more towards building up the country's external reserves, which no doubt, are quite large now. The question we ought to be really raising however is whether the cost of building up our external reserves with borrowings is justified and, if so, to what extent.

Poverty and Unemployment

It is also pertinent to bear in mind the impact of the new economic policy on poverty and employment. The government's claim of having increased employment and reduced poverty during the years of the new economic policy ring hollow. There is no evidence at all of a decline in unemployment in the country. Even during the period 1980-89, when the manufacturing output increased at the rate of 8 per cent per annum, employment in the organised private sector fell. Only the organised public sector registered increases, though modest, in employment.

While information for the recent past is unavailable, it is highly probable that employment in the organised private sector has declined much more than during the eighties. If we add to this the likely fall in public sector investment as a consequence of the new economic policy's focus on public sector disinvestment and privatisation, we will find that the overall impact on domestic investment one of deceleration rather than acceleration. So the likely scenario is that of a substantial increase in unemployment thanks to the economic policy that has been adopted.

The Planning Commission's recent estimates of the increase in employment fall far short of what was originally projected for the Eighth Plan. On the basis of these calculations, the unemployment situation should have worsened since early 1991. Also, since the budgetary provisions for anti-poverty programmes (actually released) were on the decline and the number of unemployed/underemployed was on the increase, and given the underlying demographic factors, unemployment and poverty are bound to have increased in the years since the economic reforms were introduced. And the situation will probably worsen further, given the sort of economic scenario that is evolving.

Comparison with China

It is fashionable to make comparisons of our new economic policy with the economic reforms in China. Only superficially do the economic reforms of India and China have any similarity. Most important in this context is to realise that China has pursued a vigorous policy of self-reliant development and has been able to register phenomenal growth over the past one decade while ensuring reasonable and equitable distribution of incomes. China has thus been on a very different growth path from India. The economic reforms China has introduced in recent years have been brought in from a position of great economic strength – a strong industrial and technological base, a dynamic agriculture, the virtual elimination of poverty, substantial growth in exports, and a phenomenal accumulation of external reserves. In the circumstances, China is in a position to liberalise selectively and invite foreign investment on its own terms. This is not at all the case with India where the economic base built up over the years is itself in jeopardy and economic reforms have been introduced under pressure, direct and indirect, from international lenders.

Conclusion

The question before us now, in my judgment, is *not* whether India should or can pursue the traditional policy in the context of a changed world scenario. The Nehruvian model itself needed many major changes. It should have provided for thoroughgoing land reforms, wholesale debureaucratisation, and democratic decentralisation. Unfortunately, we have pursued a suicidal economic policy since the early eighties when the Nehruvian model started getting discarded. What is being referred to as the new economic policy is really a logical extension of the course on which the economy was set in the eighties.

The option, then and as it is today, is to change the course altogether and take to the path of genuinely self-reliant, balanced, equitable growth through decentralised development. This is crucial because in the new unipolar world order, our vulnerability to pressures, particularly when it comes to the production of basic goods, will be the greater as we depend increasingly on external funds.

NOTES

1. See K.N. Raj, *Decentralised Development and Local Government in Kerala,* Sri Damodara Menon Memorial Lecture, Gandhi Peace Foundation, August 24, 1993.

2. One should take note here of a view that decentralisation of the type Gandhiji had in mind was simply not consistent with the type of centralised planning Nehru was enamoured of, namely, the Soviet type. According to Nirmal Mukarji, "Nehru was inspired by the Soviet experience of five year plans which had enabled the fledgling Soviet state to lift itself by its bootstraps" and therefore established central planning on more or less the Soviet model. "Reflections on the Status of Planning", paper presented at Seminar on Panchayat Raj/Nagar Palika Bill, 1993, Centre for Development Studies, Thiruvananthapuram.

3. "Our country made great progress establishing an adequate industrial base and also in promoting agricultural growth" and as a consequence, "we are no longer helplessly dependent on large imports of steel or the massive imports of foodgrains", Raj, Decentralised Development.

10

Development from Within:

Rethinking on an Alternative Development Path

K. V. Sundaram

The Development Paradigm in a Changing Global and National Context

AS political, social and economic circumstances, domestic as well as international change, development seeks new directions, orientations and emphases. It is now common knowledge that since the late sixties and seventies, the development paradigm has shifted its concerns from growth to redistribution and equity issues, and more recently to the added dimensions of stability and sustainability. In keeping with the new priorities and the socio-political context of the countries, the nature of the planning process has also been changing. During the fifties and sixties, many developing countries in Asia and Africa which attained independence following decolonisation, adopted a top-down planning process, with central control over all government functions. But over time, the shifts in political priorities, new socio-economic realities, and the more complex nature of administrative tasks compelled governments to devolve at least some of their policy formulation and decision making functions to their subnational levels.

Since the late sixties, concepts like "development from below" and "bottom-up planning" have come to be advocated. Many countries have responded to these developments and adopted multilevel planning procedures with the involvement of people in varying degrees. However, in most countries, the mechanisms evolved for the purpose are funded by the central government, and the local institutions set up for formulating and implementing various plans have over time, taken on the characteristics of state government departments without much independent authority or financial powers. In this process, the government has spread its tentacles into various sectors of development activity at all levels. This has brought the entire range of development functions, including those which can be conveniently managed by local communities, within the fold of the public sector. As a result, a "dependency syndrome" has grown, stifling local and regional initiatives.

Moreover, the national and global context has changed drastically. After decades of steady economic advance, in many countries, development is being thrown into reverse gear. The explanation is far from simple and it varies from country to country. In most cases, a complex interlocking set of external, internal and environmental factors are involved:

> For most of the countries of Africa, Latin America and the Caribbean, almost every economic signal points to the fact that development has been derailed. Per capita GNP has fallen, debt repayments have risen to a quarter or more of all export earnings, share in world trade has dropped and productivity of labour has declined.[1]

The New Economic Reforms and their Implications for Local and Regional Development

Important changes have been taking place in the Indian economy as well. We have been moving in the direction of liberalisation and a market-oriented system for almost a decade. This process was intensified following the macroeconomic crisis of 1991 and the introduction of policy reforms entailing economic stabilisation and structural adjustment. What this means, as far subnational affairs are concerned, is that the role of the state in local and regional development matters is declining and the responsibility of the people and local institutions is increasing. Regional and local communities must now find their own development centres of gravity in order to respond to the new policy changes that have emerged, this should be reflected in the nature and character of the planning and development responses. It means that the management of social and economic processes at the regional and local levels, which affects rural production, income distribution, equity, social security, and poverty alleviation, must now be handled in an increasingly self-reliant manner. A new work ethic, development ethos, and set of value systems, must be forged to spearhead, energise and mobilise society for the management of socio-economic transformation at the grass-roots level. This calls for recognising the discrete spatial levels below the one somewhat broadly characterised as "local". In our country this level comprises the following entities:[2]

- District
- Block
- Village
- Individual

The above hierarchy may further be broadly grouped into two categories:

A. Area (aggregate of villages) level : District and block

B. Grassroots level : Village and individual

If one were to relate the above categorisation to development planning in action, one may hypothesise that at the area level, where the line agencies have their outposts, government initiated projects predominate, with a modicum of public participation. It has been the experience in many countries that such projects are often identified at higher administrative levels and people have little or no direct say in their formulation and implementation. Of course, the line agencies as well as individual projects may differ with regard to their capacity to mobilise villagers in local level planning, elicit their participation, solicit contributions from them, and involve them in follow-up action. In most instances, success in this regard has been minimal. As many evaluation studies have shown, this has been one of the main causes for the inefficacy of these projects.

In our view, the grass-roots level is the village level, where members of the village community closely interact among themselves. At this level, people can initiate projects as well as implement them with the active involvement of their own community, and with little or no external support. In such projects, local participation is genuine and complete, and the efforts become self-organising and self-sustaining. Because of the people's stake in such initiatives, they feel responsible for the day-to-day running of and follow-up action on these projects.

Development from Below and Development from Within

The above-mentioned distinction between the area (group of villages) and grass-roots levels, with their respective initiators of development projects, allows us associate a different type of planning with each group. Thus if we refer to planning at level-A as "development from below", we may characterise the one at level-B as "development from within' (DFW). While DFW is also a kind of development from below, there is a subtle distinction, in that it reflects the nature and intensity of the people's participation and relation to government role. Here the distinction that we have made between government initiated projects and people initiated projects is significant. It may also be noted that development from within is in the nature of a capillary or "trickle-up" effect, while development from below is government controlled, albeit with an element of public participation. In its essentials, DFW is somewhat akin to the concept of autocentric development propounded by some German scientists.[3]

The reason why it is important to draw this subtle distinction is that for our subnational areas the days of "dependent development" must be deemed over. The central government, with its preoccupation with macroeconomic problems of adjustment and loan repayment, can hardly be expected to find the time and the resources to go all out for regional and local development. In this context, the regions (states) and local areas must increasingly take on a greater share of the development responsibilities in their respective domains and must be fully empowered in their tasks. In other words, decentralisation, instead of merely remaining a widely talked about concept, must now become a vibrant reality. This will entail a resurgence of the self-organising abilities of the people, the renewal of the sense of social efficacy, and enhanced opportunities for people's participation. This implies devising various institutional arrangements for effective regional and local development, a feat perhaps best achieved by restructuring and "reinventing" traditional structures and institutions. This must also be accompanied by a major redistribution of authority and financial powers. The term "subnational areas" implies a number of discrete spatial levels. The allocation of appropriate functions, powers and finances to each of these different levels and the development of self-governing institutions for them is a highly complex subject, one which we do not propose to go into here. Our limited purpose in this chapter is to discuss some key issues concerned with the concept of development from within, which we have demarcated as the sphere of action of people at the grassroots level.

Development from Within – Definition

DFW has already been advocated as a "survival strategy" for Africa.[4] This author has also elaborated the relevance of this concept to agriculture in sub-Saharan Africa.[5] But the concept is not limited to mere survival, which is only a temporary response to a crisis situation and therefore a short-term panacea, we, on the other hand, see development from within as a "sustainable development strategy" for developing countries. Nor is it seen as an isolated rural and local community development effort. Instead it vitally complements the concepts of top-down development and development from below, which have already taken root in most developing countries, to promote social and economic development. Thus DFW is meant to integrate local initiatives into the larger planning and development efforts of the government.

DFW is not a new idea. The seeds of this concept are contained in the teachings of Mahatma Gandhi in India and Julius Nyerere in Africa. Other luminaries, like Jaya Prakash Narain, Vinobha Bhave, and Ariyaratne (Sri Lanka), have also expounded particular aspects of this philosophy. In broad terms,

DFW may be defined as an endogenous development process by which people themselves assume the responsibility to manage their own resources, define their needs, goals and aspirations, and make decisions affecting their wellbeing and sustainable development. Its fundamental aim is to unleash the potential of the local community as well as meet their inner urges and preferences with regard to development through self-reliant approaches.[6]

The basic idea of DFW is that development at the local community level has to be self-generated, self-organised and self-sustained. The people, instead of seeking action from central and state bureaucracies or distant governments, must practise self-help. They must apply their resources to productive activities, as opposed to "rent-seeking" ones. The ideas on development must spring from within and must get concretised through local action.

DFW will make it possible for local and regional communities to raise more resources for themselves, assert their own value systems, have confidence in their ingenuity and skills, and be less dependent on external agencies for their development. This may sound like utopia; but in the context of the current crisis in macroeconomic management, there seems to be no option except to seriously adopt it as the dominant strategy.

If DFW is a concept worthy of adoption, how do we go about implementing it? This is a vital question. The answer is not simple, for there are no fixed or precise methodologies or rigid rules for operationalising it. It is not a normative concept, as the actors here are the individual citizens, who have to come together of their own volition to practice it. In this context, we may only state some general principles by way of guidelines, and not be able to provide any specific designs.

Localism in Scope and Content

DFW is "localism" in action. What are the kind of activities which can be promoted through a strategy of DFW? As Prof.

Dantwala observes, "Both the scope and content of planning shrinks at each successive lower level of Planning."[7] If this is so, of the bottom most level that we are considering, the residuary development functions will be quite limited.

This should not, however, be seen as a constraint because the functions which can be performed at this level are, in any case, circumscribed by the technical capabilities of the local people. Normally, such local functions should be labour-intensive, require local resources and know-how, and be either totally free of or minimally dependent on external aid or inputs. DFW concretely means relying on local judgements and creativity, as well as local raw materials, land, labour and capital for those forms of production which permit local grassroots initiative and innovation and yields results compatible with local conditions, tastes and culture. Broadly, the areas where DFW as a strategy and planning process can make a significant contribution to local development are:

- Sustainable agricultural development
- Natural resource conservation and management
- Forestry development and environmental protection
- Social provision
    - Education
    - Health
    - Rural sanitation
    - Community welfare
- Irrigation and water supply
- Maintenance of common property resources
- Development of renewable energy sources

More specifically, activities, falling within the above broad categories, which can best be carried out using a self-reliant approach are:

- Organic farming and manure production (mulching and use of compost).

- Village cleanliness including garbage removal and drainage.
- Maintenance of village roads including paving them with bricks.
- Revival of village industries and crafts.
- Education in health and hygiene.
- Primary education.
- Drinking water supply.
- Farm/social forestry.
- Establishment and management of grain golas.
- Construction and maintenance of footbridges.
- Construction and maintenance of microhydel projects.
- Development of biogas, solar energy and wind energy.
- Waste utilisation (bagasse, sawdust, cotton stalks, rice husk, manure).
- Support to informal production units (not only crafts and manufacturing, but also services and trade).
- Revival/maintenance of traditional distribution systems (e.g., periodic markets).
- Protective measures, needing group action, which increase crop yields (windbreaks, shade trees, anti-erosion measures, optimisation of tree cover on crop land, etc.)
- Community fodder banks.
- Collection and conservation of run-off water.
- Revival of relevant autochthonous (indigenous) solutions in the agroecological and socio-economic spheres.
- Establishment and management of credit institutions like *Grameen* Banks or other indigenous credit arrangements.
- Renovation of village tanks and other water bodies.
- Reclamation of saline/alkali soils;
- Construction and maintenance of small irrigation systems.
- Environmental protection.
- Watershed rehabilitation.
- Construction and maintenance of intravillage and intervillage roads.
- Self-help housing schemes.

- Uplift of the peasantry through cooperative efforts. (transformation of the "small peasant into a market-oriented farmer"[8]).
- Tribal welfare.
- Women's uplift.
- Human resource development.

The above list, with its formidable array of activities in the realm of group action, is only indicative and not exhaustive. Broadly, these action areas fall in the spheres of production, consumption and nature conservation. They constitute a set of measures to unleash a process of development of the production forces, with the objective of better satisfying the basic needs of the community and achieving sustainable development.

Following are the key components of the concept of DFW:

- Public participation
- Decentralisation and empowerment
- Self-reliance
- Self-management through collective voluntary action
- Polycentric institutional development

The salient features of these components have been dealt with below:

Public Participation

Genuine public participation where people are at the centre of development activities is the hallmark of DFW. But achieving this is not an easy task. Successful public participation in local development efforts requires repeated experimentation and trial and error. It is an inherently evolutionary process, in which activities must proceed step by step, allowing for a continuous cycle of observing, doing and learning. In the process of trying to cope with social realities, there is progression from passivity to activity.

Group action is the basis for DFW. Collective unified action is easier if society is homogeneous. However, such homogeneous structures are difficult to come by. Most rural communities are characterised by factions, with the clients of local patrons, followers of local leaders, associates of gangs, or members of both formal and informal groups all pulling in different directions and striving hard to maximise their particular interests. Such a context calls for a deep understanding of group dynamics and social engineering skills, when seeking to bring them together for collective action.

Decentralisation and Empowerment

Decentralisation and empowerment constitute the fundamental base on which concepts like development from below and development from within can thrive and be operationalized. It has been often emphasised by many intellectuals that if India's democratic polity has to be anchored in truly self-governing units at the level of panchayats, there has to be effective devolution of developmental functions and governmental authority to the different tiers of panchayati raj institutions. With the coming into effect of the 73rd and 74th Constitutional Amendments, the legislative and executive action of state legislatures and governments as regards the formation, structure, composition, powers and functions, periodicity of elections and such matters relating to panchayats have all been mandated. The states are now expected to bring these bodies into existence within the stipulated time and enable them to function as effective institutions of self-governance as well as local planning and development. The most critical aspect at this juncture is the effective devolution of powers and resources, political as well as financial, to panchayati raj institutions in consonance with the functions and responsibilities they have been entrusted with. Simultaneously, the bureaucratic system must be restructured so that the functionaries, elected or appointed, become accountable to the people whom they are required to serve. These are the essential prerequisites, not merely for establishing a strong panchayati raj system, but also for stimulating local initiatives towards development from within. The present political juncture is appropriate for introducing this strategy. One can reasonably hope that strengthened panchayati raj institutions, which will soon be in place, will not only catalyse the implementation of this concept, but also provide policy guidelines.

Self-reliance

Self-reliance is another key component of the strategy of DFW. However, it only means depending on one's own resources as much as possible and does not imply autarky or absolute self-sufficiency. It refers to the capacity for autonomous decision-making and selective control over external relations. Gandhi may be seen as one of the foremost ideologues and practitioners of self-reliance. According to him, self-reliance starts with the individual (everyone must be his own scavenger), but finds its fullest expression at the level of "Village Swaraj", "independent for its own vital wants and yet interdependent for many others in which dependence is a necessity."[9] Self-reliance makes possible the efficient and fuller use of local resources and draws on local culture, values and traditions. It stimulates creativity and innovation. Through self-reliance, important positive externalities are internalised. The principal ingredients of a self-reliant approach to development are:[10]

1. Building the long-term economic, social and political viability of rural communities. This is done by delineating an appropriate unit consisting of a federation of villages and devolving substantial and effective powers to this democratically constituted level of local governance in which the rural poor and marginalised groups have due representation.

2. Expanding opportunities for productive work in rural areas, especially for young people and women, through small-scale industrial development, including the extractive and processing sector. The intention is to raise rural incomes by providing opportunities for productive employment in non-agricultural sectors.

3. Ensuring the continuous upgradation of the health of the natural environment in the following ways:

   A. Improving basic ecological conditions, including the management of renewable resources, such as forests and groundwater supplies, the protection of watersheds from erosion, and the conservation of common pasture lands.

B. Improving agricultural technology including the construction and maintenance of small-scale irrigation systems and application of appropriate land preparation techniques, such as terracing, land consolidation, etc.

C. Improving energy supply not only through the sustained (yield) management of existing forests and reforestation of denuded areas, but also the use of biogas and solar energy.

D. Improving the human environment, a comprehensive term which includes environmental sanitation, pest and flood control, potable water supply and drainage systems, housing, community facilities (assembly hall, sports fields, nurseries for small children, etc.), and physical access (roads and railways) and communication infrastructure (radio, television and telecommunications).

4. Providing for the satisfaction of locally determined basic needs. This requires setting priorities and identifying certain target groups. They can be made productive by: (*a*) directly providing them with basic goods and services; (*b*) raising their real incomes to a level at which they can afford to meet their basic needs; and (*c*) developing their skills through human resource development efforts. Thus the provision of basic needs is regarded as a moral and reciprocal entitlement.

5. Achieving balanced rural-urban development.

6. Establishing linkages with various organisations, both above and below.

7. Encouraging group action by establishing healthy cooperative structures to manage production activities and

by promoting the formation of functional groups like farmers' associations, farm labour syndicates, user groups, women's groups, youth organisations, etc.

Self-Management

Efficient management is a basic prerequisite of all successful activities. In the context of DFW, it implies self-management through collective voluntary action. The emphasis in this form of participation is on developing the overall capability of a community to sustain itself in the present and in the future. Such collective, voluntary, bottom-up management at the grassroots level demands self-discipline or self-rule buttressed by peer pressure. It implies collective leadership and division of responsibilities by the creation of diverse functional groups.

Polycentric Institutional Arrangements

No community is monolithic. It is always differentiated into groups with varying common interests. In this context, what we need are polycentric institutional arrangements for binding, consolidating and unifying the groups and for promoting their common interests. Such groups will be in addition to the democratic decentralised institutional structures, such as the panchayati raj institutions, which are general-purpose authorities performing the various functions devolved on them. While the functional groups considered necessary for operationalising DFW will also be non-central institutions, they will perform circumscribed functions among numerous jurisdictions, and have independent rule-making and rule-enforcing powers. They can either be instruments for collective action in developing and maintaining, for instance, common property resources and providing various public facilities. Or they can be receiving mechanisms, which interact with the government's delivery system and distribute the benefits to appropriate target groups. They can also be special-purpose groups that develop, operate and maintain certain small infrastructure like roads, water supply, energy generation, community buildings and irrigation systems. However, all these collective mechanisms need not be established anew. At least some of them can be developed around existing traditional institutions, which can operate within a broader framework of local-self governance. Thus, for concretising DFW, indigenous institutions must be seen as an important source of social capital. In the past, however, in many instances, this social capital has been eliminated, creating a substantial lacuna in effective local organisation. In order to render DFW operational, these traditional institutional structures need to be revitalised as vehicles for collective action. Where indigenous informal groups or institutions are still working effectively, it is important to study their design principles and working procedures, so that they can be replicated. Capital is no doubt important for economic and social development at the grassroots level; but of equal if not greater importance is the organisational ingenuity of the community, the extent to which it can mobilise its members, and the tasks it can accomplish.

Apart from these traditional institutions, wherever necessary, the creation of user or interest groups with sufficient autonomy must also be promoted as part of the orgnizational structure for DFW. Such groups will have a strong, long-term impact, particularly in sustaining small-scale infrastructure. These user/interest groups may either be spontaneous responses of the local communities for managing their own affairs or be created and supported by governments or other agencies for specific projects. Either way, they should be formally recognised and given the right to mobilise their own resources and act independently. Thus, enabling the potential beneficiaries of infrastructure and other types of public goods to organise themselves into polycentric limited-purpose functional groups with circumscribed governmental authority should be top priority for ushering in DFW. Some studies on user or interest groups have clearly demonstrated that when users realise that the operational and maintenance costs of projects have to be borne by themselves, (the beneficiaries), they become highly motivated about keeping the costs as low as possible and monitoring the activities of producers to avoid corrupt practices. In countries like Nepal, where developmental resources are very scarce, user or interest groups and self-management enterprises have evolved to such a degree that some large-scale voluntary institutional arrangements have also come into existence and are functioning successfully. A classic example is *chhatis mauja* – thirty-six villages – a large-scale, gravity-flow farmer-managed irrigation system, irrigating almost 3,500 hectares of land, farmed by approximately 25,000 people in 54 villages.[11] Now, many donor agencies are investing in the construction of infrastructure projects only when they have is firm evidence that those who are supposed to benefit from a facility are committed to maintaining it over time and have the organisational and financial capabilities to do so. Undoubtedly, the idea of user or interest groups has great potential in developing countries where the challenges are immense.

The policy implications here for DFW are quite clear. We must: (*a*) encourage the beneficiaries into forming primary local units/provision units that can mobilise resources to acquire ownership of small-scale infrastructure over time and assume full responsibility its operation and maintenance, and (*b*) invest in general institutional facilities which enhance the capabilities of such primary local units. Such arrangements may be viewed as a form of privatisation of public services, in other words, as market arrangements that have become necessary and must therefore be encouraged by local governments. Normally, when groups of beneficiaries organise by themselves to provide or secure common benefits through joint decision-making and by accepting mutual obligations for resource mobilisation, some type of governmental authority must be created and suitable working rules be framed to ensure that these mutual obligations are met.

It is, however, difficult to specify a set of common principles that should guide the formation and working of primary local units of collective action. No single institutional arrangement will be universally applicable. It would be fruitful to study a number of such organisations that are currently operating successfully in the country and draw relevant inferences and lessons from them. This is a task which governments at higher levels (central as well as state) in India must undertake. "Successful institutional arrangements are usually complex rather than simple and that polycentric institutions that perform relatively well for some types of rural infrastructure have not been successfully fitted into a simple typology."[12] It will not be out of place to mention here that some NGOs have applied scientific knowledge to create systems that endure. They deserve to be carefully studied so that their example can be emulated. NGOs which have performed well in this field can catalyse many grassroots level projects and help in their effective implementation.

The polycentric institutions discussed earlier can be of three kinds:

- Indigenous institutions that have proven highly successful over time.
- User groups sponsored by local and other governments.
- Special interest groups, like farmer organisations, which are self-organised and self-governed.

Indigenous management systems have been particularly recognised to be effective for forest protection and management and for natural resource conservation. The experience of countries like Nepal has shown that such organisations are effective when operated within the local institutional context. In Nepal, Furer-Haimendorf has noted among the Sherpas of the Khumbu region, the presence of *shingo naua*, or forest guards, who are a part of the village organisation "in charge of the preservation of protected forests."[13] In many countries, local forest committees exist. The idea that users of natural resources should also be responsible for sustaining them has now gained widespread recognition. The participation of users, and others who have rights, in decision-making processes about the protection and management of natural resources should be encouraged. McNeely and Pitt have argued in favour of adding cultural and social dimensions to environmental planning and management for "conservation from below". They have found that cultural norms and values, including religious beliefs, act as control mechanisms, thereby aiding natural resource protection and management systems.

DFW as a Planning Tool for Sustainable Development

Sustainable development requires local initiative. The question of how to achieve sustained local action therefore becomes crucial for long-term development efforts. DFW can make a substantial contribution in this area. A scientific approach to the problem is to prepare an indicative micro-plan at the village level (ecodevelopment plan), which can distinguish between schemes emerging from the local authority and implemented by various sectoral agencies, and those that are undertaken by the people themselves through the kind of polycentric self-management institutions discussed above. The basic elements of such a plan involving active community participation are:

1. Resource inventory (land, water, biomass); assessment of the extent of resource degradation; and optimal resource use.
2. Projectisation

   A. *Class I:* Projects to halt resource degradation and promote farm development; projects for sustainable agricultural development; village forestry programmes; and programmes for income and employment generation.

   B. *Class II:* Projects for agri-support services.

   C. *Class III:* Projects for village habitat improvement and provision of social infrastructure.

3. Preparation of a village ecodevelopment plan which distinguishes between projects falling under development from below and development from within, as well as those under different funding arrangements.

This is shown in Fig. 10.1. An innovative project, Micro Level Resource Survey with People's Participation, is currently under way in the state of Kerala. It is being undertaken by the Centre for Earth Science Studies in collaboration with the Kerala State Land Use Board and other agencies and with the

Fig. 10.1
Village/Farm Ecodevelopment Planning: An Approach

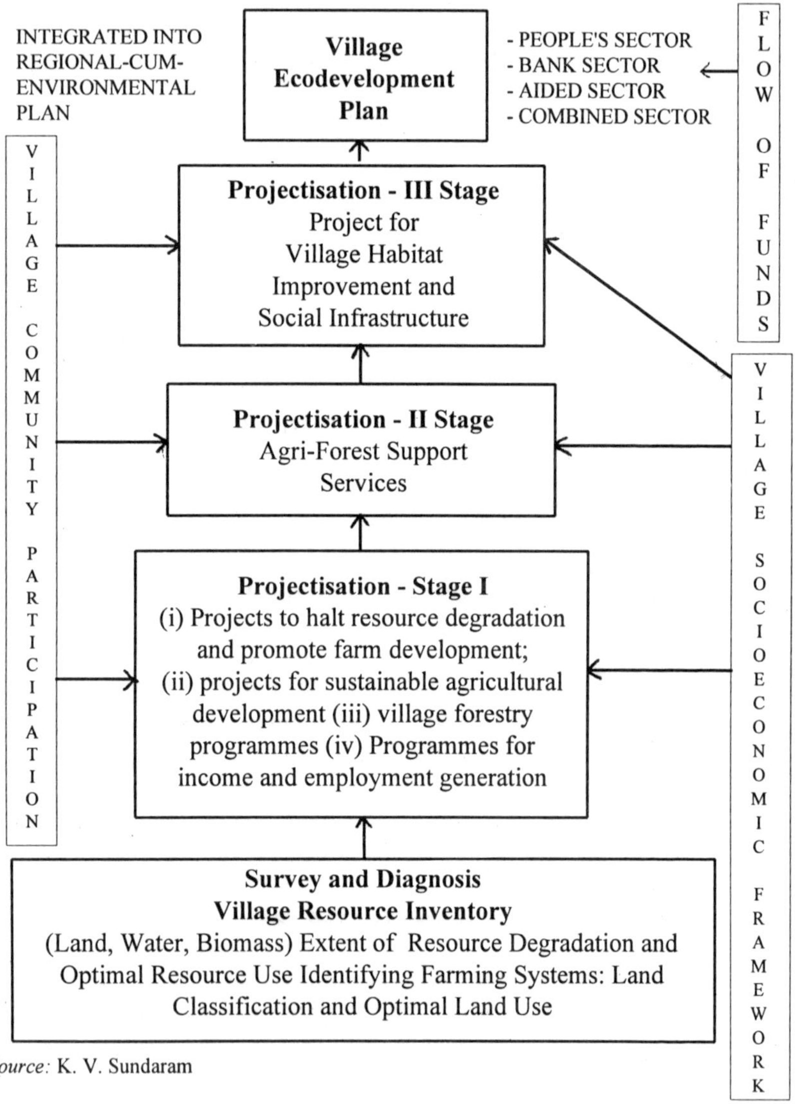

Source: K. V. Sundaram

active support of NGOs.[15] While the project will initially undertake an integrated resource survey and mapping at the panchayat level, it is expected to eventually lead to a District Development Plan, hopefully incorporating all the steps and procedures indicated in Fig. 10.1. The Kerala experiment is likely to throw up valuable lessons for DFW. Successful DFW by a community would imply that the community: (*a*) has full control over the resources in the local area; (*b*) adopts a sustainable pattern of resource use; (*c*) avails of appropriate technology; and (*d*) is able to distribute the fruits of development among all its members in an equitable manner. All these are implied in the village ecodevelopment plan.

Role of Governments, NGOs and Donor Agencies

DFW does not imply that development is initiated and sustained totally independent of government support. In fact, the government can play a great facilitating role in the following ways.

1. Develop suitable methodologies and guidelines.

2. Facilitate group formation and action, establish codes of conduct for groups, and recognise them as mechanisms receiving various forms of assistance. (Support to orgnisation development.)

3. Provide some financial support in the form of seed money or grants.

4. Imparting training and techniques, knowledge and skills appropriate to the local level and relevant to the context in which people will be organising their activities.

It should be emphasised that the government's role is essentially catalytic – one of galvanising the people to initiate development actions according to their own collectively perceived priorities and aimed at self-reliance. Assuming too interventionist a role will undermine the spontaneous and voluntary processes involved in DFW and should be avoided. What has been said about the role of government applies equally to NGOs and donor agencies, who may be involved in stimulating community efforts at the grassroots level.

Summing-Up

To pull together a diffused body of ideas and thoughts presented above, DFW is not a mere abstract idea or philosophical postulate or technical jargon. It is an aspect of bottom-up strategy calling for mass action at the local level. It has to be have a local base, which includes not only the people, but also traditional leaders and indigenous institutions. The kingpin of this approach is self-reliance. This spirit of self-reliance has to suffuse and permeate not only the economy, but also the people, collectively as well as individually. DFW implies local action in multiple aspects, which works outwards from oneself in a set of "oceanic circles" as Gandhi said. Verily, it brings Gandhi back into local development in a big way by adapting his ideas and programmes to suit our modern value systems. All these imply far-reaching changes and call for experimentation with ideas, self-help, diligence, and cooperation among the beneficiaries, as well as upgradation of the skills of the local people and adoption of new technologies. If DFW is to be successfully operationalised, systematic human resource development must follow.

According to Peter Oakley *et al*, "it is the Indian subcontinent which has the richest vein of innovative approaches."[16] Here we have many experiments on self-reliant approaches to development, thanks to the dedicated work of a few NGOs and some Gandhian institutions. Their methodological innovations still await detailed study. Methodologies of qualitative processes are often not readily apparent and need a number of key reference points before they become visible. The imperatives at this juncture are clear. It is necessary to carefully analyse the practice, review the ideas, and see what practical methodologies can emerge from them. Giving methodology a shape and form and preparing guidelines is a big task which the central and state governments must take up by setting up competent study/working groups. The urgency is great. There is no time for dithering or delaying action.

NOTES

1. UNICEF, *The State of the World's Children*, New York: UNICEF publications, 1988.

2. In some states in India, a cluster of villages below the block level, designated as the "mandal", has also been recognised as a planning level.

3. Senghass, D., and H. Elsenhans, quoted in Theo Rauch and Ael Redder, "Autocentric Development in Peripheral Rural Regions through a Strategy of Locally Integrated Economic Circuits – Theory and Methodology", *Applied Geography and Development*, vol. 35, Institute for Scientific Cooperation, Tubingen, 1990.

4. Fraser Taylor, D. R. and Fiona Mackenzie (eds.), *Development from Within–Survival in Rural Africa*, London: Routledge, 1992.

5. Sundarm, K.V., *Decentralisation of Agricultural Sector Planning in sub-Saharan Africa,* Rome: FAO/UN, 1993.

6. Galtung, Johan, *et al*, *Self-Reliance – A Strategy for Development*, London: Bogle L'overture Publications, 1980.

7. Dantwala, M.L., "Two-way Planning–Logic and Limitations, A Critical Review of Indian Experience", in FAO document, *Expert Consultation on Multilevel planning and the Two-way Process in Agriculture and Rural Development Planning,* Bangkok, 1983.

8. Raanan, Weitz, *From Peasant to Farmer – A Revolutionary Strategy for Development*, New York: Columbia University Press, 1971.

9. Gandhi, M.K., *Rebuilding our Villages*, Ahmedabad: Navajivan Publishing House, 1959, p. 5.

10. Sundaram, K.V., *An Alternative Rural Development Strategy: The Self-reliant Approach Based on Gandhian Concepts and Principles*, (Forthcoming).

11. Documented in *Institutional Incentives and Sustainable Development – Infrastrucutre Policies in Perspective*, Elinor Ostrom, Larry Schoeder, and Susanne Wynne, Oxford: Westview Press, 1993.

12. *Ibid.*

13. Furer-Haimendorf, C.Von, *Sherpas of Nepal: Buddhist Highlanders,* London: John Murray, 1964.

14. McNeely, J.A., and D. Pitt, "Culture: The Missing Element in Conservation and Development" in McNeely and Pitt (eds.), *Culture and Conservation: the Human Dimension of Environmental Planning*, London: Croom Helm, 1985.

15. Centre for Earth Science Studies, "Panchayat Level Resource Mapping – An Approach Paper", Trivandrum, December 1991.

16. Oakley, Peter, *et al*, *Projects with People – The Practice of Participation in Rural Development*, Geneva: ILO, 1991.

11

Participatory Governance: Some Issues

Christopher C. Benninger

WITH the passage of the 73rd Amendment to the Indian Constitution, decentralisation has become a widely-discussed issue. The Amendment promises more participation by people in the governance of their own private and public affairs. This chapter argues that while creating more open and active local bodies is the important first step, a number of modalities inherent in the administration of public affairs must be studied and reformed. It is not enough to reform only political decentralisation (Benninger, 1990). Who will administer what a local body decides upon? From where will the resources emerge, and how? What technical and professional staff will be available to carry out local decisions?

Panchayat raj has not been achieved by the passage of the 73rd Amendment. Only a process has been set into motion. Unless local bodies have control over their public resources, over an adequate administration to manage their plans, and over a qualified professional staff to carry out their decisions, the amendment could turn out to be a mockery of a democratic dream. Some of the issues involved are discussed below. Certain recommendations have also been made.

The chapter underlines the need to review the specific framework within which the goals of local level governance can be achieved. District, taluka and village level governance can be meaningfully discussed under the following three headings.

Decentralisation

There is wide consensus that the Indian polity will stabilise if the management, public finance and planning functions are decentralised to a greater extent. This entails new institutional arrangements. While federalism is a national issue, it is herein maintained that decentralisation is one concerning the states. The notion that every state in the country will move toward decentralisation at the same pace, and in a similar way, is untenable. Even within Maharashtra, different regions and districts may transform themselves variously, depending upon the local conditions. But some common principles underlie this transition.

Participation in Management

"Participation" is a widely used word, variously defined and interpreted. Often our panchayati raj institutions are undermined by the creation of special committees and councils for "user groups", in the name of enhanced participation. For example, *panchakroshi* mandals were formed in Ratnagiri in Maharashtra in the early eighties on the recommendation of the Centre for Development Studies and Activities (CDSA), UNICEF, and a broad-based experts group (CDSA, 1979). The idea was that since panchayats were controlled by "vested interests", who could hijack a major UN supported programme, mandals under the charge of "the poor" needed to be created. In retrospect, one wonders whether such ad hoc arrangements – creating parallel institutions – facilitate or militate against participatory development. Moreover, a myriad system of institutional interfaces evolve. Such complex public systems become even more opaque to the participating public. In this essay, therefore, by "participation" we mean the enhancement of panchayati raj institutions themselves, and the involvement of community associations, user groups, private enterprises, and voluntary agencies in these institutions. Governance herein implies the involvement of a range of actors, not just formal government institutions. These actors are referred to as "the civil society" in this chapter.

Local Level Planning

Local level planning is still an enigma. Town planners have dominated this field, focusing on the narrow physical aspect of development. Likewise, economists have overemphasised budget mechanisms to achieve macrogoals at lower levels. Their use of sectoral schemes and district allocations is effective neither for achieving socio-economic transformation, nor catalysing a desired pattern of economic growth. Local level planning is an area where mere "training" of officials will not create the adequate human resources. Just as specialised professionals are required to prepare urban land use plans, civil works investment programmes, public works and social facility plans also require professionals to coordinate, prepare, present and negotiate local level plans for rural development. Local level bodies cannot just sit down and prepare development plans. They require expert advice. Ironically, the very societies which advocate deregulation, privatisation, and the promotion of entrepreneurship for India, have highly evolved local level planning systems. Where land use and environmental planning, water and sanitation management, social inputs and economic infrastructure programming are concerned, probably no settlements are more planned, controlled and policed than those of the freewheeling West. The same may be said of Singapore and other models being suggested to us. The critical difference is the level of participation. The issue here is not one of more or less planning, but of inclusive versus exclusive institutional arrangements. In fact, the more pluralistic the development scenario becomes, the more local governance becomes focused on protecting local resources and assets. Guided investment and regulation become larger issues for *local* people. Microlevel plans will be facilitative of local economic initiatives and responsive to local entrepreneural skills. Local people protect the resources they cherish (Benninger, Aneeta, 1991). The present *mechanisms* of governance ensure that this is not possible.

Since the district will ultimately be the key intermediary tier between macro level governance and local level governance, several key aspects need to be discussed and clarified. The units of local level jurisdiction within a district, the demarcation of functions and transfer of schemes, projectisation, devolution of funds, local planning machinery, human resources development, information data base, participation modalities, and the integration of related institutional activities – all require discussion. This chapters offers no solutions. It only attempts to open the Pandora's box, so to speak, by raising certain issues and making some recommendations.

ISSUE ONE: AREA OF JURISDICTION

Recommendation

The boundaries of panchayats must be reconsidered. Revenue villages are not conducive units for effective governance. An effective local body must have the threshold population for basic services but be small enough for local institutions to be *visible* to the participants. Political and administrative *accountability* will be enhanced through such rationalization.

District as an Intermediate Tier

It is important to delineate the smallest area of jurisdiction, or the smallest unit, at which the formulation of viable projects and local activities can meaningfully be undertaken (Prasad, 1969). This may be defined as the "local level", and be seen as quite distinct from the district level, accepting that the district is one of the crucial tiers in a multilevel government structure. The district is important since it is here that all the decision-making powers of the state are concentrated. The idea inherent in the Karnataka model of locating a chief secretary within each district is worth noting. But the local level must be looked upon as a small area below the district level, where appropriate development activities and projects can be formulated and implemented. This chapter views the district rather than the development block as the intermediate tier.

Micro-level Tier

Even at the subdistrict or local level, there are different tiers which vary in their scope for decision-making, planning, and implementation (Benninger, 1984). The development block, which has been recognised as a development unit below the district level, can be taken as one such local unit. But since it can be fairly large in size, it would be desirable to think in terms of an area, say defined by a small watershed, a microtidal basin or a market town itself, which may be conceived of as the lowest of tiers below the district level for management and decision-making. Such a tier must aggregate statutory panchayat raj constituencies rather than cut across local level boundaries. Development blocks should be disbanded. Rather the taluka can be seen as an administrative unit akin to an urban ward office. Panchayat samitis are non-entities. They hold no unique deliberative place either with regard to representative government, or in terms of legal accountability to the people.

Population Threshold for Basic Services
Such local level clusters should be sensitive to the criteria of minimum population and distance thresholds, so that local activities can be economically sustained within that area and social services can be provided within easy reach of the local population (Roy and Patil, 1976). In the Integrated Rural Development Programme at Ratnagiri (noted above), a traditional unit called a *panchakroshi* was used. These units are in fact small watersheds. Large villages, with their related hamlet clusters, can also formulate their own projects and thus form a rational jurisdiction for local level governance. However, it is proposed that jurisdictions below the district should be based on nested tiers *within any environmental system.* Such tiers should be aggregated directly from existing administrative units. This multitiered system of jurisdiction can comprise the following territorial units, each with their own actors (spatial unit/actor):

1. Microwatersheds/multipurpose cooperatives

    a. Farm terraces/households
    b. Village ponds, canals, roads, pastures, temple and forest lands/user group panchayats

2. District regions/zilla parishads

3. The development block has been dropped. The taluka office is seen more as a deconcentrated ward office of the district. The samitis introduce an opaque layer between governance at the local level and that at the state level. Samiti jurisdiction boundaries often more approximate the

interests of members of legislative assembly and Parliament whose constituencies overlap with the blocks. By ridding the system of panchayat samitis, the larger village panchayats will take on their just importance.

Optimising Functional and Formal Boundaries
In the long run, such a multilevel system should be strengthened by adjusting boundaries to define ecological units, instead of attempting to carry out resource-based development within formal tax revenue boundaries defined during the colonial era.

Section (g) of Article 243 under the Amendment gives the Governor of a state reasonable powers to make this important adjustment.

ISSUE TWO: DEMARCATION OF FUNCTIONS AND TRANSFER OF SCHEMES

Recommendations

The functions of local bodies require definition. It is suggested that the goal is not autonomy but "critical regionalism", wherein microvalues are applied to implementing critically applied to the implementation of national goals in a critical manner, and vice versa.

Critical Regionalism
In an era of ethnic conflict and regional chauvinism, the concept of "critical regionalism" is proposed. It assumes a regionalism which is conscious of the local ethos, yet responsive to global values. In the absence of such a dialectical link between the two, our efforts to decentralise could lead to a kind of localised fascism, wherein locally dominant groups misuse their powers to suppress minorities or to grab local resources. At the same time, the value system of macrogovernance must be tempered by local values. Critical regionalism also holds "the state" to be the persistent value system, as opposed to "the government", which is a creature of circumstance (Kulkarni, 1979).

Desegregation of Functions

Once the jurisdictions of local governance are defined, there should be a very clear-cut demarcation of the development functions to be performed at each tier (Eleventh Schedule, Constitution of India). The kinds of programmes, supportive schemes and projects which are to be associated with these functions should then be identified and allocated to their appropriate institution. Ideally, this exercise not a subject of "final decisions," but one of open-ended negotiations between tiers. It has to be carried out in some detail, taking into account issues such as uniformity in standards and quality control within the state as a whole. For example, even in such a highly decentralised function as secondary education, certain areas of responsibility (such as core syllabi, textbooks and examinations) will have to be kept with a higher tier to ensure a minimum level of performance. Once the demarcation of responsibilities amongst the different tiers of governance is decided upon, the state government must effect the transfer of these functions, along with their component schemes and financial outlays, to the appropriate levels for decision-making. The Eleventh Schedule (Article 243G) of the 73rd Amendment clearly spells out which activities are considered purely "local".

Transparent Terms

People can only participate in a system of governance when they can define the matters they are deciding upon (Oommen, 1991). Here we would like to sharpen the definitions of projects, supportive schemes and programmes.

Projects. These are activities carried out by individuals, households, cooperative enterprises, or interested groups to achieve some desired social or economic outcome. For example, a household may do terrace bunding on its own farm to retain soil, manage water, and limit access; or a village panchayat may build a percolation tank to increase the community's water-harvesting capability. Projects are always composed of inputs and outputs which together result in certain outcomes, for example increased productivity or enhanced efficiency. Private companies and cooperatives most often carry out what they clearly conceptualise as projects.

Schemes: They facilitate projects by providing *inputs* which are not easily procurable within the project milieu. These may also be inputs which a public body, as opposed to the individual, disaggregated actors in the private sector, is in a better position to secure. These facilitative inputs represent only a small fraction of the total inputs required to reach the desired outcomes.

Programmes: There are clusters of schemes which together fill major gaps in the input systems required to reach some broad purpose through a number of outcomes, and therefore emerge out of a diversity of projects.

Localised Control

All programmes, schemes and projects which are distinctly visualised from within the local community, should come under the effective management and control of the concerned local body for their planning and implementation. A local body may or may not have the requisite capabilities or skills needed to formulate and implement some of these local level schemes and public projects. Notwithstanding these deficiencies, all local decisions with regard to publically funded actions must be left to the discretion of the local body. Moreover, activities which is not in a position to carry out can be contracted out, since often private or cooperative agencies are more capable of delivering inputs and achieving outputs.

Where personnel are deputed, they must work under the direction of, and be accountable to, the local body.

The Manager

At the local level, the dual control of technical personnel is unavoidable, but the problems inherent in such an arrangement can be minimised through personnel management practices. Within a microwatershed, or other local level planning unit, a chief coordinator should be employed by the local body. For example, a PHC doctor works under the administrative control of the Directorate of Health Services and under the functional control of the district health officer, but is expected to respond to the needs of the people in a particular group of villages. Such a doctor should be under the functional control of a Chief Coordinator during the hours of his scheduled visit to the local area. On his part, the chief coordinator must arrange a place for the doctor and facilitate patients' appointments.

Development Management Committee

The chief coordinator is expected to manage technical officials operating in the local jurisdiction. He or she must direct the work of ANM's and village level workers and see to routine tasks. A local development management committee will be responsible for horizontal coordination. Such a committee should be composed from amongst the elected representatives of the local panchayat. The chief coordinator must be administratively senior to the various sectoral functionaries working at the local level. His powers and functions should be carefully defined. It should not be that executive orders are issued by the state government. For example, a village level worker cannot simply be redesignated Chief Coordinator in the name of a transformation in governance. The local body must employ its own manager.

Gradual and Diverse Model

The emplacement of chief coordinators must be a gradual process. In about 10 per cent of the local bodies a well-known NGO may be deputed to take up the responsibility on a contract basis. In 30 per cent of the cases, they may employ coordinators with high education levels and who belong to the private sector – either a manager, management consultant, or local professionally qualified graduate. In another model, a local college may be engaged to take up this assignment in the initial stage, though colleges are not insulated from external interests and have other focal concerns. This transition must come about gradually, as and when local bodies themselves feel the need for local planning and management. But there will be administrative responsibility *only* when a manager is hired by the local body.

ISSUE THREE: PROJECTISATION

Recommendation

The "schemes" through which state governments allocate funds sectorally and districtwise should be dispensed with. Block grants to local bodies to carry out their own programmes and statutory duties is alternatively suggested.

Functional Linkage Networks

Currently, district planning and development is not an integrated activity (Gaikwad and Parmar, 1980). Since the large number of schemes that are being implemented within districts are financed, controlled and operated by external agencies at different levels, having their own organisational structures and lines of command, the coordination between and integration of these schemes, and their appropriate linkages and sequencing in space and time, have never been achieved (*ibid.*). One characteristic of top-down governance is the multitude of sectoral schemes through which it operates. This effectively spreads resources so thinly that no one scheme has a high enough investment level to achieve significant results. Participatory modes of governance usually vacilate between populist schemes (which suffer from dissipation) and more focused promotive ones (related to local economic potential). As noted above, schemes which have been defined by state level departments should be scrapped, and economic development councils at the district level be awarded block grants to support "lead sector" investments at the local level.

The CDSA (Poona) has developed a functional linkage matrix (FLM) technique through which the interdependence of local level schemes can be analysed and more highly linked schemes be identified and prioritised. Poorly integrated schemes should be dropped at the earliest as they do not have an impact. A logical, phased system of scrapping schemes, based on linkage hierarchy, can be implemented. It suggests a logic for both block grants as well as toward functions which justifiably need public support.

Economic Lead Sectors

Projectisation around an identified lead sector will ensure a three-way integration of sectoral, spatial and operational public administration. The lead sector strategy ensures the optimum utilisation of available local resources and encourages production specialisation in the area. It is a means of achieving developmental objectives appropriate to a given context. If scarce resources are distributed too thinly across many sectors and subsectors, effective economic infrastructure cannot be installed, nor can economies of scale for processing, packaging, marketing and transport be achieved. Specialisation through the lead sector strategy ultimately fosters intradistrict complimentarities in production and consumption systems, and in the long run, encourages a narrowing of interdistrict disparities in development. It is suggested that local bodies be given block grants under two categories: (*a*) to meet statutory responsibilities (primary education and public health); and (*b*) for economic development. Since about a thousand ineffective state government schemes, under about ten departments will be scrapped once the FLM technique is applied, these block grants will be sizeable. Therefore, the identification of lead sectors by local communities is a vital aspect of the decision-making by local bodies.

Agency Integration

The schemes under the Integrated Rural Development Programme, Jawahar Rojgar Yojana, etc. are all presently "remote controlled". Ultimately, they fall short of their objectives and do not have the desired impact. As presently implemented, they remain isolated, with each department concentrating on its own targets, both physical and fiscal (Reddy, 1979). This is done in utter disregard of other schemes and projects with the same objectives, but organized and implemented by other agencies and departments. Unless all the schemes and projects impinging on an area are brought under the effective operational control of the local body, the necessary coordination and integration will be difficult to achieve.

The Employment Guarantee Scheme (EGS) is a key activity funded from a higher tier but implemented at the local level. Under such a scheme, the blueprint of works is prepared by the district public works department for the district revenue machinery. It should, in fact, be prepared by the chief coordinators and the development management committees at the local level. Such schemes will then contribute to the development of local water harvesting structures, marketing facilities, and other investments supportive of a lead sector activity.

Reach of the District Plan

The district planning exercise, as currently practiced, is confined to a small fraction of the district economy. Many developmental activities are not within its purview. Numerous private sector initiatives have a direct or indirect bearing on a district's progress, which the district plan does not reflect. There are, of course, many constraints in preparing a strategy which covers the entire development spectrum and encompasses all the "stakeholders" of civil society impinging on a particular district's space. But key entrepreneurs and lead sector consortium representatives should be involved in the development of districts. For example, the Venketeshwara Hatcheries consortium can play a key role in the introduction of finance, infrastructure, veterinary services, processing, packaging, transport and marketing for poultry development in particular areas of a district. To attract such conglomerates, the district development councils and local development management committees will have to invest in infrastructure and services supportive of the activity. Local committees can tailor beneficiary-oriented inputs under IRDP so as to link below poverty line (BPL) households to effective systems like the Venketeshwara Hatcheries network. Similarly, in the dairy sector, the Chitale Group can be involved; in cattle development, joint ventures can be worked out with the Bharatiya Agro-Industries Foundation (BAIF) (Srivastava and George, 1977). Local bodies can reconceptualise their entrepreneurship in terms of designing "investment packages" with other potential stakeholders once the wasteful schemes are scrapped. Banks, investment firms, support NGOs and enterprises can be facilitated by district development councils. Thus, comprehensive district planning can be dropped in favour of demand-based, disjointed incrementalism. The statutory responsibilities of district governments can be carried out with the district block grants extended to zilla parishads.

Categories of Inputs
Currently, the agencies implementing programmes, schemes and projects in a district belong to the following categories: (*a*) district body; (*b*) sectoral agencies and departments of the state government; (*c*) centrally sponsored/assisted, or controlled by the central government ministries and departments; (*d*) the cooperative sector; and (*e*) non-governmental, voluntary and private welfare agencies.

Integration Strategy
The integration different activities and coordination of investments can be visualised as follows:

Activity I: Identification of lead sectors which need to be initiated or further catalysed. Various stakeholders at the local level propose investment packages based on their interests and what they can deliver.

Activity II: Integration of project inputs and investments with local level, corporate and/or co-operative sector activities.

Activity III: Integration of projects with the voluntary sector and community-based organisations.

Basically, local bodies should use their schemes and block grants to design investment plans which can attract outside capital. The different activities noted above need not be undertaken in a fixed sequence. They may be gone through synchronously or consecutively depending on the situation. In each activity, the focus should be on the desired outcome (measurable change expected, area covered, participants targeted), schedule of transition, outputs required, inputs needed and their sources, roles and actors. But the programmes of action must emanate from CBOs, NGOs, entrepreneurs, cooperatives *and* the local government. The motto should be, "People Decide, Government Supports". Such proposed investment packages should be prepared at the local level and negotiated with outside investors and the district economic development council for investment participation.

ISSUE FOUR: DEVOLUTION OF FUNDS

Recommendation

Allocation of funds to a district must be based on two criteria. First, the health, education and social welfare needs of the district's population. Second, its performance in local revenue mobilisation; effective management should be rewarded. The Gadgil formula used in interstate allocations at the Centre and inter-district allocations by several states is a system which awards funds based on weighted "backwardness criteria". It does not reward efficiency or effective development management. Similar criteria should govern the allocation of district block grants to local governments. The Gadgil formula which is the basis for the allocation of central plan must be dropped.

Interdistrict and Intradistrict Allocation of Development Funds
Allocation of development funds must fulfil the tests of social and spatial equity as well as take into consideration the special problems faced in particular areas. Using indicators like population, area covered, poverty levels, resource endowment, special problems, and the degrees of backwardness in specific sectors, each state government must develop such criteria. In addition, sizeable incentives should be given for mobilising local resources. Here it may be noted that it is not the gross funds mobilised which should be rewarded, but the *recent performance* in mobilisation of funds. This will mitigate the discrepancies between zones rich in resources and those which are poorly endowed.

Interdistrict allocations should be the responsibility of state governments. The state level finance commission can hammer out a revised formula periodically. Intradistrict allocations should be left to district bodies (zilla parishads). If they carry out their district planning exercises within a bottom-up framework which recognises crucial local concerns as well as critical macrovalues, they will be able to identify which activities in the district need to be given priority. This will systematise intrasectoral allocation to a great extent. District governance is concerned primarily with a limited list of statutory duties to the people. But to fulfil even these, the budget is often inadequate. District bodies should focus on these "unavoidable" areas and leave economic development activities to local bodies and the more open district development councils. If such intradistrict allocations turn out to be suboptimal, then it will normally be due to a skewed political base. Local bodies can perform well only if constituencies begin to link their participation levels with the costs and benefits of skewed development. Without the active participation of civil society, no one will blow the whistle on skewed, irrational investments. Two kinds of block grants should be extended. Those for fulfilling statutory obligations must be appropriated on a *need* basis. But block grants for development projects should be based on *performance* criteria, in which the resource mobilisation history of local bodies will figure prominently.

Integration with the Lead Bank's Credit Plan

Several rounds of credit plans have been formulated and some useful experience has been gained in development finance (Rao and Mehta, 1990). Yet, it has not been possible to integrate credit plans with district plans. The banks' annual action plans are announced in advance of the district plans. They have no idea of the credit requirements of districts.

One way of obviating this problem is to ensure that no, or only marginal, changes are effected in the district's draft annual plans. But such rigidity will stifle creative economic initiative. Therefore, only the quantum of investment required may be fixed. If credit plans are to be formulated well in advance, and yet be in consonance with district plans, changes will have to be made in the plan calendar and the manner in which the state plan and district plan outlays are determined. If each local body has a lead sector and is seeking investment partners, lead banks become part of a more flexible negotiating process. The present assumption is that lead banking plays a "social role" by making investments in areas which perform well socially, but not necessarily in the market. Lead banks then can negotiate in favour of projects with greater social impact – like local employment generation and enhanced environmental sustainability. But they should drop "schemes" in favour of "blocks of funds" for investment in packages which are "socially attractive". They may seek partnerships with local bodies whose goals they support: poverty alleviation, sustainable environment, higher productivity and enhanced management. In such a scenario, the banks will be in a position to know which components of district development require credit support before finalising their action plans. But again, they should not attempt to be comprehensive, with an exhaustive list of schemes and allocations. Instead, the action plans should identify "fertile areas" for negotiation as well as packages where firm commitments can be made. Our subsequent discussion with regard to schedules is appropriate in this regard.

Most of the credit plans formulated at present confine themselves to extending credit to beneficiary-oriented programmes, such as the Integrated Rural Development Programme. For the rest of the programmes, no serious effort is made to explore the possibilities of linking credit with an economic lead sector build-up. On the contrary, banks engage in lending without reference to contextual development strategies. Presently, most district credit plans look suspiciously alike.

When attempts will be made to formulate credit plans in tandem with district plans, it is likely that there will be a clash between the style of functioning of the banking world and the new milieu of local governance. These two cultures will have to be integrated if the process of decentralised planning is to be streamlined. The considerable expertise within the banking community has to be harnessed and complimented by the skills and experience of those working in zilla parishads and local government offices. Lead bank managers can play a constructive role in educating local communities about "investment packaging". This may call for the sharpening of their managerial skills.

Policy decisions made by the Reserve Bank of India to implement the service area approach (SAA) need to be considered in this regard. Under the SAA, the branch manager is supposed to examine the credit requirements of an area and the potential investment possibilities in each village and accordingly formulate the service area credit plan. Actual borrowers are identified and the bottom-up aggregate credit requirement is calculated for each tier – village, service area, block and district. In such a bottom-up aggregation process, a proper liaison will have to be kept with other credit agencies of the government, cooperatives and the private sector. Such steps will enhance the integration of local level development plans with a more appropriate credit back-up. The lead bank will be a partner in the local investment plan right from the start.

Ad hocism prevails in the credit system as the cooperative leadership is generally in the hands of the rural elite. Such interests may resent the actual targeted borrowers in the area. Thus the credit delivery system remains in the hands of unintended borrowers. The banking community still carries an impression that SAA is a *bank programme*. They see their role as one of extracting grassroots contributions to achieve corporate goals such as deposit mobilisation, overall priority sector advances, and housekeeping. Such attitudes have to be overcome as credit plans should be seen as tools which aid the participatory process; wherein both credit requirements and the quality of delivery evolve through continuous interaction with the ultimate users and their leaders at different levels. Since the banking system has demarcated blocks into smaller service areas, the earlier issue of local jurisdictions of governance should be seen in this context so that possible mismatches can be avoided.

Forms of Allocation

The state may devolve development funds in the following three forms:

1. Funds for implementing on-going schemes and projected sectoral schemes in the district, which are currently being channellised through different sectoral departments and agencies, can be directed to *local bodies*.

2. A lump sum grant in the nature of untied assistance may be made to the *local body,* which can be spent at its discretion towards meeting the priority needs of the people.

3. A part of the untied assistance may be earmarked as incentive outlay which is to be released, subject to a certain proportion of funds required for a project being mobilised by the *local community*.

Self-reliance

In the ultimate analysis, it is envisaged that local communities should become more self-reliant, generating a major portion of the resources needed for local development works. But there are limitations to this approach owing to resource scarcity in the areas that require the most attention, and the fact that the best taxes often lie in urban areas (Reddy, 1979). In any case, whether funds are devolved to, or mobilised from the local level, they should be controlled by the local body. This body, in turn, must be a decision-making authority, with powers to allocate these funds among various sectors, programmes, schemes and projects according to their requirements. Usually, the "easier to collect" taxes are kept with progressively higher levels of government, leaving the dryer tax well to the local bodies.

Intradistrict Allocation and Reappropriation of Development Funds

In the local governance paradigm advocated, local bodies should be the sole agency for: (*a*) allocation of development funds, and (*b*) monitoring of expenditure performance. The district technical departments may give an initial technical sanction for larger projects. Subsequent minor modifications in schemes during the implementation stage, as well as the administration of project funds, should be left totally to the local bodies. These administrative tasks will be repeated at the end of every semester. At this stage the performance lags can be monitored, and local bodies should be able to issue appropriate directions to the defaulting agencies and reallocate funds if necessary. Once block grants are given to local bodies, all functions relating to financial sanctions, releases, and monitoring of performance will vest with them, and sectoral departments will be relieved of these routine tasks. In this way, a more expeditious implementation of programmes, projects and schemes will ensue. The procedure outline here is a departure from present practice, but if effected, it will go a long way towards overcoming implementation delays and bringing about a better execution of development activities.

Accountability

The accountability of local bodies can be enhanced through a system of public performance audits (Khera, 1979). In this way they will be given a chance to grow into a responsible governing agencies, ensuring speedy and effective implementation of local schemes and projects. Audits constitute the most opaque and deceptive mechanism of reviewing governance. External auditing hides the facts from participants, rather than controls irregularity. A simple "notice board", listing funds received, expended, account expended on, and at whose discretion funds have been released, will regularise fiscal management in a more significant manner than any "external audit". If the lead bank in an area is holding the local body's account, it can be given the job of recording and verifying the "notice board".

Schemes

Again, it is important that programmes, projects and schemes a clear distribution be made between the agencies implementing Mesotier or intermediate level bodies such as districts will plan, finance and manage *programmes*. In agriculture and roads, these would focus on lead economic activities. Each microtier local body will plan, finance and manage its own *projects*, either through user groups or households. Schemes are to be seen specifically as *some* of the inputs required by projects (which emanate from programmes) which cannot be provided by the local people owing to management requirements, technical reasons, or because economies of scale can be achieved only at a larger tier. A scheme may be sponsored by the government, a cooperative, or a private sector agro-based industry. Where public-purpose concepts are to be applied and social subsidies given, the government may be the appropriate implementer. But each district council will have to decide on the social relevance of various schemes to its people and whether or not they wish to transfer sueh *expenditures* to *investments.* Where efficiency and market forces are critical to a scheme's efficacy, the private sector may well be the implementer. Where user group interests are clear and strong, cooperatives may be very appropriate implementing agencies.

Role of Cooperatives

Thus far, there have been few attempts by district planning authorities to raise capital for investment, or to attract private or cooperative capital to particular investment packages. In Maharashtra, for example, it is the cooperatives who have taken the lead by making deductions per tonne of sugarcane supplied, and using a part of these funds for irrigation and other projects of interest to their members (Namjoshi, 1985). Thus, they have spontaneously developed an interest in taluka-level planning. Many government development programmes have been implemented more efficiently in sugar factory command areas because of the cooperative development structure. Cooperative primaries at the village level in sugar factory areas are generally prosperous in Maharashtra, unlike those in non-sugar factory areas. Turning to the private sector, it is true that a few large-scale units have shown an interest in supporting schemes of infrastructure development and even general rural development. However, while private managements try to maximise profits, cooperative managements, being semi-political bodies, are also interested in maximising services to members and voters in their respective constituencies.

The tax concessions and financial incentives offered by the government for the location of economic activities in industrially underdeveloped areas are important instruments of decentralisation. This aspect of policy therefore needs to be integrated with other suggestions made with regard to allocation of public funds. Cooperative banks can facilitate the development of agricultural processing units of diverse types. There are also excellent possibilities for developing innovative schemes in the sphere of leasing finance, utilisation of surplus funds with cooperative banks, and the financing of agricultural exports. The possibilities of attracting investment from non-residents and international developmental organisations also deserves to be explored in this context. This can be taken up by the proposed district development councils.

The role of cooperatives in local level planning will vary from district to district depending on the degree of development of the cooperative sector. It is necessary to evolve mechanisms for mobilising different forms of capital and encouraging the emergence of complex forms of organisations involving private, cooperative and public authorities in development projects of mutual interest.

Methods of Resource Mobilisation

It is not possible to fully consider here the pros and cons of transferring to local authorities taxes such as land revenue, income tax, etc. However certain broad points relevant for effective development from below can be indicated. The government taxation machinery, and even public enterprises and cooperatives, can contribute in important ways to the mobilisation of local capital and its distribution so as to make development from below possible. Districts and talukas have to be treated differently in terms of their potential for development and taxation, as well as their capacity to attract private and cooperative enterprises to different local tiers within them. Weightages will have to be assigned and typologies accordingly defined before we can visualise the full potential of fiscal reforms and financial innovations in the public and cooperative spheres. The increasing importance being given to local level governance will be a leap in the dark unless we indicate not only the ways in which proposed projects can be prepared, but also how finances are to be made available for each project. They can come from taxation, local contributions matched by grants, or by assisting the private and cooperative sectors through joint sector arrangements. Banking and cooperative reforms related to financial procedures and governmental reforms related to local taxation must go hand in hand. Subsidies, incentives and regulations impinging on production cost factors must be coordinated to open up investment possibilities that would otherwise not exist. Direct allocation of sales tax to districts and of enhanced land tax to local bodies must be explored.

Redistribution of Finances among Districts

Districts may be classified into those that are highly developed, moderately developed and poorly developed. Inevitably the more developed districts will be able to raise more resources, both through taxation and by persuading private and cooperative institutions to invest within their territories. In the matter of matching grants, it is possible, however, to give larger (proportionate to local share) grants to investment proposals coming from the less developed districts. This may be particularly recommended in fields such as local irrigation for which a uniform cut-off point for different districts is not necessary. It is also possible to use the surplus funds from the already developed districts to finance development in the backward districts. For example, sugar factory profits can either be used to diversify production in the same district, or be channelised through appropriate federations into developing districts. Such joint ventures can apply the experience of profitable cooperatives to less developed areas, introducing both their managerial and technological innovations. Similar joint ventures between local producers in less developed areas and private companies can also be negotiated. Realistically, such a proposal should not depend on incentives, but on the saturation of potential in the presently developed districts. Incentives may only be given in the form of assistance in project and programme design, and implementation management. But it would be wise for a "development hungry" local body, or district, to direct its own investments in a manner which attracts capital to its lead sectors.

A hierarchy of criteria for the allocation of government resources would be a useful device in this context. Thus, central government allocations can be guided by very few principles, based on population, potential for development, poverty and tax effort. At the state level a larger number of criteria would be necessary. In particular, the extent of urbanisation, levels of economic infrastructure development, and local resource potential would be important factors. At even lower levels, additional criteria such as wasteland utilisation, unemployment level, irrigation potential, etc., will become necessary. The central, state, district and local level development strategies may suggest different criteria of allocation for each subclass of investment. However, these should not be seen as neutral or "clean" criteria which allow one to scientifically assess the level of "backwardness". They must ultimately *support* development strategies. A particular district development council may see investment in roads as the key to developing its lead sector. Its distribution criteria would then emphasise various aspects of roads relating to the production of its lead sector products. For instance, milk collection and chilling plants routes may be given priority in one kind of road network, while tourism may dictate a different road pattern.

Multilevel Disaggregation Formula

While distributing funds among the districts, some states rely on the Gadgil formula. This formula was basically meant for allocating resources amongst the states. Its application at the substate level has contributed to inter-regional and district imbalances, which is contrary to the very objective of local level development. Against this background, we moot three kinds of formulae for addressing backwardness and enhancing performance at different tiers.

The first set of formulae addresses regional disparities. They will help determine how funds should be distributed among the different regions within a state. These regions will consist of groups of districts, and their delineation should be based on similar contextual indicators. For example, in Maharashtra, they will comprise Vidarbha, Marathawada, Khandesh, Western Maharashtra, the Bombay Metropolitan Region and Konkan. Appropriate regionwise indicators should be identified and carefully weighted. Indicators selected should address the causal factors in the backwardness of regions. This is a political rationalisation process. In fact, they can be seen as tools which make visible the extent to which the strong use their power at the expense of the weak, within a consensual framework. Such an approach will enable areas with a cumulative deficit in public investment to get their fair share.

Once the regionwise allocation is made, the quantum of resources that should be distributed amongst the various districts of each region need to be determined. This can be done using the second formula. This vitally important criterion will address the interdistrict imbalances within a region. It will channel funds into the lagging sectors of particular districts, with a view to rectifying distortions in local conditions. Physical quality of life indexes may be the most relevant measures here. Emphasis should be placed on sectors which have been neglected on account of poor governance (such as potable water supply infrastructure). Too often economists have attempted to balance the climatic vulnerability of drought prone areas with compensatory development investments. This is not only inefficient, but leads nowhere. In principle, scarce resources should go where they get results. Only when "transparency" in governance is achieved and elightened public welfare is given precedence, will public investment cease to be viewed emotionally as "theirs" versus "ours". Enhancing opportunities to migrate toward greener pastures may be more cost-effective than making every village a green pasture. Such an approach will temper various negative trends in the districts such as growing shortages in basic services.

The third tier formula will address the very gravity of a district's backwardness, intradistrict imbalances, and those local issues, problems and opportunities which have been overlooked at the regional and other higher levels. Such a formula should take into consideration the local context and reflect the needs and aspirations of the local community. In-depth and focused in character, it will require periodic review and updating to ensure the timely channelisation of funds. The third tier formula will emphasise factors such as employment rates, access to basic services, common resources management, the development of local institutions, and social indicators.

Thus, the disaggregation of plan funds should be seen in a multitier framework where regional, district and local level issues and problems are addressed at their respective levels. This approach is also supportive of "critical regionalism", which tempers local values with macro concerns. But a word of caution. Such formulae have become ends in themselves. They must be means which create visibility in the process of allocation. They must not become the central focus of governance, but remain simple mechanisms which facilitate accountability.

ISSUE FIVE: PLAN SCHEDULE

Recommendation

Concepts such as the financial year, budget lapses, and timebound development projects must be redefined.

Basic Plan Period

We have become used to the notions of Five Year Plans and annual plans (Frankel, 1978). It will be more fruitful to convert the financial year into a "basic plan period" which runs over two or more calendar years. Thus, three such basic plan periods would make up a Six Year Plan. Plan periods must be loosely defined. Allocations under certain block grant headings may take place according to a fiscal year schedule, but once the funds are notionally deposited in an account, there is no logic in their necessarily being expended within one calendar year. They may be used sooner and an early call forward for new funds may be placed, or they can be used later without lapsing. The expenditure of funds should be evaluated at the next higher tier, but monitored locally. No particular calendar day should end an expenditure period (like the 31 March). Plan periods should not merely be phases during which expenditures are made, but be time-frames over which funds are accumulated and deposited in block grant accounts. Actual project gestation periods may have their own rationale. Let the centre and the states have their fixed plan periods, and the districts and local bodies can choose a "rolling plan", or some other more flexible arrangement.

Shift to Participatory Efforts

There must be a fairly strict schedule with regard to public meetings, elections, submission of reports by officials, and decisions on action to be taken. The advantages of a basic plan period are that certain plan formulation operations will take place less often, and thus more effort (with roughly the same expenditure and personnel) can be devoted to the participatory management aspects of governance. While the first phase of a basic plan period should concentrate on spillover activities and the start-up of new projects, the second phase can focus on the completion of objectives. Greater emphasis should be placed on scheduling in such spheres as listing local level voters, holding local elections, having meetings, and presenting reports on expenditures and activities.

Statutory Deadlines

Statutory deadlines must be fixed for passing down expenditure ceilings from tier to tier and for the presentation of reports. Similarly, there must be clear directives on the types and compositions of councils and committees which can take decisions. Their functions and powers must also be specified.

Defined Roles and Actions

The expected output of each council and committee should be well-defined (Reddy, 1979). Otherwise, deliberation will dominate these bodies and the final decisions will be made by technocrats at higher levels. The stretched basic plan period will also make the convening of these bodies more feasible and their decisions more tenable. They will discuss expenditures twice as large as that envisaged in the current annual plans.

Over the past four decades, participation has been restricted to certain, limited allocation procedures. Not much emphasis has been placed on either the management of services and facilities, or the implementation of projects. This "planning fixation" has exacerbated the opaque nature of local level governance. No doubt, the plan decision is the moment of truth. But it is a very small slice of the cake in terms of what needs to be done.

ISSUE SIX: PLANNING MACHINERY

Recommendation

The district plan, as presently conceived, must be dispensed with. A more representative district development council composed of "stakeholders" must replace the district planning and development council. Parastatal development institutions must be dissolved, or redefined.

Instead of a comprehensive budget allocation in a taluka scheme, it should take the form of banked funds from which resources can be drawn upon to make block grants to local bodies under specific conditions of negotiation. In the need-based social sector, the transfer of such block grants will be (more or less) automatic. In the economic sector, the district development council will look for "offers" from local bodies in the form of investment packages. The local body must state its contributions and investments, and what it plans to raise from outside (loans from development finance institutions, commercial investments, and block grants). Each district should lay down minimum performance standards on the basis of which specific applications for block grants can be assessed. For example, a local body may claim a grant that the grant which it is seeking will not only improve livelihood security of the poor but also increase the gross income of the community.

As noted earlier, the local level must be appropriately defined. There must be a chief coordinator and a development committee at this level. Project formulation and implementation should take place at the local level supported by district schemes and other programmatic strategies. In order to support and coordinate local development activities, as well as assess the investment environment and initiate strategies, a district development council is required. Given the new emphasis on deregulation and privatisation, such an entity will play an even wider role. Presently, the district planning and development councils are totally government centred. Only the lead bank manager is from the "risk taking" sector. The Lead Bank Manager, collector, CEO, guardian minister, MLAs and other members of the present DPDCs are not locally elected representatives.* Most of them have *no stake* in the performance of the local economy! A district development council will be relevant only when it is composed of the real stakeholders. Voting members should be representatives of various groups of stakeholders. The council meetings should be open to any interested participant, though only statutory members will be allowed to vote.

* These agencies relate mostly to Maharashtra, a state which the author is familiar with.

District Planning Cell

There has been a great deal of discussion on issues related to the planning machinery both within the states and at the centre. Some working groups appointed by the central government have stressed the need to set up a small multidisciplinary cell at the district level. The central government has assisted this process through a scheme intended to strengthen the planning machinery at the district level. But the implementation has suffered owing to a lack of appropriate personnel. Trained professionals have not been appointed to district planning cells. There has also been a certain ad-hocism in the recruitment, management and training of planning personnel. It must be recognised that the formation of planning cells at the district level is intended to inject a certain degree of professionalism into the planning process at the intermediate level.

Planning functions include specialised tasks such as analysing situations, carrying out a development diagnosis, formulating programmes using appropriate techniques, and adopting a scientific approach to the monitoring and evaluation of district investment plans. Only properly trained development planners, aided by some sectoral specialists, can adequately discharge these functions. Hence the planning team at the district level should consist of members who are professionally trained, or have a postgraduate education, in the relevant disciplines so that they are equipped with the requisite knowledge and skills.

As the secretariat of the district development councils, these cells will focus a great deal of their efforts on the attraction and management of *private sector capital.* Investment management will be the key function through which private sector resources are brought into a focused development process. It is therefore emphasised that when forming planning cells at the district level, great care must be taken to induct personnel of the right calibre and ability. The team must be composed of persons on limited contracts or deputation. Permanent government employees should not comprise a "planning cadre". Alternatively, the work may be contracted out to a professional consultancy group. But merely changing the designation of the district statistical officer to "district planning officer" is of no avail.

Development Planning and Management Professionals
It is not adequate merely to install a young highly qualified team. The members must be experienced and professionally competent. Planning and management teams must be able to deal with private investors, NGOs, trade unions, leaders of cooperatives, as well as formal government at several levels. Without this capability, the personnel recruited into the district planning cells will retard the planning and development process and kill initiative. Career advancement and ambitions about moving from the lowest institutional tier to the highest should not be on their agenda. Younger professionals with ideals and ambitions will be suitable at the local level. A blanket approach towards personnel deployment is not advisable since every local body is not prepared to initiate local level planning.

Minority Interests
Decentralisation does not mean that the centre abandons minorities and economically disadvantaged groups (Rao, 1969). Nor does it make such groups the dictators over smaller, more advantaged groups. In fact, the macro-micro planning paradigm hinges around this issue. How strong is the danger that elite, local level representatives will pander to their own families and constituencies as opposed to serving public interest? In a feudal society, where entrenched interests completly control microlevel institutions, all the constitutional powers of the state cannot be devolved to local bodies. The success of local level governance clearly depends on a strong separation of state and governmental functions. The state must guarantee equity, access and human rights. This will be taken up later with regard to the roles of the collectorate and the chief executive officer of zilla parishads. Certain schemes and mechanisms deemed to be instruments of equity will be monitored more closely by the collectorates.

Organisation of Development Administration at the District Level and Role of the District Collector
Public administration has become an increasingly complex process (Gaikwad and Parmar, 1980). It must take into

consideration both technical as well as public participation aspects. The growing diversification of development activities under the administration has increased the work load of the senior administrator of the district, the district collector. He is already overburdened with regard to revenue administration, magisterial, and law enforcement functions. It is recommended that the development administration of districts be handled independently by a separate official holding position equal to the district collector. Such an arrangement will contribute to the efficient planning and implementation of the district's development. It will also enhance the management of on-going programmes. This proposal does not imply that the district collector should be excluded from development planning and management. However, his role should be limited to overseeing mechanisms which guarantee human rights, environmental protection, law administration, and land tenure – all of these are more suited to the work of an officer having some functional distance from the local milieu. The senior officer handling development functions and on-going services, on the other hand, must be directly responsible to an elected body.

The functions and activities of these two district officials may be effectively coordinated at the divisional level by the divisional commissioner. As noted above, the collector need be involved only in roles which protect the Constitution and the state's goals. These would be more in the form of limited review operations rather than control of line functions. But roles in land tenure and environmental protection cannot be easily demarcated from those in "development".

Research Support

The district investment plan should be based on appropriate analytical studies. Field surveys should be conducted. District planning should not be a mere compilation exercise, which is the case with the *District Statistical Abstract*. Neither the National Sample Survey, nor the various census activities can provide the appropriate information for programme design, promotion or monitoring. Once a development promotion unit and qualified professionals are in place, it will be possible to introduce an element of analysis into the district planning exercise.

But the plans will no longer be perspective, they will be promotive. They will identify key gaps in infrastructure and services which retard potential development. Profitable options will be identified along with their impact on employment generation, sustainable environment and other social aspects. These options should be evaluated by assessing the comparative costs of differential inputs sets and assessing the differential outcome sets. Variable performance standards such as employment generation, resource sustainability, productivity, value added in the local economy, etc., can be used. Monitoring or checking is a normal management function. But evaluation must consider outcome achievement, internal and external factors resulting in over- or underachievement, and possible course correction measures. Thus, research which can be associated with meso- and microlevel planning has wide scope. A training and research institute in a district can support the basic research objectives of the district development council, including research related to impact and outcomes.

All the issues related to private sector initiatives require analysis. Linkages between public investments, regulations and incentives must be studied so that the use of these measures in attracting and coordinating a variety of investments could be assessed.

ISSUE SEVEN: PEOPLE'S PARTICIPATION

Recommendation

The practice of members of Parliament and members of the legislative assembly sitting as members on district decision-making bodies must cease. As also the allocation of discretionary grants to MLAs for expenditure in their constituencies. The practice of deputing a guardian minister from the state cabinet to "look after" a district must also be brought to a halt.

Sanctity of Membership

The local body should be compact and manageable – in which mutual interactions can take place in a meaningful manner.

District and local level development councils should be organised and managed solely by elected representatives. Experts from academia and research and training institutions must also be involved, albeit only as advisors. Major voluntary organisations from the area should also be consulted on various issues. Most importantly, district development councils must involve the key stakeholders – the local entrepreneurs. These are the actors who will make and nurture investments.

Prominent local leaders elected to the legislative assembly, legislative council, and Parliament should *not* be included as district development council members, as their legitimate roles in the political system lie elsewhere. There is no logic in members of Parliament sitting on state level bodies, and the same principle operates for district level bodies. This equally true of state cabinet members becoming guardian ministers. Often they do not even hail from their "ward" districts! Various types of discretionary allocations made to MLAs to expend in their constituencies must be done away with. Where necessary, assistance of such elected officials may be availed of on an advisory basis. It is only in this way that "localism" can be encouraged and the local level political leaders be empowered to play their legitimate roles. Such institutional arrangements will make public service in elected capacities more attractive.

Community Based Planning

People's participation should not be confined to their formal representation in district or local level development management councils (Singh, 1982). It has to operate through several formal and informal channels and the different stages of planning and implementation. At the local level, households should be encouraged to state their production expectations, input requirements, expected outputs, and hoped for profit margins. These can then be grouped into user group projects at the local tier. Thus, local objectives can be supported through credit plans, economic infrastructure created under the Employment Guarantee Scheme (EGS), and district plan outlays. Community-based planning requires local leadership and participation through open meetings. The local level chief coordinator must convene planning and implementation meetings of user groups at the local level in order to integrate these aspects. The blue prints of works prepared for the EGS can thus be dovetailed with locally planned outcomes.

Non-governmental Organisations
Voluntary groups involved in grassroots development must be specially encouraged to participate in planning and development activities at the local level in a meaningful way. Where NGOs have gained the confidence of the local people, the development management committee may designate them as chief coordinators. Such organisations can provide user group training, input coordination, and assist in the formation of local level participatory institutions. They can support local households, entrepreneurs, and cooperative primaries in formulating projects.

Scope of People's Participation
Participation at the local level is a process through which the people are able to organise themselves and identify their own needs. The various elements of participation at the local level are: decision-making at various stages, project planning, control over implementation, management of funds, review of expenditure audits, as well as maintenance of the assets created (Benninger, Aneeta, 1991).

ISSUE EIGHT: SIGNIFICANCE OF LOCAL GOVERNANCE

Recommendation

Local bodies must have control over the use of their own land, location of polluting activities, and the protection of local physical assets. Related environmental, conservation and worker protection acts must be so amended.

In the context of economic deregularisation and privatisation, local level governance takes on greater significance. One of the myths of development studies is that the world is divided into freewheeling, unplanned economies and regulated, planned ones. Unfortunately, this political rhetoric has to some extent been accepted as descriptive reality. A corollary of this illusion is the belief that owing to deregulation, planning now has a lesser role to play. In fact, the most industrialised countries, the ones we use as models of free enterprise, have carefully carved out the territories, both distinct and shared, of public and private interests. The more localised an issue becomes, the more public interest emerges as a determining factor. What are the spheres of such local level plans within more deregularised contexts? The following domains are suggested:

1. Land use (and other non-renewable resources) planning.
2. Transport and communications management.
3. Public works investment.
4. Conservation, ecology and environmental protection.
5. Water supply and waste disposal.
6. Social services access.
7. Special problem area planning, with relation to floods, coastal degradation, earthquakes, fire prone areas, etc.
8. Economic infrastructure planning.
9. Building, urban design and settlement planning.

These plans usually focus on both the attraction of certain types of economic activities as well as the exclusion of some others. Even in the so-called capitalist countries, local plans have strong anti-poverty components. These have often been promoted by higher tiers offering various grant schemes and other incentives. Similarly, town councils and local country bodies hold open meetings in which local interest groups play a strong role in planning. Such programmes as the Model Cities Programme in America have handed over a great deal of power to local communities in every sector, ranging from land use and transport planning to social services, social welfare and employment generation programming. In the emerging system of governance, we should be sensitive to the fact that one of the key reasons why opening up of the Indian economy to foreign investment is in the interest of corporations of industrialised countries is that it allows them to escape the costs brought into their productive operations through their own strict local planning practices. Environmental protection, land use control, occupational safety, building regulations, and hygiene controls are closely monitored by citizen's groups, local bodies, and special interests. Local unions are quick to detect minimum wage violations. Thus, in the name of deregulation, we must not throw the baby out with the bathwater, nor become a dumping ground for transnational corporations. Local level governance, in the ultimate analysis, is the only feasible protector of the nation's resources.

REFERENCES

Benninger, C.C., "Institutional Strategies for Decentralization," *The Administrator*, 36:3, 1991.

Benninger, C.C. "District Planning Methods and Techniques – An Overview", D.N. Yugandhar and Amitava Mukherjee (eds.), *Readings in Decentralized Planning,* New Delhi: Concept Publishing, 1991.

Benninger, C.C., *New Institutional Arrangements for Regional Development,* Nairobi: UNCHS (Habitat), 1990.

Benninger, Aneeta, "Rural Development and Decentralization Planning: Who should Participate and How?", *The Administrator,* 36:3, 1991.

Centre for Development Studies and Activities (CDSA), "Integrated Rural Development Programme: Ratnagiri", UNICEF, 1979.

Divekar, V.D., *Planning Process in Indian Polity,* Bombay: Popular Prakashan, 1978.

Faludi, Andreas, *Planning Theory*, Oxford: Pergamon Press, 1976.

Frankel, Francine, *India's Political Economy, 1947-1977: The Gradual Revolution*, New Jersey: Princeton University Press, 1978.

Gaikwad, V.R., and D.S. Parmar, *Rural Development Administration under Democratic Decentralization*, Delhi: Wiley Eastern, 1980.

Khera, S.S., *District Administration in India,* Delhi: National Publishing House, 1979.

Kulkarni, P.D., *Social Policy and Social Development in India,* Madras: Association of Schools of Social Work in India, 1979.

Mathur, M.V., and Iqbal Narain (eds.), *Panchayat Raj, Planning and Democracy,* New Delhi: Asia Publishing House, 1969.

Mishra, Jagannath, and R.K. Sinha, *Financing of State Plans: Problems and Prospects,* New Delhi: Sterling Publishers, 1984.

Mosher, A.T., *Thinking about Rural Development,* New York: Agricultural Development Council, 1976.

Oommen, M. A., (1991), "Towards Evolving a Methodology for District Planning with People's Participation: Some Experiences from Kerala's Kannur District", *The Administrator* 36:3, July-September, 1991.

Roy, Prodipto and Patil, D., *Manual for Block Level Planning*, New Delhi: Council for Social Development, 1976.

12

Statutory Transfers and Interstate Disparities in India

K. N. Reddy

REGIONAL imbalance has been the concern of most of the finance commissions in the past. The First Finance Commission (1952) stated that "the scheme of distribution should attempt to lessen the inequalities between States."[1] The Second Finance Commission (1957) supported and hailed this objective as "unexceptionable."[2] The Fifth Finance Commission (1969) noted that "the progress of the nation depends, in a real sense, on the development of weaker states and there is a danger that larger and persistent disparities in the basic service levels of different States would weaken national unity and strength."[3] The Sixth Finance Commission (1973) went a step further and declared that the "correction of disparities comes clearly within the purview of the Finance Commission...and difference in levels of public expenditure on vital social services can be eliminated within a shorter time span than the differences in per capita incomes which are determined by various factors, not so easily amenable to control."[4] The Seventh (1978) and the Eighth (1984) Finance Commissions endorsed the same.[5] The Ninth Finance Commission (1989, 1990) noted that "distribution of revenues among the states, should be equitable so that every State is enabled over time to provide a specified minimum standard of basic public services."[6]

It is beyond doubt that almost all the finance commissions were concerned with interstate disparities and did their best to remedy them. Did they succeed in reducing these disparities? If not, why was this so? An attempt is made to address these questions in this chapter.

Interstate Disparities

Interstate disparities may allude to a variety of inequalities. It could refer to disparities in per capita revenues, in per capita income (level of development), in human development (quality of life indicated by literacy, infant mortality, life expectancy at birth, etc.), in basic public services (e.g., education, health and water supply), in employment, or in infrastructure. We shall discuss below the kinds of disparities we should be concerned with.

To start with, should reduction of disparities in revenue be attempted? A laudable objective, it is one which would be difficult to implement, since it depends upon a number of factors beyond the purview of finance commission. Per capita revenue is the function of tax and non-tax revenue effort, per capita income, efficiency of tax administration, tax handles available, and scope for the exploitation of those tax handles. At the most, the finance commission can equitably distribute revenues, to enable each state over time to provide a specified minimum standard of basic public goods.

Next, should we strive towards reduction of disparities in income. This is the objective which is mentioned most often. Some of the previous finance commissions had tried to keep it, though the Sixth Finance Commission had reservations about meeting this objective. Again, disparities in income hinge on various factors – states' economic structure, tax structure, expenditure policy, economic philosophy, and socio-cultural aspects of the people – and are not just the result of financial transfers from the centre.

Yet, it is worth verifying, empirically, whether interstate disparities in income have decreased over a period of time both due to statutory transfers (at the behest of the finance commissions), and statutory and non-statutory transfers combined (at the behest of the finance commissions, the Planning Commission and the central ministries). In 1990-91, Bihar's per capita income was the lowest (Rs. 2,539) and Punjab's the highest (Rs. 8,281); this was the case in 1974-75 and 1980-81 as well (Table 12.1). The only difference is that the per capita NSDP disparity between the two states was much smaller in 1974-75 (Table 12.2). The interstate disparity in income among the 15 major states increased from 0.2669 in 1974-75 to 0.3281 in 1980-81 and to 0.3552 in 1990-91. Thus, contrary to professed objectives, disparities in income have widened continuously. The hypothesis that the per capita income of states is dependent on transfers (statutory transfers and total transfers separately) has not stood up to empirical scrutiny. It has been clearly found that transfers have a negligible impact on the per capita incomes of the states. It can be seen from Table 12.3 has been extremely low and not at all significant for 1974-75 and 1980-81. It was only for 1990-91 that R^2 was somewhat reasonable, but not to the extent of indicating that the transfers had a significant impact.

Can reduction of disparities in expenditure on essential social sectors like primary education and health be an objective? Yes. In fact, most of the finance commissions from the Sixth Finance Commission onwards, have given weightage to this objective in their recommendations. They have pleaded that left to themselves, the poor states may not be able to raise resources for these important sectors; and disparities in levels of literacy and health may widen further and threaten the very foundations of our federal polity. Have the disparities in expenditure on essential social sectors come down? Table 12.4 shows that the per capita expenditures on education and health are still low in the poor states and that interstate disparities are quite wide. In 1990-91, Bihar's per capita expenditure on education (Rs. 140) was the lowest and Kerala's (Rs. 226.50) was the highest. This was the case in 1974-75 as well – Bihar's per capita expenditure on education was Rs. 14.70 and Kerala's was Rs. 45.68. Similarly, with respect to health care, Bihar's per capita expenditure in 1990-91 (Rs. 42.41) and 1974-75 (Rs. 4.56) was the lowest. The positive aspect is that relative disparities among the states have come down over time. For example, although the disparity index for expenditure on education increased marginally from 0.304 in 1974-75 to 0.315 in 1980-81, it decreased to 0.240 in 1990-91. Similarly, with respect to expenditure on medical and public health, the disparity index declined from 0.2796 in 1974-75 to 0.2493 in 1990-91 (Table 12.2).

Does the reduction of disparities in per capita expenditure on essential social sectors imply that interstate disparities in indicators of human development – literacy, infant mortality and life expectancy at birth – have also come down? It is feared that such a thing has not happened. It can be seen from Tables 12.5 and 12.6 that interstate disparities in literacy, infant mortality rate and life expectancy at birth have continued to remain wide. This is because an improvement in the indicators of human development depends on a variety of factors. The increase in the literacy rate depends on: (*a*) the priorities accorded to elementary, secondary, technical and higher education, (*b*) salary and non-salary components of the education expenditure, (*c*) investment in education by non-government agencies, (*d*) historical context, and a host of other factors. Again, a decrease in infant mortality and increase in life expectancy depend upon: (*a*) priorities accorded to curative, preventive and other categories of health expenditure, (*b*) within each of these categories, the salary and non-salary components, (*c*) investment in health by non-government agencies, (*d*) socio-cultural habits of the people, (*e*) nutrition levels (*f*) environment, and (*g*) other health-related expenditure (e.g., on water supply and welfare of the handicapped) by government and non-government agencies.

It may be hypothesised that literacy and life expectancy at birth will improve as per capita expenditures on education and health services go up, (in turn, are the result of an increase in transfers from the centre to the states). Based on this hypotheses, a simple regression analysis has been done, with per capita essential social sector expenditures and human development indicators (literacy and life expectancy at birth) as the dependent variables, and per capita transfers (statutory as well as total) from the centre to states as the explanatory variables. It appears that neither statutory transfers nor total transfers have had a significant effect on per capita essential social sector expenditures and human development indicators. It can be seen from Tables 12.7, 12.8 and 12.9 that R^2 is very low in all the three years – 1974-75, 1980-81 and 1990-91 – under study. One may improve the firmness of the results by using a lagged model for transfers and expenditures, but in our view this does not make a significant difference for a simple inference.

In brief, interstate disparities in income have widened over the period under study. Statutory transfers during 1974-75 to 1990-91 have had no impact on economic development (per capita income) and very little effect on social sector expenditure (education and health) and human development indicators.

Some Suggestions

If interstate disparities are to be reduced, then two issues need to be addressed. *The inter-se distribution of revenues (horizontal equity problem) and devolution of revenues from the centre to the states (vertical equity problem).* The latter is equally important since a larger share in the central revenues will enlarge the cake available for distribution.

Let us take up the second problem first. What proportion of the shareable proceeds from personal income tax (under Article 270) should go to the states? What proportion of shareable proceeds from union excise duties (under Article 275) should go to the states? What share of the central kitty (under Article 275) should go to the states in the form of grants-in-aid? There is not hard and fast rule for determining how much of the revenue needs of the states are to be met through shares in the central taxes (personal income tax and union excise duty) and how much through grants-in-aid. The various finance commissions have taken different approaches.

One suggestion in this regard is that the finance commission should follow an approach which results in the growth of revenues to the states as central tax revenues grow. The reason is that so far the sharing of tax proceeds has been restricted to two taxes while the proceeds from other important sources of revenue – e.g., corporation income tax and customs duties – have been left out. If the income tax paid by companies had not been abolished in 1959 and the rates of corporation tax not raised, made non-shareable with the states since then, the divisible pool would have been much larger and the story would have been different. And now, with a major share of the personal income tax proceeds being allotted to the states, union excise duty alone has to be manipulated for sharing with the States. What share of union excise duty should go to states will depend upon the judgement of the finance commission (it can be 45, 50, or 55 per cent). This, in turn, depends upon the assessment it makes about the revenue needs of the central government. It has often been observed that the reassessment of central government forecasts has not been as rigorous as that of the states. Suspicions exist that finance commissions settle on a percentage indirectly indicated by the Finance Ministry. This allegation seems to have some substance. Between 1974-75 to 1977-78, the states' share in the gross tax revenue of the centre was around 20 per cent. In 1980-81, it rose to 28.77 per cent (peak level). Since then, it has been falling gradually – from 26.13 per cent in 1985-86 and to 23.04 per cent in 1991-92 (Table 12.10). It cannot be mere coincidence that the states' share of central taxes has hovered around 25 per cent. Given this trend, why should any finance commission devote its limited energies to reassessing the central government forecasts. It may as well decide, in consultation with the Finance Ministry, what share of the central tax revenue it should assign to the states. One advantage in such a negotiation is that the finance commission can work with a clear conscience and it can convince the states that it had no secret understanding with the Finance Ministry.

Alternatively, the finance commission itself should fix the percentage of central taxes that is to be shared with the states. It may be based on: (*a*) past record, (*b*) its own assessment, (*c*) experience of other federations, and (*d*) consensus prevailing among the experts. In our opinion, the share should be 26 per cent of central taxes[7] (the average of the past 12 years, from 1980-81). The commission should not hesitate to suggest a constitutional amendment to this effect so that succeeding finance commissions would be free from such a problem.[*]

---

* These recommendations have been accepted by the Tenth Finance Commission.

The next issue is that of regional imbalances or interstate disparities. This issue has to be faced with clarity and vision. When it comes to reduction of disparities in income, there is not much that a finance commission can do. As the Sixth Finance Commission observed, it is better to give up such an objective and concentrate on the improvement of essential social sector services – elementary education, primary health care, water supply and sanitation, nutrition, etc. Unlike the Sixth Finance Commission, the Tenth Commission does not specifically refer to these essential sectors. Instead, it highlights the need for "computerization of land records and providing faster channels of communications above district level, and for upgrading the standards in non-developmental sectors and services and the manner in which such expenditure can be monitored", which may have to be covered under grants-in-aid (Article 275). Therefore, interstate disparities in essential social sector services may have to be brought in the *inter se* distribution of the divisible pool of income tax and excise duties.

It will be in order if the *inter se* distribution of the divisible pool of union excise duties and personal income tax for reducing regional disparities is guided by population, per capita essential social sector services, (i.e., elementary education and public health and clinical services), and tax effort measured in terms of non-agricultural income. What weightage should be given to these various factors is a matter for detailed investigation. It must be understood that by reduction in regional disparities we mean a decrease in inequalities in the provision of essential social sector services and not in any other sense of the term. As discussed earlier, it is beyond the scope or the purview of a finance commission to reduce *inter state* disparities in income as several factors, stated above, influence it. Of the four criteria mentioned for *inter se* distribution, population should be given the maximum weightage – say 70 per cent – for, it indicates the needs of a particular state and is neutral to its level of development. Per capita income, per capita essential social sector services, and tax effort measured in terms of non-agricultural income should each be given a weightage of 10 per cent, so that the needs of the states for economic and social development, on the one hand, and fiscal efficiency on the other are taken into account.

Conclusion

1. Interstate disparities in income have been the concern of almost all the finance commissions. Unfortunately, this concern has not translated into a reduction of disparities in income. The disparity indices for 15 major states indicate that disparities have in fact widened.

2. Interstate disparities, in certain essential social sector services (education and health) have declined marginally.

3. The hypothesis that increasing the statutory transfers can help reduce interstate disparities does not stand up to empirical scrutiny.

4. To reduce interstate disparities – defined in terms of income, social sector services, revenues, or human development – the current finance commission may have to allocate to the states a higher share (around 26 per cent compared to the previous average of 25 per cent) of the central tax revenues. A constitutional amendment to this effect may be proposed and made before the next finance commission is appointed.

In the *inter se* distribution of the divisible pool of union excise duties and personal income tax, a weightage of 70 per cent may be given to population and 10 per cent each to per capita income, per capita expenditure on essential social sector services, and tax effort measured in terms of non-agricultural income.

Finance commissions should ensure that their recommendations have a certain relationship to the overall receipts (revenue and capital accounts combined) of the centre, so that the temptation of central government to opt for deficit financing and unnecessary borrowing is kept under check. This step may ward off the criticism that assessment of the states' forecast is a matter of reality, while that of the centre forecast is a matter of make-believe.

Table 12.1
Per Capita Net State Domestic Product at Current Prices (Rupees)

Sl. No.	*States*	*1974*	*Rank*	*1980-81*	*Rank*	*1990-91*	*Rank*	*Percentage increase (1990-91) over 1974-75*
1.	Andhra Pradesh	1,010	6	1,380	9	4,722	7	367.52
2.	Assam	822	12	1,200	13	3,427	13	316.90
3.	Bihar	683	15	868	15	2,539	15	271.74
4.	Gujarat	1,033	5	1,951	4	6,060	4	486.64
5.	Haryana	1,299	3	2,370	3	6,936	3	433.95
6.	Karnataka	1,000	7	1,623	5	4,737	6	373.70
7.	Kerala	910	8	1,513	7	3,843	10	322.31
8.	Madhya Pradesh	840	10	1,183	14	3,614	11	330.24
9.	Maharashtra	1,360	2	2,427	2	7,409	2	344.78
10.	Orissa	715	13	1,231	11	3,180	14	344.13
11.	Punjab	1,634	1	2,690	1	8,281	1	406.79
12.	Rajasthan	895	9	1,222	12	3,983	9	347.03
13.	Tamil Nadu	826	11	1,498	8	4,428	8	436.08
14.	Uttar Pradesh	752	14	1,278	10	3,553	12	372.47
15.	West Bengal	1,092	4	1,580	6	4,750	5	334.98

Source: Government of India, Department of Economic Affairs, Ministry of Finance, Economic Division, *Economic Survey, 1982-83*, p. S-11.
Government of India, Department of Economic Affairs, Ministry of Finance, Economic Division, *Economic Survey, 1992-93*, p. S-12.

Table 12.2
Unweighted Index of Interstate Disparities (VUW) for Per Capita NSDP, Per Capita Expenditure by Government on Education and Health (Disparity Index)

Year	*Disparity Index (VUW) (15 Major States)*		
	Per capita NSDP	*Education, art and culture, scientific services, and research*	*Medical, family planning, public health, sanitation, and water supply*
	1	2	3
1974-75	0.2669	0.3040	0.2796
1975-76	0.3131	0.3326	0.3138
1976-77	0.3514	0.3660	0.2544
1977-78	0.3406	0.2970	0.2678
1978-79	0.3540	0.2997	0.2668
1979-80	0.3792	0.3134	0.2577
1980-81	0.3281	0.3150	0.2412
1981-82	0.3346	0.2904	0.2643
1982-83	0.3309	0.2559	0.2486
1983-84	0.3050	0.2635	0.3214
1984-85	0.3104	0.2651	0.2615
1985-86	0.3145	0.2691	0.2824
1986-87	0.3139	0.2820	0.2417
1987-88	0.3267	0.2791	0.2278
1988-89	0.3357	0.2412	0.2206
1989-90	0.3552	0.2380	0.2475
1990-91	0.3552	0.2400	0.2493

Note: VUW is an unweighted index of variation.
VUW = (Y1-Y)2 / N-1 y, where
n = number of states
Y_i = per capita net state domestic product (NSDP) in the ith state.
Y = average of per capita NSDP of 15 states.
VUW = 0 indicates perfect equality.
VUW = 1 indicates perfect inequality.

Table 12.3
Regression Results of Per Capita Income and Transfers from Centre to States

	Constant	*Regression Co-efficient*	R^2	*F*	*DW*
(1) Per Capita Income = f (Statutory Transfers)					
1974-75	1260.3 (6.141)	-9.382* (1.385)	0.128	1.919*	2.489
1980-81	2193.3 (1.812)	-10.303* (0.493)	0.018	0.243*	2.369
1990-91	8435.1 (7.126)	-21.099 (3.245)	0.448	10.529	2.639
(2) Per Capita Income = f (Total Transfers)					
1974-75	1186.7 (5.1660	-5.138 (0.892)*	0.058	0.796*	2.523
1980-81	1187.9 (2.626)	-3.351 (0.408)*	0.013	0.167*	2.256
1990-91	8044.0 (6.189)	-11.659 (2.639)	0.349	6.965	2.269

Notes: Figures within brackets are 't' values.
* The coefficients are not significant.
All other coefficients are significant at 5 per cent level.
DW = Durbin-Watson Statistic.

Table 12.4
Per Capita Expenditure on Education and Health (Rupees)

Sl. No.	States	Education*				Health**			
		1974-75	1980-81	1990-91	Percentage change (1974-91)	1974-75	1980-81	1990-91	Percentage change (1974-91)
1.	Andhra Pradesh	20.14	43.37	163.67	712.45	8.58	21.09	65.54	626.74
2.	Assam	26.42	48.76	200.70	659.74	8.80	18.14	93.85	966.57
3.	Bihar	14.70	33.99	140.00	852.20	4.56	9.61	42.44	829.72
4.	Gujarat	25.45	53.45	220.74	767.23	9.94	21.83	72.30	627.47
5.	Haryana	28.23	55.98	197.39	599.23	10.93	28.70	78.16	615.14
6.	Karnataka	25.75	46.79	178.33	592.50	10.2	19.15	67.56	548.71
7.	Kerala	45.68	84.40	266.50	483.47	14.19	25.50	95.71	574.33
8.	Madhya Pradesh	29.92	61.17	262.03	775.89	14.45	25.97	103.40	615.79
9.	Maharashtra	20.56	33.04	219.79	460.82	9.50	22.73	55.20	481.28
10.	Orissa	20.09	40.93	142.68	610.33	7.75	20.98	55.39	614.55
11.	Punjab	37.36	82.74	252.67	576.28	13.40	29.39	101.18	654.96
12.	Rajasthan	23.99	42.98	183.80	666.22	12.38	23.53	91.07	612.81
13.	Tamil Nadu	26.28	49.53	229.86	774.58	11.43	21.80	92.80	733.99
14.	Uttar Pradesh	17.77	31.74	151.18	750.75	5.29	13.60	59.28	923.07
15.	West Bengal	21.99	45.35	201.94	818.25	10.38	24.84	73.86	611.75

* Education, art and culture, scientific services and research.
** Medical, public health, family planning, sanitation and water supply.
Source: *Reserve Bank of India Bulletin* of various years.

Table 12.5
Interstate Disparities in Literacy and Infant Mortality Rates

Sl. No	*States*	*Infant mortality rates per 1000 live births*		*Percentage of literacy to estimated population aged 7 years and above*	
		1977-79	*1987-89*	*1981*	*1991*
1.	Andhra Pradesh	116	81	35.66	45.11
2.	Assam	112	97	N.A.	63.42
3.	Bihar	110 *	97	32.03	38.54
4.	Gujarat	128	91	52.21	60.91
5.	Haryana	107	86	43.85	55.33
6.	Karnataka	83	76	46.20	55.98
7.	Kerala	44	25	81.56	90.59
8.	Madhya Pradesh	145	119	34.22	43.45
9.	Maharashtra	92	64	55.83	63.05
10.	Orissa	143	123	40.96	48.55
11.	Punjab	105	64	48.12	57.14
12.	Rajasthan	130	101	30.09	38.81
13.	Tamil Nadu	103	73	54.38	63.72
14.	Uttar Pradesh	169	123	33.33	41.71
15.	West Bengal	87	73	48.64	57.72

* Average of 1981 and 1983

Source: CMIE, *Basic Statistics Relating to Indian Economy*, 2:September, 1991.

Table 12.6
Interstate Disparities in Life Expectancy at Birth (Years)

	1975		*1981*		*1988*	
States	*Male*	*Female*	*Male*	*Female*	*Male*	*Female*
Andhra Pradesh	43.24	43.34	50.10	51.22	50.99	53.45
Assam	N.A.	N.A.	47.52	44.45	49.59	47.32
Bihar	42.20	43.07	47.22	48.15	49.63	50.63
Gujarat	50.84	45.93	51.05	48.72	53.49	51.53
Haryana	45.11	43.49	43.71	45.52	54.18	55.08
Karnataka	49.78	49.61	53.20	53.24	53.36	55.31
Kerala	54.41	56.59	57.18	61.45	59.69	63.30
Madhya Pradesh	40.34	37.60	42.56	41.19	46.08	44.32
Maharashtra	49.56	50.12	52.44	52.75	53.58	55.93
Orissa	41.03	40.04	46.62	46.62	48.30	48.52
Punjab	52.05	51.60	54.48	55.04	54.94	56.01
Rajasthan	41.71	40.36	44.68	44.40	45.09	44.59
Tamil Nadu	44.81	44.88	48.64	48.94	53.73	53.67
Uttar Pradesh	37.42	33.03	43.92	41.01	47.40	45.88
West Bengal	N.A.	N.A.	49.18	49.94	54.22	54.36
Disparity Index	42.41	43.32	8.77	11.14	7.59	9.99

Source: A.K. Dev and D.N. Rao, "Determinants of Impact of Policy Variables on Health Status – An Inter-State Study", a study conducted for WHO by Institute of Public Administration, Shimla, 1992.

Table 12.7
Regression Results of Essential Social Sector Expenditures and Transfers from Centre to States (Expenditure on Social Sectors are the Function of Transfers)

	Constant	*Regression Co-efficient*	R^2	*F*	*DW*
Per Capita Income = f (Statutory Transfers)					
1974-75	24.889	0.026	0.001	0.014*	1.880
	(3.856)	(0.119)*			
1980-81	105.067	-0.952	0.172	2.705*	2.144
	(3.133)	(1.645)**			
1990-91	234.436	-0.245	0.099	1.431*	2.475
	(6.292)	(1.196)*			
Per Capita Expenditure on Education = f (Total Transfers)					
1974-75	23.356	0.0596	0.009	0.117*	1.838
	(3.366)	(0.342)*			
1980-81	75.009	-0.288	0.103	1.486*	1.848
	(3.628)	(1.219)*			
1990-91	235.371	-0.155	0.101	1.461*	2.466
	(6.253)	(1.208)*			
Per Capita Expenditure on Health = f (Statutory Transfers)					
1974-75	11.050	-0.29	0.011	1.480*	1.575
	(4.688)	(0.384)*			
1980-81	34.451	-0.220	0.84	1.185*	1.718
	(2.943)	(1.089)*			
1990-91	79.204	-0.018	0.003	0.041*	2.296
	(4.892)	(0.202)*			

Table 12.7 Contd...

Table 12.7 Contd...

	Constant	*Regression Co-efficient*	R^2	*F*	*DW*
Per Capita Expenditure on Health = f (Total Transfers)					
1974-75	10.567	-0.010	0.002	0.024*	1.556
	(4.145)	(0.154)*			
1980-81	24.104	-0.027	0.008	0.107*	1.756
	(3.342)	(0.320)*			
1990-91	75.701	0.001	0.000	0.005*	2.303
	(4.616)	(0.023)*			

Notes: Figures within brackets are 't' values.
* The coefficients are not significant.
** The coefficients are significant at 10 per cent level.
All other coefficients are significant at 5 per cent level.

Table 12.8
Regression Results of Literacy Rates and Transfers from Centre to States
(Literacy Rates are the Function of Transfers)

	Constant	*Regression Co-efficient*	R^2	*F*	*DW*
Literacy = f (Statutory Transfers)					
1974-75	30.476 (3.091)	0.193 (0.594)*	0.026	0.353*	2.678
1980-81	26.568* (0.891)	0.326* (0.633)	0.030	0.409*	2.695
1990-91	62.400 (5.109)	-0.047 (0.694)*	0.036	0.482*	2.834
Literacy = f (Total Transfers)					
1974-75	31.901 (2.985)	0.108 (0.404)*	0.012	0.163*	2.691
1980-81	54.654 (3.082)	-0.109 (0.537)*	0.022	0.288*	2.647
1990-91	64.312 (5.255)	-0.036 (0.855)*	0.53	0.731*	2.802

Notes: Figures within brackets are 't' values.
* The coefficients are not significant.
All other coefficients are significant at 5 per cent level.

Table 12.9
Regression Results of Life Expectancy at Birth (LEB) and Transfers from Centre to States

	Constant	*Regression Co-efficient*	R^2	*F*	*DW*
LEB (Male) = f (Statutory Transfers)					
1974-75	62.581 (5.141)	-0.805 (2.003)	0.236	4.013**	1.420
1980-81	46.871 (4.713)	0.034 (0.199)*	0.003	0.039*	2.918
1990-91	56.052 (16.166)	-0.025* (1.334)	0.120	1.778*	3.103
LEB (Male) = f (Total Transfers)					
1974-75	63.929 (4.844)	-0.642 (1.940)	0.225	3.764**	1.213
1980-81	52.659 (9.082)	-0.045 (0.673)*	0.034	0.453*	2.810
1990-91	56.830 (12.102)	-0.028 (1.074)	0.082	1.154**	2.957

Table 12.9 Contd..

Table 12.9 Contd...

	Constant	*Regression Co-efficient*	R^2	*F*	*DW*
LEB (Female) = f (Statutory Transfers)					
1974-75	59.652 (4.782)	-0.733 (1.780)**	0.196	3.167**	1.435
1980-81	43.396 (3.454)	0.095 (0.436)*	0.014	0.191*	2.668
1990-91	56.830 (12.102)	-0.028 (1.074)*	0.082	1.154*	2.957
LEB (Female) = f (Total Transfers)					
1974-75	51.433 (4.574)	-0.599 (1.778)**	0.196	3.163**	1.236
1980-81	51.606 (6.923)	-0.032 (0.378)*	0.011	0.143*	2.676
1990-91	59.086 (13.096)	-0.025 (1.638)**	0.171	2.683*	2.829

Notes: Figures within brackets are 't' values.
* The coefficients are not significant.
** The coefficients are significant at 10 per cent level.
All other coefficients are significant at 5 per cent level.

Table 12.10
Statutory Transfers as Percentage of Centre's Resources

Year	*States share of taxes as percentage of gross tax revenue of the centre*	*Statutory transfers* as percentage of gross revenue receipts of the centre*	*Statutory transfers as percentage of total receipts of the centre*
1974-75	19.36	22.36	17.08
1975-76	21.02	22.17	16.68
1976-77	20.43	21.41	15.51
1977-78	20.30	21.05	15.70
1978-79	18.59	20.39	14.40
1979-80	28.45	25.44	17.41
1980-81	28.77	25.35	16.18
1981-82	26.97	23.84	16.23
1982-83	26.22	22.95	15.17
1983-84	25.31	22.86	14.53
1984-85	24.61	21.53	13.18
1985-86	26.13	24.09	14.49
1986-87	25.81	22.79	13.45
1987-88	24.48	23.35	14.27
1988-89	23.99	22.16	13.71
1989-90	25.63	22.69	14.20
1990-91 (RE)	24.67	24.99	15.15
1991-92 (BE)	23.04	23.03	14.69

* States' share of taxes plus grants-in-aid.

Source: Government of India, Ministry of Finance, *Indian Economic Statistics*, various issues.

NOTES

1. Government of India, *Report of the First Finance Commission*, New Delhi: Finance Ministry, 1952, p. 10

2. Government of India, *Report of the Second Finance Commission,* 1957, pp. 23-24.

3. Government of India, *Report of the Fifth Finance Commission,* 1969, p. 14.

4. Government of India, *Report of the Sixth Finance Commission,* 1973, pp. 8-9.

5. Government of India, *Report of the Eighth Finance Commission,* 1984, p. 8.

6. Government of India, *Report of the Ninth Finance Commission,* 1989, p. 10

7. For an elaborate reasoning, see K.N. Reddy, "Ninth Finance Commission – Biased Recommendations", *Business Standard,* 1 February 1989; and Raja J. Chelliah, *Towards a Decentralised Polity,* Fourth L.K. Jha Memorial Lecture, Fiscal Research Foundation, 1991, p. 19.

13

State Policy and the Socially Deprived in India: Situating the Religious Minorities

T. K. Oommen

THE state in the contemporary world is no longer a police state; it is a "reformist" or "welfare" state. Consequently, the erstwhile private worries of individuals have become contemporary public issues. Further, the state has taken upon itself the task of inspiring and institutionalising social transformation. But in a multiparty democratic polity, wherein a large number of interest groups indulge in intense bargaining, the state becomes vulnerable to the dictates of sizeable collectivities which tend to behave as vote banks. And yet, it is necessary that the underlying rationale of any state policy should be accepted as legitimate by the public at large. This is the dilemma which formulation of state policy in the context of the socially deprived in India poses.

I

Generally speaking, deprivation in a complex society such as India stems from several sources, some of which are universally recognised and others which are hotly contested. Thus economic assistance to the poor, that is, those who are below the *poverty line,* is accepted as legitimate by all. But when the absolute size and proportion of the population which qualifies for this category is substantial, the limited state resources will not permit adequate measures. This is the case in India – 40 per cent of the population, currently estimated to be over 350 million, falls below the poverty line. In such a situation, the state can provide only very basic economic assistance and that too just to the destitutes.

The matter is further complicated because there are several sources of deprivation. For example, though women are distributed across races, age groups, castes and classes, they are deprived as women. Their deprivation is specifically gender-based and rooted in the structure of patriarchy. All women experience powerlessness, which was not recognised even by women until recently. But currently, feminists pursue empowerment as an important goal. Logically, one can speak of a section of the population (not only women) below the *power line*.

Thirdly, one can refer to the *pollution line*, a phenomenon peculiar to a caste society. Thus, according to traditional caste stratification, the population is divided into two polar opposites – the ritually clean and the ritually unclean. The latter are believed to be permanently in ritual pollution and consequently excluded from social interaction and stigmatised for ever. These "untouchables" of India number over a hundred million, constituting 14 per cent of the population. Designated as Scheduled Castes (SCs) by officialdom, the deprivation of these *Dalits*, as they prefer to call themselves, is primarily rooted in the social stigma attributed to them.

The case of Scheduled Tribes (STs) or the *Adivasis*, who claim to be the pre-Aryan settlers of India (as do the SCs) is different. They are not perceived as Untouchables unless they attempt to get incorporated into Hindu society and in the process acquire such a status. The primary disability of the STs emanates from the fact that they are inhabitants of hilly tracts and are physically isolated. Consequently, modern facilities are relatively inacessible to them. The STs number over 50 million, accounting for little over 7 per cent of India's population.

The Other Backward Classes (OBCs) are another deprived category. They belong to the fourth *varna* (the ritually clean *Sudras*) who fall in between the twice-born caste Hindus drawn from the top three *varnas*–Brahmin, Kshatriya and Vaishya – and the Panchamas, those of the fifth order (the Untouchables). OBCs account for over 50 per cent of India's population. Some of the castes in this category succeeded in crossing the pollution line around the 1930s, thanks to the social reform movements and/or because they converted to other religions. However, it is important to note that a substantial section among the OBCs were tenants, sharecroppers and small peasants who benefited from the two measures taken by the Indian state. First, land reforms leading to the abolition of intermediaries made the tenants and sharecroppers land-owning cultivators. Second, the package of subsidies provided to them to increase agricultural productivity brought about the green revolution which rendered them prosperous farmers. Notwithstanding the new economic prosperity, they suffer from several disabilities as they are mainly inhabitants of rural India.

Viewed in terms of the availability and accessibility of transportation, communication, health and education facilities, particularly higher education, the vast majority of the rural people of India, constituting nearly 80 per cent of the total population, is deprived. The much talked about divide between India and Bharat is based on the perception of this reality. However, such a dichotomy is misleading in that it clubs all the people of rural India into one homogeneous category and those of urban India into another. As noted above, there is a growing category of the rural rich and middle class. Their deprivation is not based on non-affordability of goods and services but their non-availability in rural areas. The answer to their problem is expansion of the relevant facilities and making them available in the rural hinterland. On the other hand, a substantial proportion of the rural population which cannot afford even the most basic amenities required for bare survival. Their problem is non-affordability and non-availability.

There is another aspect to the deprivation of the well-off in rural India. Although they have experienced an upward mobility in material and political terms in the recent past (since the OBCs constitute a substantial proportion of the population, large numbers belonging to these castes get elected to legislative bodies), there is no commensurate change in their representation in urban occupations, particularly in full-fledged professions.

That is, they lag behind in terms of prestige. This status incongruence is the basic source of deprivation suffered by the economically prosperous and politically powerful OBCs.

Numerous others drawn from the religious and linguistic minorities are deprived because of cultural disabilities, in addition to other deprivations. For example, if a particular mother tongue is not accorded constitutional recognition (only eighteen out of over a thousand spoken in India have been given this status), is not the medium of instruction even in primary schools, is not the medium of communication by All India Radio and/or Doordarshan, and is not the language of the print media, its speakers are bound to feel disadvantaged.

Needless to say, the vast majority of Indians are deprived on one or another count. Therefore, in evolving an appropriate policy, the state has to take into account two factors: multiple deprivations suffered by some of the collectivities and the hierarchy of factors contributing to deprivation. Pursuantly, the policy measures ought to be different for different categories, depending on the nature and sources of deprivation. To prescribe the same package of benefits for all is not only irrational but also economically unviable.

The nature of policy prescription should also be tempered by one's definition and the preferred instrument of development. Development ought to be viewed as a process of social transformation brought about through the active participation of the people; one which attends to their specific needs and is particularly geared to the welfare of the disadvantaged and deprived. The policy package and its application, therefore, should vary from category to category.

As it stands, there is no consensus with regard to the policy of protective discrimination as an instrument of development. The articulated positions are as follows:

1. The policy should be abolished as it inhibits incentives and initiatives. At any rate, it was originally intended to be a time-bound measure and it has continued far beyond the

promised time period. Its continuation only perpetuates dependence.

2. The policy should continue only for SCs and STs since they continue to suffer from specific disabilities, and it is a constitutional obligation in their case.

3. The policy should continue but its basis should be changed from caste to income. That is, (*a*) the only criterion of reservation ought to be the level of income and, (*b*) all those who belong to a specified income category should be brought under the purview of the policy irrespective of their social background.

4. The policy should not only continue but the social base of the potential beneficiaries should be expanded so as to include the OBCs and religious minorities. This position suggests that income should not be the only criterion for providing benefits, and that the social deprivation of beneficiaries ought to be given due weightage as well.

5. Finally, the policy should continue but the basis should be a *combination* of caste and class; the economically well-off originally from the traditionally socially disadvantaged should be excluded and the poor from the traditionally socially privileged should be included.

In spite of the multiplicity of articulations, the arguments remain incomplete because of two vital omissions. First, the need to dereserve from among the SCs and STs, those who are or have become well-off so that the benefits can seep vertically downwards instead of being monopolised by an entrenched upwardly mobile SC/ST bourgeoisie which has developed a vested interest in backwardness. Second, a differential application of the policy depending on the nature and sources of deprivation. That is, the policy should not be viewed as a package equally applicable to all types of the deprived. Thus, what well-off sections from among the linguistic minorities, rich OBCs, or urban middle class women need is not economic benefits in the form of job reservation, etc., but safeguards against the erosion of their culture and identity, appropriate opportunities for development, and adequate representation on decision-making bodies.

Not only is the vast majority of the Indian population deprived one way or another, it is also internally differentiated. The Scheduled Caste elite, the Westernized tribes, the economically dominant among the OBCs, the well-off from among the religious and linguistic minorities, the rural elite, the upper- and upper-middle class urban women, etc., are not as deprived as their less fortunate brothers and sisters. Given this situation, the way out seems to be to concentrate on those who suffer *simultaneously* from several disabilities, that is, on victims of *cumulative deprivation*. One can postulate a *hierarchy* of the deprived and advocate a policy of *graduated* and *contextually relevant* assistance. That is, the victims of cumulative deprivation should be extended the maximum and a wide variety of assistance while those who suffer from *dispersed deprivation* need be given only the critical minimum and sectoral assistance. Such an approach will not be excessively burdensome on the exchequer. Moreover, it will enable the implementing agencies to resort to the peeling-off mechanism. That is, as and when particular individuals and households have moved out of the defined level or context of deprivation, the assistance can be shifted to another category/sector, reduced or withdrawn.

All available evidence suggests that the cumulatively deprived in India are composed of: (*a*) poor SCs living in rural areas, (*b*) poor STs of central India, and (*c*) Scheduled Caste converts to Buddhism, Islam and Christianity. In what follows, I shall focus primarily on the Dalit Christians and Dalit Muslims and spell out the rationale behind extending the policy of protective discrimination to them.

II

Secularism as defined in the Indian Constitution can mean either (*a*) equal respect for all religions and/or (*b*) equal distance from all religions. But this doctrine is not consistently applied to all religious collectivities which in turn has implications for the application of the policy of protective discrimination.

The inconsistency begins with the mode of defining religious collectivities. Both in the Indian Constitution and in the Hindu Code Bill, "Hindus" include Jains, Buddhists and Sikhs. This constitutional and legal *expansionism* cuts at the very root of Indian secularism. But this definition was not upheld in the implementation of the policy of protective discrimination with regard to the above religious collectivities. While both the Scheduled Caste Hindus and Scheduled Caste converts to Sikhism are entitled to all the benefits of this policy, until recently, neo-Buddhists (Scheduled Caste converts to Buddhism) were given only limited benefits; that too if they lived in Uttar Pradesh and Maharashtra, where they are mainly concentrated and hence have some political clout. But this anomally was done away with in 1990 by the V.P. Singh government. And it is but logical to bring the Scheduled Caste converts to Islam and Christianity also under the policy of protective discrimination, which has not been done so far. (As for Scheduled Caste converts to Jainism, either they are too few or they are not as depressed as the converts to other religions.)

There is another context in which the official definition of religion poses a problem. From 1871 to 1931 the British Indian census had a specific religious category which variously labelled as "primitive", "animist", or "tribal" the religion of the Scheduled Tribes. Most sociologists and social anthropologists, on the other hand, considered the tribes as backward Hindus. From the census of 1951, the first census of independent India, the category of "tribal religion" was dropped. It is important to recall here that (*a*) the religious practices of SCs and STs have many features in common and (*b*) both these categories claim that they are the pre-Aryan peoples of India. In fact, several movements of the Scheduled Castes explicitly reject Hinduism as their religion. Yet, the Scheduled Castes are automatically counted as Hindus, while the Scheduled Tribes are not. Only if the latter have not converted to one of the world religions such as Islam, Christianity, or Buddhism are they categorised as Hindus. That is, the religion of the tribes of India is not recognised as a religion, while the religion of the Scheduled Castes is reckoned as Hinduism.

The contradiction is further compounded when one notes that all the Scheduled Tribes are entitled to the full benefits of the policy of protective discrimination, irrespective of their religion. In contrast, as noted above, Scheduled Caste persons who convert to Islam and Christianity are denied these benefits. Thus, the salient defining criterion is different in the two cases: tribes, in the case of STs; and religion in the case of SCs. This means that the conversion of SCs and STs to Islam and Christianity has different consequences for the converts. While it affects the SCs adversely, it is neutral with regard to STs. Once again we find inconsistency, both in principle (denial of freedom of religion to SCs) and in practice (application of secularism).

It is necessary to examine here the argument advanced in favour of the differential application of the policy of protective discrimination to the converts to Sikhism and Buddhism, on the one hand, and Islam and Christianity on the other. The policy, it is argued, is enunciated and applied on the basis of the evils of the caste system; and since Islam and Christianity do not recognise the caste system, it is illogical to extend the policy to the Scheduled Caste converts to these religions. But a moment's reflection would reveal that the argument is untenable on several counts.

First, both Buddhism and Sikhism emerged as the result of revolts against the Hindu caste system, particularly upper-caste oppression and Brahminical dominance. That is, these religions too do not accept the caste system. Therefore, if non-acceptance of the caste system by Islam and Christianity is the basis for disallowing the benefits to those who convert to these religions, by the same token, the benefits should not be given to Mazbhi Sikhs and neo-Buddhists.

Second, the practice of untouchability is not accepted as a part of genuine Hinduism; it is viewed as an aberration. In fact, one of the refrains of Mohandas Karamchand Gandhi was that untouchability is the greatest blot on Hinduism. At any rate, numerous Hindu reform movements strived to cleanse Hinduism of this evil practice. That is, even if one accepts that untouchability is an essential part of Hinduism, it is sought to be eradicated by neo-Hinduism.

Third, the argument is naive in that it seems to endorse the isomorphism between doctrine and praxis. It is true that neither Islam nor Christianity endorse the values of the caste system. Yet, the adherents of these religious faiths get incorporated into the caste system and becomes victims of caste discrimination. There is enormous evidence to show that neo-Christians and perhaps even neo-Muslims (that is, recent converts to these religions from Scheduled Castes) are treated as Untouchables, not only by caste Hindus but also by their co-religionists who claim upper-caste origin. That is, the practice of untouchability persists vis-a-vis lower-caste converts to Christianity and perhaps Islam as well. Therefore, there is no logical basis in denying the benefits of the policy to neo-Christians and neo-Muslims.

There is also an unstated assumption and a popular belief behind the denial of these benefits to Scheduled Caste converts to Islam and Christianity – those who convert to these religions experience sudden upward mobility in socio-economic terms. The assumption is unwarranted and the belief is false because they are based on what may be called the conquest/colonial syndrome. The presence of Islam in India is attributed to conquest and that of Christianity to colonialism. But the fact is that both pre-conquest Islam and pre-colonial Christianity existed in India. Further, the uninformed assumption that because of the support from the state during the medieval and British periods, Muslims and Christians experienced substantial upward mobility is not borne out by facts. It is true that a tiny elite supported by the then regimes did emerge from these religious collectivities, but it consisted of either foreign migrants or upper-caste converts. The vast majority of Indian

Muslims and Christians were/are converts from not only the lowest castes, but also the lowest class. In fact, the disparaging epithets used to describe the converts to Christianity – rice Christians, the milk powder Christians, etc. – clearly indicate that they were really the poorest.

However, this is not to deny that the Scheduled Caste converts to Christianity did experience limited upward mobility during the colonial period. But the beneficiaries were those who succeeded in crossing the pollution line, like the Ezhavas of Kerala and the Nadars of Tamil Nadu. Those who remained Untouchables rarely experienced any collective upward mobility even after they got converted to Christianity. That is, upward mobility due to conversion was essentially a function of crossing the pollution line. The vast majority did not succeed in doing so in spite of conversion. Given this context, to exclude the Dalit Christians and Dalit Muslims from the purview of the policy of protective discrimination is logically untenable and factually unsustainable.

Thus far, I have argued that denial of the benefits of reservation to Dalit Christians and Muslims is legally inconsistent, unsustainable in terms of the doctrines of reformist Hinduism, and not supported by empirical evidence. If so, why is it advocated and practised? I suggest that the advocacy and practice smacks of deep-rooted prejudices and is politically motivated.

It is clear that the application of the policy of positive discrimination divides the people of India into "insiders" and "outsiders". Those who profess religions of "Indian" origin are insiders', and while the followers of religions of "alien" origin are outsiders. Islam and Christianity are widely perceived not only as alien religions, but are also stigmatised as products of conquest and colonialism in India. Not only are these widely held popular beliefs historically incorrect, but the vast majority of those who profess these faiths are native, indigenous pre-Aryan people of India, converted from Scheduled Castes and Scheduled Tribes. Only their religion is "alien". Moreover, Christianity came to India in the first century AD, while Islam has been in India for twelve centuries. This begs the following questions: What is the time-frame within which a cultural item – be it technology, religion or language – gets nativised or indigenised; in the present context Indianised? If the people of a region, country, nation, change their faith/religion, do they become non-natives or aliens? Whichever way one argues, it is specious to consider Islam and Christianity as alien to India after so many centuries of their presence in the country and to treat the Muslims and Christians of India as alien to the Indian soil. This being the case, the exclusion by the Indian state of Muslims and Christians from the purview of the policy of protective discrimination is irrational. It smacks of the politics of expediency pursued in deference to the cultural mainstream, the Hindus.

There is another reason which renders Indian Christians politically insignificant. An overwhelming majority of them, 90 per cent, are drawn from three geographical enclaves: South India, North-East India, and the tribal belt of Central India. On the other hand, the vast Hindi heartland, accounting for 40 per cent of India's population and the citadel of political power, contributes barely 10 per cent of Indian Christians. And an overwhelming majority of the Christians from the Hindi heartland are absolutely marginalised due to their numerical inferiority, low-caste social origin, and appalling poverty. Thus not only is Christianity stigmatised as an alien religion in India, but Christians, particularly from the Indian mainland, occupy a marginal position in the Indian polity.

Moreover, although Christians are the second biggest religious minority in India, with a population of nearly 20 million, they are dispersed all over the country. Thus, Indian Christians are not only an obscure minority but also a diffuse minority. To change their existential condition, it is imperative that the Dalit Christians be brought under the purview of the policy of protective discrimination.

III

I began my argument by suggesting that in an economically backward, culturally plural, and socially totalitarian society like India, there are several sources of deprivation. Admittedly, a staggering number of people are deprived, and it is not possible to attend to the deprivations of all of them, not at any rate with equal commitment. Therefore, it is necessary to recognize that (*a*) a hierarchy of deprivations exists and (*b*) a selective application of the policy of protective discrimination to particular categories, in terms of the source of their deprivation, is necessary and also feasible. I have also suggested that if one places the multiplicity of the deprived on a continuum, at the one end one can locate the cumulatively deprived who are victims of economic exploitation, socio-cultural discrimination, and political oppression.

The cumulatively deprived in India are mainly the poor Dalits irrespective of their religious faiths. A cursory analysis of the existential conditions of Dalit Christians and Muslims reveals that they too are cumulatively deprived. Yet, they are not entitled to the benefits of the policy of protective discrimination. This is because of the deep-rooted prejudices prevalent in India against Christianity and Islam. These religions have become associated with colonialism and conquest. Unfortunately, this prejudice is articulated not only in everyday life, at the popular level, but is also reflected in the Indian Constitution and in state policies. The Indian state is secular in that it purports to extend equal treatment to all its citizens, irrespective of their religious faith. In pleading for the extension of the policy of protective discrimination to Dalit Christians and Dalit Muslims, one is only arguing for the fulfilment of the constitutional promise and the removal of contradictions and inconsistencies which have crept into the practice of state policy.

14

Communities and Community Politics in Kerala

George Mathew

THE *National Geographic* had carried a special article on Kerala in its May 1988 issue. It began with the observation: "Kerala became the first destination in India for Christians, Jews and Muslims whose descendants have added a cosmopolitan flavour to the state's 29 million people, who are predominantly Hindu." Has the state lost its cosmopolitan flavour?

Kerala was not only the first destination in India for several religions, it also developed a unique model of community living. Is that model on the wane if not already broken down? Or, in the light of events since 1900, will Kerala's social history follow a different trajectory? These are some of the questions we have to address in dealing with the Kerala's community dynamics.

The term "community" in its sociological sense means a group with distinctive racial or cultural characteristics, and thereby implies a religious bond in terms of belief systems, values and ritual practices. In the Indian semantic context, "communal" is often not a value-neutral term. D. E. Smith is nearer this truth when he says: "Sometimes communal has a neutral objective form as used in communal representation, but it is generally associated with a narrow, selfish, divisive and aggressive attitude on the part of a religious group."

According to Louis Dumont, the religious element that enters into the composition of communalism is but a shadow of religion, i.e., religion taken not as the essence and guide of life in all spheres, but only as a sign of the distinction of one human group against others, with political overtones. Communalism can then be explained as "an attitude which emphasizes the primacy and exclusiveness of the communal group and demands the solidarity of members of the community in political and social action." (K'earney, 1967). It is important to underline here that community has a relation to primordiality which is a state of intense and comprehensive solidarity through a common territory of origin and residence, common place of work, or ties of blood, and sexual connection, etc. This is characterised by an intense attachment to symbols, particularly religious ones, which play an important part.

I have argued elsewhere (Mathew, 1989) that communalism bereft of its negative religious overtones is "communalisation". A community with religious identities devoid of transcendent, ritual or spiritual significance, and hostility or contempt towards other religious or caste groupings, and organising itself to bargain for a larger or proportionate share in wealth and power, commensurate with its numerical strength, is communalisation. Increasing commercialisation, quest for enhanced status, consciousness of deprivation, realisation of the importance of political power, recognition of a rival reference group are all its causes and consequences. Communalisation acquires a respectable status through its close affinity and attachment to non-religious (secular) instrumentalities. Here hostility gives way to healthy competition.

The hundred years of Kerala's history – here the focus is primarily on Travancore – starting from 1891 – the year of the Malayalee Memorial – are a fascinating instance of this communalisation. The closing decades of the nineteenth century in Travancore were ripe for awakening the people to demand their rights from the state. In a social context where members of particular communities were discriminated against on the basis of their birth, organisations realised that in order to protect and wrest the legitimate rights of the communities they represent, members would have to be mobilised on the basis of their primordial loyalties.

Organisations such as Malayali Sabha (1885), Nazrani Jathaikya Sangham (1885), SNDP (1903), Sadhujana Paripalana Yogam (1905), Vaala Samudaya Parishkarani Sabha (1912) and

NSS (1914) sprang up on Kerala's soil within a span of three decades. Later on, struggles were launched by Sri Narayana Dharma Paripalana Sangham (SNDP), Nair Service Society (NSS), AKCC (1930), and its predecessor, Keraliya Catholic Mahajana Sabha (KCMS). All these movements mainly aimed to protect the self-interests of the respective communities. Thus, the communal organisations were used as a convenient instrument for securing primordial loyalty to achieve an optimum congruence between social standing and economic status vis-a-vis other contending communities.

In the pre-capitalist society which existed in Travancore at the dawn of the twentieth century, the indices of high status were government jobs and the size of landholdings. But when feudalism began to crumble, status was attributed to economic achievements. In the changed economic context, mere ownership of land or government employment were not sufficient to acquire status. Newer economic enterprises began to emerge as the prerequisites for upward social mobility.

The Movement for Civil Rights and the formation of the Civic Rights League in 1919 were notable steps in the politicisation of communities in Travancore. Only 20 per cent of the citizens of Travancore enjoyed true civic rights based on ascription (social and religious considerations). Since equality was crucial for benefiting from the new economic forces, the movement won the support of all the communities which were at the receiving end. As P. K. K. Menon (1972) had observed, the Civil Rights Movement "was not a request for the favour of appointments but a demand for the recognition of the elementary right to equality of opportunity." The secular demand (civic right) and its secular consequence of participation in the new economy (equality of opportunity) were promoted through a primordial medium. The movement was secular in substance but communal in form.

The period 1932-47 was significant. The first half saw a heightening of the activities of community organisations; these declined in the latter part, more or less giving way to political parties. In the early thirties, the level of popular consciousness rose to newer heights through the work of community organisations. The abstention movement of 1932 was the best example of traditional primordial instrumentality (communal demands) giving rise to modern secular values (political consciousness). But soon people realised the inadequacy of communal traditional instrumentalities in achieving secular goals. Community organisations became conscious of the fact that political power was crucial for enhancing and consolidating their status. This led to the formation of political parties. In 1938 the Joint Political Congress, which had spearheaded the abstention movement, was dissolved, making way for the Travancore State Congress. This political consciousness was the result of the latent secularising process which paradoxically gathered momentum through the "communal" struggles of different communities for their social rights. Communal organisations themselves became a threat to the theocratic administration. As the Regional Records Survey Committee (1972) put it aptly, "The abstention movement, grossly communal in complexion, represented yet a challenge to vested interests in administration."

The period after independence and before the formation of Kerala state in 1956, the state of Travancore-Cochin saw communities influencing state politics through political parties. Travancore's freedom struggle was led by the leaders of three main communities Nairs, Ezhavas and Christians. To achieve their goal of "responsible government" they came together. Once they achieved it, differences in opinion sharpened and the communities began vying with each other for a larger share of the national resources cake – social, economic, political – to be distributed by the state.

The Congress Party's move towards communal forces during this period was the most disturbing aspect, with far-reaching consequences. It began to appease some of the communal organisations which had opposed responsible government and even wanted to destroy the state Congress unit. These organisations had allied with the Dewan in the crucial days of the struggle, but when power was in sight, they shifted their positions with ease.

However, a countervailing force was emerging within Kerala society – growing class consciousness. It was a counter move to the communal consciousness. The emergence of a militant working class as well as an organised agrarian movement (it was stronger in Malabar than in Travancore) contributed in no small measure to the growth of class consciousness. It acquired a new form and received an added impetus through party politics which had become an accepted norm.

From 1956, when Kerala state came into existence, till 1990, the broad political process was woven around two distinct streams. Class politics became the axis of one group of political parties and communal politics of another set. LDF and UDF must be seen in this light – the emergence of almost a two-party system within multiparty coalition arrangements. Differentiation within communities, the hallmark of a secular society, was clearly evident. Thus, a fascinating feature of Kerala's social development has been the process of secularisation on the one hand and continuing communal loyalties on the other. It cannot be understood without appreciating the role played by the community organisations at various levels of Kerala society in different phases.

The secularisation role was not one which communal leaders consciously played. It was a spin-off of their activities and programmes. The community leaders' and organisations' strong emphasis on modern education opened the avenues for radical thinking, encouraged a universal outlook, and promoted enduring human values. It also helped in the development of the Malayalee culture and language which gave to all the people of the state an overarching identity – one which subsumed the identity of the community to which they belonged. In almost all life situations, the Malayalee identity could overlook other differences. The working class, intellectuals, writers, artists, social reformers, professionals, those who migrated to various parts of the country and the world, and political activists of secular hues all made a positive contribution to building this predominant Malayalee identity. This was another positive aspect of communities and community politics in Kerala.

This trend was visible till 1990. Since then, certain developments have taken place which raise the question whether the Kerala model changed and the post-1990 social development will take a different course.

We will consider three incidents which, in our view, suggest that a paradigm shift may be taking place.

In October 1990, at the time of L.K. Advani's Rath Yatra, there were riots between upper-caste Hindus and Muslims. On 14 October, a Muslim religious teacher was hacked to death at Kattoor in Trichur district. The riots coincided with the state BJP President K. Raman Pillai's Jan Sakthi Ratha Yatra. The Kattoor incident had repercussions in number of places and two persons were killed in police firing near Cochin.

On 16 December 1991 at Palghat, following clashes between Hindus and Muslims, a 11-year-old girl, Sirajuneeza, was killed in police firing, several were injured and shops in the town set ablaze. This coincided with Murli Manohar Joshi's Ekta Yatra.

On 1 April 1992 there was a blast in a mosque in Faizabad. While this created no disturbance in any other part of the country, in Kerala there were wild rumours that the mosque in Ayodhya had been destroyed. Normal life was affected in southern parts of the state – buses were stoned, and shops downed their shutters.

Is it correct to think that the process of "communalisation" peculiar to Kerala has begun to falter since the early nineties and communalism has started raising its head? Several reasons have been cited to explain this shift.

The most important reason is the entry of forces and issues which were alien to the state's ethos. They had a negative impact on the state's polity and society. For instance, the RSS, Bajrang Dal, Vishwa Hindu Parishad, or even BJP and the kind of militancy in politics they propagated was alien to Kerala. When the militant elements of any religious community are determined to capture political power, it generates considerable tension. Every action has an equal and opposite reaction. This rule of physical science is true for society as well. Therefore, when the RSS and its allied organisations with political overtones began to appear on the scene, Islamic militancy (e.g., Islamic Sevak Sangh) was not far behind.

The role of external forces in fomenting trouble in Kerala was evident even before 1990. The Nilackal conflict of 1983 between Hindus and Christians on the question of an ancient church believed to be founded by St. Thomas the Apostle of Jesus Christ, is a case in point. After visiting Kerala, during this conflict the veteran socialist thinker and writer, Dev Dutt, observed, "The Kerala Hindu has an instinctive affinity for the essential Hinduism and not ethnicised Hinduism. Therefore, left to himself he is inclined to take to a broad, accommodative position. But the entry of 'outsiders' under RSS made the Kerala Hindu vulnerable and his original stamina weakened."

Secondly, the affluence of certain sections has been used to the detriment of societal peace. The *nouvea riche* of all the communities seem to be fuelling the fire for their own advantage – to control organisations so as to enhance their power and status. For them, the front organisations of political parties of all hues are convenient covers for carving out their spheres of influence or settling old scores with their rivals through newfound money.

All the three major religious communities in the state have departed in the recent times from their earlier practice of establishing schools, colleges, technical institutions, hospitals, etc., which used to compete as centres of excellence for the entire community. Now the money flowing from outside into each community's hands is being diverted to erect structures and symbols which flaunt their wealth and glory to the envy and anger of others. Naturally, they become targets of ire at the slightest provocation.

Another aspect of the post-1990 scenario in Kerala is that the issues which made the Kerala model possible have either lost their relevance today or new issues have sprung up, with the state having reached a different stage of development.

Kerala can take pride in several aspects of its development. Its development experience is basically one of high physical quality of life, comparable to that attained by some developed countries, but with a low per capita income. Economists have also characterised its development pattern as one low per capita income and high per capita consumption. Prof. M.A. Oommen (1987) has noted that "the failure to create meaningful employment is the most tragic failure of development." Kerala has the highest share of unemployment – while accounting for just 3.4 per cent of India's population, its share of the unemployed is 16 per cent. There was negative growth in employment during 1971-81. This is creating a social crisis which, if not handled properly, will become a recruiting ground for all kinds of chauvinistic and fascist groups in the post-1990 period.

There is a paradox in Kerala's education system. Unlike the rest of the country, Kerala has achieved universal literacy. It is commendable that 73 per cent of the total expenditure on education in the 1989-90 budget was earmarked for primary and secondary education alone. But as regards direct expenditure on students, especially at the higher education level, Kerala ranks one of the lowest. A study by Moonis Raza and others found that "Kerala is well ahead of all States in the country about [*sic*] institutions, teachers, enrollment of students. But in terms of direct expenditure per student it is on the lowest rung of the ladder, next to Bihar" (Raza, 1984).

This reflects on the quality of technical and higher education as well. Advanced research in the physical and social sciences has not achieved the desired level of excellence. The new social atmosphere as a result of this crisis in education is breeding negative social attitudes, which communalism may capitalise on. These factors and the militancy of outside forces have the potential to destroy the Kerala model of communalisation, mentioned earlier.

I would like to argue that the process of communalisation leading to a secular society in Kerala is still valid in spite of the upsurge of fundamentalist forces all over the country. In other words, the state is still on the path of secularisation. So far, the extreme provocations from communal elements belonging to all religious communities have not disastrously affected the social fabric of the state. Certain positive factors have offset their negative impact on Kerala society.

First, the size of the state is an important factor. Small states are less prone to the communal virus as they are manageable. In bigger states like UP, Madhya Pradesh and Maharashtra, the writ of the government does not run in several areas and they are more vulnerable to communal disturbances.

Second, the local communities, local bodies and panchayats in Kerala are alert and dynamic. They act as early warning systems. Community organisations like SNDP or NSS, Christian parishes and other associations and organisations, as well as the single-tier panchayats have all played an important role in welding together Kerala society on a firmer, communitarian basis and alerting the authorities about potential troubles and tensions in localities. In the last several decades, secular political parties have played an important role. Perhaps, in future, the new generation of vibrant panchayat bodies will further strengthen the secular fabric of Kerala society.

Third, for a society to be secular, there must be a strict separation between religion and the state. In Kerala, there is an interesting, contradictory situation. The leaders at the helm of governance, unfortunately, deliberately violate this principle. They participate in religious observances under the public gaze using money from the exchequer. But the ordinary people do not allow religious practices to intrude into public places. Unlike several other states, in Kerala even religious pictures and symbols are kept away from the workplace and state transport buses. This is an important aspect.

Fourth, the secular and political forces are extra vigilant in times of crises and people respond positively to social problems.

They make efforts for conflict resolution. The high level of literacy the state has achieved, the large number of newspapers and magazines it publishes (highest in the country), and the excellent communications network throughout the length and breadth of the state have strengthened its capacity for conflict resolution. The high level of political awareness as well as people's participation in mass organisations have also contributed to creating a congenial climate, which allows for positive responses in times of social crises.

As a result of all these positive influences, the communities and their organisations are setting new agenda for themselves. Issues like environmental protection, survival of humankind, wider questions of justice like gender and caste equality, and the liberating elements in its culture, rather than religious identities, are being accorded priority. This is going to be the next phase in the continuous evolution of a secular outlook of the people of Kerala.

REFERENCES

K'earney, Robert N., *Communalism and Language in the Politics of Ceylon*, Durham: Duke University Press, 1967.

Mathew, George., *Communal Road to a Secular Kerala*, New Delhi: Concept Publishing, 1989.

Menon, P. K. K., (ed.), *The History of Freedom Movement in Kerala*, Vol II, Regional Records Survey Committee, Trivandrum: Government of Kerala, 1972.

Oommen, M. A., (ed.) *Issues in Teaching of Economics in Indian Universities*, New Delhi: Oxford IBH Publishing, 1987.

Raza, Mooniz, *et al.*, 'Higher Education in India–An Assessment' in J. Veera Raghavan (ed.), *Higher Education in the Eighties*, India International Centre, New Delhi.

15

Kerala's Development, Constraints and Options

K. K. George

KERALA'S economy today resembles a freak baby with abnormal growth of some organs and stunted growth of others. Like bizarre phenomena elsewhere, this too has attracted a good deal of attention from researchers, both national and international. Many of them have acclaimed the Kerala model of development for its phenomenal growth in the spheres of education, health care, population control, and physical quality of life. However, despite the continuing euphoria about near universal literacy, falling death and birth rates, gender equality, and absence of rural-urban disparity, the fact that the economy is basically unhealthy is surfacing. It is also being realised that this model of development cannot sustain the state much longer, in view of the near stagnation in the commodity producing sectors. Besides, the very success of Kerala in the social services sectors has generated a large number of secondary problems, for solving which the state is not in a position to generate enough resources on its own. Since national planners are still grappling with some of the first-generation problems like illiteracy, high death and birth rates, it is unlikely that enough resources will flow from the national kitty for solving the state's twin difficulties – success-induced secondary problems in the social service sectors and the problem of stagnation in the commodity producing sectors. In a way, Kerala's present economic crisis can be traced to the dichotomy between the state's priorities and national priorities in the past as well as at present.

Decelerating Growth of the Commodity Producing Sectors

Few remember today that at the beginning of the planning era in India, the erstwhile Travancore-Cochin state had attained a level of per capita income (that too of industrial origin) which was higher than the national average. But ever since planning commenced, Kerala's relative position in per capita income has been slipping almost continuously due to the low growth of its state income. Lower than the national average throughout, Kerala's growth rate of state income has shown deceleration from the mid-seventies onwards. Among the three sectors, only the tertiary sector showed a higher growth rate during this period than during the previous decade. In fact, during the decade covering the second half of the seventies and the first half of the eighties, income from the primary sector actually showed a negative growth. Growth in the secondary sector was also low; it was lower than the national average. In other words, it was only the tertiary sector which contributed to whatever little growth the economy has achieved in recent years. This growth in tertiary sector, unrelated to growth in the commodity producing sectors, was facilitated by the large-scale remittances from outside the state, particularly from the Gulf.

Further disaggregation of the growth rates reveals the increasingly narrow, fragile, and unsustainable economic base of the state. In the primary sector, growth was recorded not in agriculture proper but in allied activities like animal husbandry, fisheries and forestry. Production of crops, particularly food-grains, showed an absolute decline. Even among cash crops, only rubber and coffee registered an increase in production. In the secondary sector, whatever little growth took place, was contributed to largely by electricity generation and construction rather than by manufacturing. The manufacturing sector in Kerala continues to be dominated by the household and unregistered subsectors. And traditional "sunset" industries still account for a major share of the industrial sector. Even after four and a half decades of planning, the state's industrial base continues to be narrow.

The sluggish growth of Kerala's economy has made it impossible to absorb the increasing number of unemployed in the state. The state today accounts for about one-tenth of the country's unemployed. In the past, this problem was mitigated to some extent by outmigration. With the spread of education and increase in unemployment in other states, employment opportunities in India are no longer widely available to Kerala's unemployed. Fortunately, from the mid-seventies, the Gulf labour market opened up, providing a partial escape route.

Instability of Kerala's Economy

The narrow base of the state's economy renders it highly vulnerable to changes taking place in other parts of the country as well as in the world. The slender production base of agriculture and industry has made the state extremely dependent on imports of both food articles and industrial products. Due to its geographical location at the tip of the subcontinent, the frequent increases in transportation charges affect the state's cost and price levels more severely. This is one of the reasons for the clamour for higher money wages in the state. Kerala's agriculture as well as industry are oriented towards exports, either to the rest of the country or to the rest of the world. Most of its plantation crops are sold outside the state. The prices of these few commodities on which the state's agriculture relies so heavily are determined largely by national policy considerations or by international market forces. This also contributes to the instability of Kerala's economy. Finally, international political developments, through their impact on inward remittances, can also be destabilising.

Options for the State

The problems latent in the Kerala model of development have not only surfaced but are threatening to assume crisis proportions. As noted earlier, income from the primary sector declined during the second half of the seventies and the first half of the eighties. The growth in the earlier years, though small, was made possible to a large extent by an extension of the area under crops. In this process, the state's forest areas were encroached upon. It was also possible in the past to bring large areas under major irrigation projects. But these soft options are no longer available. In fact, the environmental degradation wrought by the growth process in the earlier decades has now started retarding agricultural growth. The fisheries sector, which grew at a rapid pace during the sixties and the seventies, has also reached the limits of its growth. Overexploitation of marine resources in the past has now resulted in the decline in fish catches. The animal husbandry sector, particularly the dairy sub-sector, was another source of growth. The decline in grazing land and fall in paddy cultivation, with the resultant reduced availability of roughage, are now limiting the further development of this sector.

The industrial sector in the state continues to be dominated by traditional industries like coir, handloom, *beedi* and cashew. While some of these industries face raw material bottlenecks, others face demand constraints. All these industries are showing a tendency to migrate to neighbouring states to take advantage of the cheap labour there. Modernisation and upgradation are absolutely necessary to make them competitive and retain them within the state. But the fear of aggravating the already severe unemployment problem has resulted in resistance to technological change. Such a myopic attitude may in the long run lead to the virtual extinction of these industries in the state.

Even the modern segment of the industrial sector is characterised by the domination of a few industry groups like electricity generation, chemical and chemical products, food products, rubber and plastic products, and wood and forest-based products. All these groups, except perhaps the rubber-based ones, are facing growth constraints today. Electricity generation is the largest single industry group in the state, accounting for nearly one-fourth of the total value added in Kerala's factory sector. This industry has been relying exclusively on the state's hydel potential. With mounting resistance from environmental groups, tapping of the remaining hydel potential is proving to be difficult. Due to high population density, limited land availability, and distance from supply sources, coal-based thermal stations in the state are costly to run, both economically and environmentally. For environmental reasons, the atomic option is also not an acceptable one. The only environmentally benign option for meeting Kerala's energy needs in the short run is gas-based thermal power. This however remains a far cry.

Till 1983, the state was exporting electricity to the neighbouring states. During this period, many chemical units with little forward or backward linkages in the state's economy were established only because of the abundant availability of cheap electricity. Such energy-intensive units have now become a drag on the state's growth. In fact, Kerala must consciously steer clear of such industries in future. In view of the very limited forest cover remaining in the state, its forest-based industries too have very limited growth prospects. In other words, Kerala will have to change its industrial priorities. It has got to jettison a large number of industries which were consciously promoted in the past. Entirely new type of industries will have to be planned for. Given the high wage expectations and educational attainments of Kerala's labour, the skill- and knowledge-intensive and high value adding industries will have to be given priority.

The commodity producing sectors failed to grow fast enough to absorb the increasing number of unemployed in the state. This problem is more acute in Kerala than in other states. Besides, the nature of unemployment in this state is qualitatively different from that of other states, thanks to its success in the field of education. The problem of unemployment in Kerala is largely that of educated unemployed. Moreover, unlike in other states, educated women also enter the labour market in large numbers as a result of the increasing gender equality in educational attainments.

Role of Education in State's Future Growth

Despite the problem of educated unemployment generated by the universalisation of education, Kerala's investment in education in the past has come to its rescue, especially during the last two decades. It is this investment which has made it possible for Kerala's youth to obtain high-wage employment in the Gulf. And it is these remittances from the Gulf which have propped up the sagging economy in recent years. An inadequate appreciation of this contribution of education to the state's economic development has, of late, generated a demand for curtailing expenditure on education. In fact, in recent plans, the share of education in total expenditure has been brought down. This, in the long run, is likely to adversely affect economic development by reducing the exportability of manpower. If the educational system in the state fails to cope with the fast changes taking place in the fields of science, technology and management, it will not be able to respond to the emerging opportunities in the job markets in India and abroad. This will also pose a constraint on the state's future course of industrialisation, if it is to be based on skill- and knowledge-intensive industries. In fact, the need of the hour is not to reduce Kerala's investment in education, but to channelise it into the frontier areas of technology and management.

Success-Induced Problems of Kerala

The success achieved in the sphere of medical care has brought about a phenomenal decrease in birth and death rates. Life expectancy in the state has increased substantially. These have led to certain changes in the demographic profile, such as an increasing proportion of aged persons in the population. Because of the higher life expectancy of women, the proportion of widows among the aged has also risen. These changes, in turn, have increased the dependency burden of Kerala households. The working people today have to shoulder not only the burden of their unemployed brothers and sisters, but also that of aged parents. Because of their low incomes, many households find it difficult to sustain themselves. It is in this context that the state had assumed the responsibility of sharing a part of this burden by implementing social security schemes targeted at the elderly, widows and the unemployed. The increasing proportion of the aged has also led to prolonged periods of pension payments to retired government employees and teachers, adding to the burden on the exchequer.

The growing share of the elderly in the population has started straining the medical facilities in the state. The health care system has to increasingly cope with the diseases of old age. This calls for higher investment per patient and therefore a higher budgetary outlay on health care.

State's Perennial Fiscal Crisis

While the expenditure requirements are going up to meet the problems generated by the underdevelopment of the commodity producing sectors and a relatively higher development of the social services sector, the state government is confronted with the worst ever resource crunch. Though Kerala's record of resource mobilisation is one of the best among Indian states, the resources which it is able to mobilise are limited in volume as the resource base is not growing. A hike in tax rates to mobilise resources is neither feasible nor desirable as the present rates in Kerala are much higher than those in the neighbouring states. Diversion of trade resulting in a fall in tax collections is already a serious problem. Any further increase in tax rates will only aggravate the migratory tendency of economic activities.

Centre-State Relations and Kerala's Development Crisis

In a way, Kerala is caught in the vicious circle of low growth-low resources, low investment-low growth. To break this vicious circle, a massive injection of funds from the central government is absolutely essential. But the flow of central investments to the state's industrial sector has been steadily coming down. With regard to central assistance for state plans under the Gadgil formula, Kerala has been receiving some preference, though only marginal. But large chunks of central assistance flow outside this formula, on the recommendations of the finance commission, Planning Commission, and the various central ministries. As noted earlier, the priorities of most of these agencies are different from those of Kerala. This prevents the state from getting adequate funds from the centre. While Kerala's achievements in the social sectors are taken cognisance of by the central agencies while allocating funds, stagnancy in its economy has not received the same attention. As a result, growth in the state's plan expenditure lags behind. This is not only retarding its development, but also continuing to widen the economic disparity between Kerala and other States.